An Ecosystem Approach to Economic Stabilization

'A very ambitious and innovative project to establish an alternative formalism for economic modelling using methods from statistical mechanics and information theory. The author's concise presentation of the mathematics is complemented by illustrative case studies and carefully considered reflections on the interpretation and the limits of the models.'

Torsten Heinrich

The creation of economic institutions that can function well under substantial uncertainties – Black Swans – is analogous to the dilemmas confronting our hunter-gatherer forefathers in the face of large-scale ecological unpredictability. The ultimate solution was not the development of a super hunter-gatherer technology that could ride out repeated catastrophe, but rather the invention, in neolithic times, of culturally adapted 'farmed' ecosystems constructed to maximize food yield and minimize risks of famine.

Recent advances in evolutionary and ecosystem theory applied to economic structure and process may permit construction of both new economic theory and new tools for data analysis that can help in the design of more robust economic institutions. This may result in less frequent and less disruptive transitions, and enable the design of culturally specific systems less affected by those that do occur.

This unique and innovative book applies cutting-edge methods from cognitive science and evolutionary theory to that program. At the book's core is the construction of a statistics-like toolbox for the study of empirical data that is consistent with generalized evolutionary approaches and that can be used to address problems of economic stabilization and control.

Rodrick Wallace is Research Scientist in the Division of Epidemiology, The New York State Psychiatric Institute, USA.

Routledge Advances in Heterodox Economics

Edited by Wolfram Elsner of University of Bremen and
Peter Kriesler of University of New South Wales

Over the past two decades, the intellectual agendas of heterodox economists have taken a decidedly pluralist turn. Leading thinkers have begun to move beyond the established paradigms of Austrian, feminist, Institutional-evolutionary, Marxian, Post Keynesian, radical, social, and Sraffian economics—opening up new lines of analysis, criticism, and dialogue among dissenting schools of thought. This cross-fertilization of ideas is creating a new generation of scholarship in which novel combinations of heterodox ideas are being brought to bear on important contemporary and historical problems.

Routledge Advances in Heterodox Economics aims to promote this new scholarship by publishing innovative books in heterodox economic theory, policy, philosophy, intellectual history, institutional history, and pedagogy. Syntheses or critical engagement of two or more heterodox traditions are especially encouraged.

This series was previously published by The University of Michigan Press and the following books are available (please contact UMP for more information):

An Ecosystem Approach to Economic Stabilization

Escaping the neoliberal wilderness

Rodrick Wallace

Routledge
Taylor & Francis Group

LONDON AND NEW YORK

First published 2015 by Routledge

2 Park Square, Milton Park, Abingdon, Oxfordshire OX14 4RN

52 Vanderbilt Avenue, New York, NY 10017

Routledge is an imprint of the Taylor & Francis Group, an informa business

First issued in paperback 2020

British Library Cataloguing in Publication Data
A catalogue record for this book is available from the British Library

Library of Congress Cataloging-in-Publication Data
Wallace, Rodrick.
An ecosystem approach to economic stabilization : escaping the neoliberal wilderness / Rodrick Wallace.
      pages cm. – (Routledge advances in heterodox economics)
   1. Evolutionary economics. 2. Ecology – Economic aspects. 3. Economic stabilization. I. Title.
   HB97.3.W35 2015
   330.1–dc23   2014026987

ISBN: 978-1-138-83186-5 (hbk)
ISBN: 978-0-367-59978-2 (pbk)

Typeset in Times New Roman
by HWA Text and Data Management, London

Contents

Figures

About the author

Rodrick Wallace received an undergraduate degree in mathematics, and a PhD in physics, from Columbia University. He worked in the property insurance industry, and then as technical director of a public interest group, examining the impacts of policy and socioeconomic structure on public health, safety, and order. These efforts involved adaptation of analytic methods from ecosystem theory to the study of administrative data sets. After postdoctoral studies in the epidemiology of mental disorders, he received an Investigator Award in Health Policy Research from the Robert Wood Johnson Foundation. His peer-reviewed publications have been largely in the social sciences and public health, with more recent books and papers focused on evolutionary process and cognition, at and across various modes, scales, and levels of organization. He is presently a Research Scientist in the Division of Epidemiology at the New York State Psychiatric Institute, associated with the Columbia University Medical Center.

Preface

The creation of economic institutions that can function well under the impact of substantial 'non quantifiable' Knightian uncertainties – Black Swans – is analogous to the dilemmas confronting our hunter-gatherer forefathers in the face of large-scale ecological uncertainties. The ultimate solution was not the development of a super hunter-gatherer technology that could ride out repeated catastrophe, but rather the invention, in neolithic times, of culturally adapted 'farmed' ecosystems constructed so as to maximize food yield and minimize risks of famine.

Farmed, as opposed to hunter-gatherer, ecosystems permitted, in turn, a transition to village, city, and larger-scale human communities. From that perspective, our current boom-and-bust 'globalized' economy might be seen as primitive indeed, and may not permit long-term maintenance of current levels of human population.

Recent advances in evolutionary and ecosystem theory applied to economic structure and process may permit construction of both new economic theory and new tools for data analysis that can help in the design of more robust economic institutions. This may result in less frequent and less disruptive Knightian transitions, and enable as well the design of culturally specific systems less affected by those that do occur.

Generalized evolutionary theory has emerged as central to the description of economic process (e.g., Aldrich et al. 2008; Hodgson and Knudsen 2010). Just as evolutionary principles provide necessary, but not sufficient, conditions for understanding the dynamics of social entities, so too the asymptotic limit theorems of information and control theory provide another set of necessary conditions that constrain socioeconomic evolution. These restrictions can be formulated as a statistics-like toolbox for the study of empirical data that is consistent with generalized evolutionary approaches, but escapes the intellectual straitjacket of replicator dynamics. The formalism is a coevolutionary theory in which punctuated convergence to temporary quasi-steady states is inherently nonequilibrium, involving highly dynamic information sources – 'languages' – rather than system stable points.

From this perspective, the self-referential character of evolutionary process noted by many can be restated in the context of economic process through the language model. The underlying inherited and learned culture of the firm, the short-time cognitive response of the firm to patterns of threat and opportunity that is sculpted by that culture, and the embedding socioeconomic environment, can be represented as interacting information sources interfaced by artifacts of niche construction. If unregulated, the larger, compound, source that characterizes high probability evolutionary paths of this composite then becomes, literally, a self-dynamic language that speaks itself. Such a structure is indeed, for those enmeshed in it, more akin to a primitive hunter-gatherer society at the mercy of pathological internal dynamics than to a neolithic agricultural community in which an ordered, adapted, ecosystem is deliberately farmed so as to match its productivity to human needs.

Recent results linking information and control theory – the Data Rate Theorem – suggest that stabilizing such an inherently unstable structure requires a minimum of imposed control information. That is, below a threshold of regulatory authority, the system will inevitably crash.

All this being said, however, like 'ordinary' statistical inference, the theory presented here does not, by itself, do the science for us – the vain hope of mathematical equilibrium economics and analogous game theory approaches. Rather, the theory can provide a new set of tools for the empirical comparison of similar systems under different, and different systems under similar, observational (or experimental) conditions. And unlike dynamic game theory, the generalization to spatially, temporally, or socially structured systems, falls within standard (if difficult) methodologies.

Chapter 1 examines something of the crisis in current economic theory.

Chapter 2, based on Wallace (2013a), introduces the general approach, adapted from recent theoretical developments in evolutionary theory (Wallace 2010a, 2011a).

Chapter 3 restricts the formalism to short time periods in order to explore Black Swan events.

Chapter 4 examines niche construction in short-time fitness – lies, bribery, extortion, insider trading, consumer fraud, advertising, and related strategies – as a kind of lubrication between environmental demands and the 'phenotypic' responses possible to the firm.

Chapter 5 explores the 'farming' of economic systems for maximal productivity and stability and introduces the Data Rate theorem.

Chapter 6 examines economic forms of evolutionary 'Cambrian explosions' and 'mass extinction' events, an application of Wallace (2014).

Chapters 7, 8 and 9 – exemplary counterexamples – are taken from material written in close collaboration with John Ullmann, Robert E. Fullilove, and Robert G. Wallace. Chapter 7 examines the collapse of the US industrial base as a consequence of improper economic 'farming,' the massive Cold War diversion of technological resources from the US civilian economy into what Seymour Melman has called Pentagon capitalism. Chapter 8 studies the failure of the standard economic model of criminal behavior developed by Becker and colleagues that contributed to the policy of mass incarceration in the US. Chapter 9 examines the literal farming of human pathogens under the economic impetus of large-scale agribusiness and its political clients. Chapter 10 summarizes the overall argument.

The mathematical demands vary, but most material should be accessible at the upper undergraduate level, with specialized tutorials in a mathematical appendix. Some familiarity is assumed with the standard approaches to stochastic differential equations.

This book does not attempt to provide a coherent picture of the development of economic theory, or even of the branching off of institutional and evolutionary economics. Many standard references will be missing, many (socially constructed) 'important' topics not addressed. Others have already plowed these fields well, and the recent book by Hodgson and Knudsen (2010), *Darwin's Conjecture* provides a good overview. Beinhocker's (2006) *The Origin of Wealth* outlines of a 'complexity' approach to economic theory, and Diamond's (1997) *Guns, Germs and Steel* and his 2011 book *Collapse* give a different ecosystem perspective.

A novel feature of this work is a cognitive paradigm linking 'replicator' and 'interactor' with the embedding environment, producing a complicated self-referential evolutionary dynamic intermeshing that confounds simple compartmentalizations and description using sufficient conditions mathematical models. For some, this will be hard to digest, and the first chapter is dedicated to exploring these matters in the particular context of the current crisis in economic theory.

1   The crisis in economic theory

1.1 Introduction

While this volume is not a history of economic thought and its current evolutionary branching – many such already exist (e.g., Beinhocker 2006; Nelson and Winter 1982; Boschma and Martin 2010; Diamond 1997, 2011; Hodgson and Knudsen 2010) – a powerful influence during the author's conversion from a physical to a social scientist was a letter from the Nobel prizewinning economist Wassily Leontief that appeared in a 1982 issue of *Science* to the effect that

> Page after page of professional economics journals are filled with mathematical formulas leading from sets of more or less plausible but entirely arbitrary assumptions to precisely stated but irrelevant theoretical conclusions. ... Year after year economic theorists continue to produce scores of mathematical models and to explore in great detail their formal properties and the econometricians fit algebraic functions of all possible shapes to essentially the same sets of data without being able to advance, in any perceptible way, a systematic understanding of the structure and the operations of a real economic system.

Tony Lawson, extending Lawson (2009a, b), at the 2010 INET Conference in London, quotes Leontief and a long stream of recognizably similar complaints from well-regarded 'mainstream' economic and econometric theorists: Rubenstein (1995), Milton Friedman (1999), Ronald Coase (1999), Mark Blaug (1997), and so on. These are not criticisms made by marginalized 'heterodox' academics, but by central practitioners of the modern discipline.

Lawson's (2006) earlier manifesto on the nature of heterodox economics explains some of the underlying problems. It focuses, first, on characterizing the essential features of the mainstream tradition as involving explicitly physics-like, deductive mathematical models of social phenomena that inherently require an atomistic perspective on individual, isolated 'economic actors.' Lawson (2006) explains the need for isolated atomism in mainstream theory as follows:

> Deductivist theorizing of the sort pursued in modern economics ultimately has to be couched in terms of such 'atoms' just to ensure that under conditions

x the same (predictable or deducible) outcome *y* always follows. The point then, however unoriginal, is that the ontological presuppositions of the insistence on mathematical modelling include the restriction that the social domain is everywhere constituted by sets of isolated atoms.

In Lawson's (2006) view, post Keynsianism, (old) institutionalism, feminist, social, Marxian, Austrian and social economics, among others, are part of a generalized social science in which

> The dominant emphases of the separate heterodox traditions are just manifestations of categories of social reality that conflict with the assumption that social life is everywhere composed of isolated atoms.

Lawson (2012) concludes that the only consistent 'ideology' identifiable in mainstream economic theory is the compulsive adherence to an atomistic mathematical model strategy.

Although there is criticism of Lawson's perspective (e.g., Fullbrook 2009), many of his basic ideas seem to hold up well, but there is something deeper operating than simple constraints driven by formal mathematical limitations.

Since ecosystem theory was discovered by the physicists (e.g., May 1973), the field has been bedeviled by just the kind of mathematical modeling that Lawson decries. In reply to May and similar practitioners of physics-like modeling in biology and ecology, Pielou (1977, p. 106) writes:

> [Mathematical] models are easy to devise; even though the assumptions of which they are constructed may be hard to justify, the magic phrase 'let us assume that' overrides objections temporarily. One is then confronted with a much harder task: How is such a model to be tested? The correspondence between a model's predictions and observed events is sometimes gratifyingly close but this cannot be taken to imply the model's simplifying assumptions are reasonable in the sense that neglected complications are indeed negligible in their effects …
>
> In my opinion the usefulness of models is great [however] it consists *not in answering questions but in raising them.* Models can be used to inspire new field investigations and these are the only source of new knowledge as opposed to new speculation.

That is, mathematical modeling in biology, ecology, and social science is at best a junior partner in an ongoing dynamic relation with empirical or observational study. Under such circumstances, models can sometimes help. A little. Infrequently.

One is, however, usually inclined to prefer, as an alternative to yet another mathematical thicket, a clearly thought-out verbal model, illustrated by a few equally clear flow diagrams, followed by an appropriate number of elegant, clever, data-rich, observational or experimental case histories. Science then follows.

But there is even more going on here: recently, criticism has emerged of gene-based 'replicator dynamics' versions of evolutionary theory that suffer similar atomistic model constrictions (e.g., Lewontin 2000, 2010). Much of the debate in evolutionary theory has revolved around the 'basic' target of selection, with the Modern Evolutionary Synthesis heavily invested in the atomistic, gradualist theory of mathematical population genetics (e.g., Ewens 2004). Heterodox, non-atomistic, heavily contextual, evolutionary theories have emerged that materially challenge and extend that Synthesis, most often through focus on how selection pressures operate at scales and levels of organization beyond the individual organism (e.g., Gould 2002; Odling-Smee et al. 2003; Wallace 2010a).

These are, then, two similar case histories. Is atomism simply a 'requirement' of 'physics-like' mathematical modeling, or are deeper constraints at work, in contrast with Lawson's conclusions?

1.2 The psychology of atomism

Economics and evolutionary theory are not the only biological/social sciences to come under the same gun. The cultural psychologist Steven J. Heine (2001) writes:

> The extreme nature of American individualism suggests that a psychology based on late 20th century American research not only stands the risk of developing models that are particular to that culture, but of developing an understanding of the self that is peculiar in the context of the world's cultures.

The explanation of 'atomism' goes deeper than ideology, into the very bones of Western culture: Nisbett et al. (2001), following in a long line of research (Markus and Kitayama 1991, and the summary by Heine 2001), review an extensive literature on empirical studies of basic cognitive differences between individuals raised in what they call 'East Asian' and 'Western' cultural heritages, which they characterize, respectively, as 'holistic' and 'analytic.' They argue:

1. Social organization directs attention to some aspects of the perceptual field at the expense of others.
2. What is attended to influences metaphysics.
3. Metaphysics guides tacit epistemology, that is, beliefs about the nature of the world and causality.
4. Epistemology dictates the development and application of some cognitive processes at the expense of others.
5. Social organization can directly affect the plausibility of metaphysical assumptions, such as whether causality should be regarded as residing in the field vs. in the object.
6. Social organization and social practice can directly influence the development and use of cognitive processes such as dialectical vs. logical ones.

Nisbett et al. (2001) conclude that tools of thought embody a culture's intellectual history, that tools have theories built into them, and that users accept these theories, albeit unknowingly, when they use these tools.

In their famous paper 'Culture and Change Blindness' Masuda and Nisbett (2006) find:

> Research on perception and cognition suggests that whereas East Asians view the world holistically, attending to the entire field and relations among objects, Westerners view the world analytically, focusing on the attributes of salient objects ... Compared to Americans, East Asians were more sensitive to contextual changes than to focal object changes. These results suggest that there can be cultural variation in what may seem to be basic perceptual processes.

As Nisbett and Miyamoto (2005) put the matter:

> There is recent evidence that perceptual processes are influenced by culture. Westerners tend to engage in context-independent and analytic perceptual processes by focusing on a salient object independently of its context, whereas Asians tend to engage in context-dependent and holistic perceptual processes by attending to the relationship between the object and the context in which the object is located. Recent research has explored mechanisms underlying such cultural differences, which indicate that participating in different social practices leads to both chronic as well as temporary shifts in perception. These findings establish a dynamic relationship between the cultural context and perceptual processes. We suggest that perception can no longer be regarded as consisting of processes that are universal across all people at all times.

Wallace (2007), who uses methods similar to those of this volume, writes:

> A recent 'necessary conditions' mathematical treatment of Baars's global workspace consciousness model, analogous to Dretske's communication theory analysis of high level mental function, [can be] used to explore the effects of embedding cultural heritage on inattentional blindness [which is analogous to change blindness]. Culture should express itself quite distinctly in this basic psychophysical phenomenon across a great variety of sensory modalities because the limited syntactic and grammatical bandpass of the rate distortion manifold characterizing conscious attention must conform to topological constraints generated by cultural context.

As this book will show, a new class of statistical and analytic models likely to be useful as subordinate partners in the experimental and observational study of economic pattern and process can be developed that is not mathematically constrained to an underlying atomism.

Profound, culturally based, 'ideological' constraints abound across a plethora of Western scientific disciplines, including economics. Empires, however, do not always successfully construct their own realities, and models and policies based on those constraints can fail catastrophically. Several case histories will be given in later chapters.

1.3 The self-referential dynamic

A centrality of Lawson's (2010) critique regarding the current use of mathematical models in economics is that

> [T]here is a basic mismatch between the sorts of mathematical methods economists employ and the nature of the social, including economic, phenomena that economists seek to illuminate ... Most fundamentally, [economists'] methods can be seen to be restricted to closed systems systems ... [T]o date such closures have been found to occur only very rarely in the social realm... [and] we have good reason to suppose they will remain uncommon. Only for a closed system can one easily impose 'entropy maximization' or similar variational strategies in a search for equilibrium or long-time limit configurations. Open systems may be better addressed using Onsager-like formalisms abducted from nonequilibrium thermodynamics, at least as an empirical starting approximation.

One of the advantages of the (broadly) evolutionary perspective taken in this volume is that evolutionary, as opposed to mainstream economic, theorists have long understood the deeply self-referential form of complex, inherently open, natural phenomena. As Goldenfeld and Woese (2010) put the matter,

> [T]he genome encodes the information which governs the response of an organism to its physical and biological environment. At the same time, this environment actually shapes genomes through gene transfer processes and phenotype selection. Thus, we encounter a situation where the dynamics must be self-referential: the update rules change during the time evolution of the system, and the way in which they change is a function of the state and thus the history of the system self-referential dynamics is an inherent and probably defining feature of evolutionary dynamics and thus biological systems.

Others have repeatedly observed the recursive, self-referential nature of evolutionary process, and postulated something approaching a 'language of evolution' (Langton 1992; Sereno 1991; Von Neumann 1966). Language dynamics – the product of an information source – are, of course, inherently open, and not subject to deductive mathematical stricture.

It can be argued that self-referential dynamics are equally a feature of most social – and hence economic – enterprise and interaction, raising, among other things, profound questions regarding the utility of 'sufficient' game-theoretic formulations beyond the simplest of toy representations of reality, as well as putting the cap on the large-scale utility of deductive mathematical theory for such phenomena.

Here, we explore self-referential dynamics from the perspectives of Wallace (2010a, 2011a), recognizing that the representation of fundamental socioeconomic processes in terms of information sources restrains, somewhat, the inherently nonequilibrium nature of open systems. Although information sources are both nonequilibrium and irreversible (continuously using resources and having few palindromes), the asymptotic limit theorems of information theory, and their extension to control theory via the Data Rate Theorem, permit the study of quasi-stable nonequilibrium steady states under broad necessary conditions constraints that permit construction of statistical models useful in data analysis.

2 Evolutionary economics

2.1 Introduction

Aldrich et al. (2008) make a compelling case that Darwinian principles cover the evolution of social or economic entities. They find that, although there are important differences between biological and cultural domains and the selection processes that affect them, and the particulars of Darwinian mechanisms of variation, inheritance, and selection differ in important ways, yet the overarching general principles remain. They argue that we must regard institutions as cohesive entities having some capacity for the retention and replication of problem solutions, and that innovation is about the creation of new variations, while selection is about how these are tested in the real world. An essential strain in their argument is a paradigm of program-based behavior that requires an explanation of emergence through both natural selection and individual development, in the context of Eldredge's and Gould's 'punctuated equilibria' (Gould 2002).

A more recent, broader scale, study by Hodgson and Knudsen (2010) argues that

> Darwinism as such provides no single model or axiomatic system. Instead, it is a metatheoretical framework that stimulates further inquiry and provides a repository for contingent auxiliary theories and models … The construction of a new Darwinian theoretical system capable of generating powerful predictive models to rival established alternatives in the social sciences is a long way off. As with the application of Darwinian principles to biology, the first and principal achievement is to build a conceptual engine that is capable of guiding specific inquiry into detailed causal mechanisms. The secondary process – of showing how these principles operated in specific contexts – required a century of detailed empirical and experimental study before Darwinism triumphed in the 1940s. The task of applying Darwinism to the social sciences is much younger and has far to go.

Here, we will attempt to shorten this development period by introducing a series of necessary conditions statistical models based on the asymptotic limit theorems of information theory that might well show how these principles operate in specific empirical contexts.

The starting point is a recent expansion of the classic Modern Evolutionary Synthesis that takes into account the critical role of interaction in the real world (Wallace 2010a), a matter of current interest in economics from dangerously simplistic perspectives (e.g., Johnson 2011).

Lewontin (2010), reviewing the book by Fodor and Piatelli-Palmarini (2010), describes the Modern Evolutionary Synthesis as having four basic metaphorical principles:

1   *The principle of variation:* Among individuals in a population there is variation in form, physiology, and behavior.
2   *The principle of heredity:* Offspring resemble their parents more than they resemble unrelated individuals.
3   *The principle of differential reproduction:* In a given environment, some forms are more likely to survive and produce more offspring than other forms.
4   *The principle of mutation:* New heritable variation is constantly occurring.

Lewontin, however, finds this structure lacking, in that 'there is an immense amount of biology that is missing,' largely involving interactions within and across structures and entities at various scales.

To address this lack, Wallace (2010a) introduces a fifth principle:

5   *The principle of environmental interaction:* Individuals and groups engage in powerful, often punctuated, dynamic mutual relations with their embedding environments that may include the exchange of heritage material between markedly different organisms.

The central innovation of this approach is to describe embedding ecosystem, genetic heritage, and (cognitive) gene expression in terms of interacting information sources whose dynamics are driven by the homology between information source uncertainty and free energy density in a series of regression-like relations similar to the empirical Onsager equations of nonequilibrium thermodynamics. Taking much the perspective of Champagnat et al. (2006), the resulting theory is inherently coevolutionary, in the largest sense, so that there is no single 'natural' scale at which 'selection' takes place. There is, rather, a set of interactive quasi-steady states subject to often highly structured large deviations representing the punctuated equilibria of Eldredge and Gould (1972), as well as possibly larger, hierarchical, conformations.

Here we adapt these results to the program of Hodgson and Knudsen (2010), and begin by restating some familiar phenomena as information sources, leading to a formal structure that expresses these extensions in terms of familiar coevolutionary models. See the Mathematical Appendix for a brief summary of basic results from information theory.

2.2 Ecosystem as information source

Firms interact with – and affect – embedding environments. Here we re-express social and economic 'ecosystems' in terms of the rough regularities of their behavior, essentially a grammar and syntax, without demanding dynamic or stochastic simplicity: we characterize them as information sources – generalized languages – capable of structured output within broad constraints.

First, consider a simplistic picture of a predator/prey ecosystem Let X represent the appropriately scaled number of 'predators,' Y the scaled number of 'prey,' t the time, and ω a parameter defining their interaction. The model assumes that the ecologically dominant relation is an interaction between predator and prey, so that $dX/dt = \omega Y$ and $dY/dt = -\omega X$.

Thus the predator populations grows proportionately to the prey population, and the prey declines proportionately to the predator population.

After differentiating the first and using the second equation, we obtain the simple relation $d^2X/dt^2 + \omega^2 X = 0$ having the solution $X(t) = \sin(\omega\ t)$; $Y(t) = \cos(\omega t)$. Thus $X(t)^2 + Y(t)^2 = \sin^2(\omega\ t) + \cos^2(\omega\ t) \equiv 1$.

In the two dimensional phase space defined by $X(t)$ and $Y(t)$, the system traces out an endless, circular trajectory in time, representing the out-of-phase sinusoidal oscillations of the predator and prey populations.

Divide the X–Y phase space into two components – the simplest coarse graining – calling the halfplane to the left of the vertical Y – axis A and that to the right B. This system, over units of the period $1/(2\pi\ \omega)$, traces out a stream of As and Bs having a single very precise grammar and syntax: *ABABABAB*.

Many other such statements might be conceivable, e.g.,

AAAAA, BBBBB, AAABAAAB, ABAABAAAB,

and so on, but, of the obviously infinite number of possibilities, only one is actually observed, is 'grammatical': *ABABABAB*.

More complex dynamical system models incorporating diffusional drift around deterministic solutions, or even very elaborate systems of complicated stochastic differential equations, having various domains of attraction, that is, different sets of grammars, can be described by analogous symbolic dynamics (Beck and Schlogl 1993, Ch. 3).

Rather than taking symbolic dynamics as a simplification of more exact analytic or stochastic approaches, it is possible to generalize the method. Social, economic, or biological ecosystems may not follow physics-like 'laws,' but, under appropriate coarse-graining, may have recognizable sets of grammar and syntax over the long term that are constrained by asymptotic probability theorems, leading to empirical statistical models analogous to regression equations.

The turn-of-the seasons in a temperate climate, for many natural communities, looks remarkably the same year after year: the ice melts, the migrating birds return, the trees bud, the grass grows, plants and animals reproduce, high summer arrives, the foliage turns, the birds leave, frost, snow, the rivers freeze, and so on.

In a social setting, interacting actors can be expected to behave within fairly well defined cultural and historical constraints, depending on context: children's birthday party behaviors are not the same as cocktail party behaviors, but both will be characteristic.

Suppose it possible to coarse-grain the ecosystem at time t according to some appropriate partition of the phase space. Each division, A_j, represents a particular range of numbers of each possible fundamental actor in the generalized ecosystem, along with associated larger system economic or other parameters. What is of particular interest is the set of longitudinal paths, that is, ecological or social system statements of the form $x(n) = A_0, A_1, ..., A_n$ defined in terms of some natural time unit of the system. Thus n corresponds to an again appropriate characteristic time unit T, so that $t = T, 2T, ..., nT$.

To reiterate, the central interest is in the *serial correlations along paths.*

Let $N(n)$ be the number of possible paths of length n that are consistent with the underlying grammar and syntax of the appropriately coarse-grained eco- or social system.

The fundamental assumptions are that – for this chosen coarse-graining – $N(n)$, the number of possible grammatical paths, is much smaller than the total number of paths possible, and that, in the limit of (relatively) large n,

$$H = \lim_{n \to \infty} \frac{\log[N(n)]}{n} \tag{2.1}$$

both exists and is independent of path.

This is a critical foundation to, and limitation on, the modeling strategy and its range of strict applicability, but is, in a sense, fairly general since it is *independent of the details of the serial correlations along a path.* That is, something like Equation (2.1) can hold even in the circumstance of a strong path dependence, for which 'history matters' (Carlaw and Lipsey 2012).

These conditions are the essence of the parallel with parametric statistics. Systems for which the assumptions are not true will require special nonparametric approaches. One is inclined to believe, however, that, as for parametric statistical inference, the methodology will prove robust in that many systems will sufficiently fulfill the essential criteria.

Nonetheless, not all possible ecosystem coarse-grainings are likely to work, and different such divisions, even when appropriate, might well lead to different descriptive quasi-languages for the ecosystem of interest. The example of Markov models is relevant. The essential Markov assumption is that the probability of a transition from one state at time T to another at time $T+\Delta T$ depends only on the state at T, and not at all on the history by which that state was reached. If changes within the interval of length ΔT are plastic, or path dependent, then attempts to model the system as a Markov process *within* the natural interval ΔT will fail, even though the model works quite well for phenomena separated by natural intervals.

Thus empirical identification of relevant coarse-grainings for which this body of theory will work is clearly not trivial, and may, in fact, constitute the hard scientific core of the matter.

This is not, however, a new difficulty in natural ecosystem theory. Holling (1992), for example, explores the linkage of ecosystems across scales, finding that mesoscale structures – what might correspond to the neighborhood in a human community – are ecological keystones in space, time, and population, and drive process and pattern at both smaller and larger scales and levels of organization.

In this spirit, Levin (1989) argues that there is no single correct scale of observation: the insights from any investigation are contingent on the choice of scales. Pattern is neither a property of the system alone nor of the observer, but of an interaction between them. Pattern exists at all levels and at all scales, and recognition of this multiplicity of scales is fundamental to describing and understanding ecosystems. In his view there can be no 'correct' level of aggregation: we must recognize explicitly the multiplicity of scales within ecosystems, and develop a perspective that looks across scales and that builds on a multiplicity of models rather than seeking the single 'correct' one.

Given an appropriately chosen coarse-graining, define joint and conditional probabilities for different ecosystem paths, having the form $P(A_0, A_1, ..., A_n)$, $P(A_n | A_0, ..., A_{n-1})$, such that appropriate joint and conditional Shannon uncertainties can be defined on them. For paths of length two these would be of the form

$$H(X_1, X_2) \equiv -\sum_j \sum_k P(A_j, A_k) \log[P(A_j, A_k)]$$
$$H(X_1 | X_2) \equiv -\sum_j \sum_k P(A_j, A_k) \log[P(A_j | A_k)]$$

(2.2)

where the X_j represent the stochastic processes generating the respective paths of interest.

The essential content of the Shannon-McMillan Theorem is that, for a large class of systems characterized as information sources, a kind of law-of-large numbers exists in the limit of very long paths, so that

$$H[X] = \lim_{n \to \infty} \frac{\log[N(n)]}{n}$$
$$= \lim_{n \to \infty} H(X_n | X_0, ..., X_{n-1})$$
$$= \lim_{n \to \infty} \frac{H(X_0, X_1, ..., X_n)}{n+1}$$

(2.3)

Taking the definitions of Shannon uncertainties as above, and arguing backwards from the latter two equations (Khinchin 1957), it is indeed possible to recover the first, and divide the set of all possible ecosystem temporal paths into two subsets, one very small, containing the grammatically correct, and hence highly probable paths, that we will call 'meaningful,' and a much larger set of vanishingly low probability.

Basic material on information theory can be found in any number of texts, for example, Ash (1990), Khinchin (1957), and Cover and Thomas (2006). A summary is given in the Mathematical Appendix.

2.3 Corporate heritage

Adami et al. (2000) make a case for reinterpreting the Darwinian transmission of genetic heritage in terms of a formal information process: genomic complexity can be identified with the amount of information a sequence stores about its environment. Thus genetic complexity can be defined in a consistent information-theoretic manner. Most particularly, in their view, information cannot exist in a vacuum and must be instantiated. For biological systems information is instantiated, in part, by DNA. To some extent it is the blueprint of an organism and thus information about its own structure. More specifically, it is a blueprint of how to build an organism that can best survive in its native environment, and pass on that information to its progeny. Adami et al. assert that an organism's DNA thus is not only a 'book' about the organism, but also a book about the environment it lives in, including the species with which it co-evolves. They identify the complexity of genomes by the amount of information they encode about the world in which they have evolved.

Ofria et al. (2003) continue in the same direction and argue that genomic complexity can be defined rigorously within standard information theory as the information the genome of an organism contains about its environment. From the point of view of information theory, it is convenient to view Darwinian evolution on the molecular level as a collection of information transmission channels, subject to a number of constraints. In these channels, they state, the organism's genome codes for the information (a message) to be transmitted from progenitor to offspring, subject to noise from an imperfect replication process and multiple sources of contingency. Information theory is concerned with analyzing the properties of such channels, how much information can be transmitted and how the rate of perfect information transmission of such a channel can be maximized.

Adami and Cerf (2000) argue, using simple models of genetic structure, that the information content, or complexity, of a genomic string by itself (without referring to an environment) is a meaningless concept and a change in environment (catastrophic or otherwise) generally leads to a pathological reduction in complexity.

The transmission of genetic information is thus a contextual matter involving operation of an information source that, according to this perspective, must interact with embedding (ecosystem) structures.

The essential analogy, at the level of the firm, is that there will be a persistent, temporally transmitted, corporate culture, a transmitted backbone of learned habit, that, while modifiable in the long term, will strongly constrain short-term behaviors. We do not invoke replicator dynamics or the description of this corporate culture, but characterize it as another information source, a quasi-language, having recognizable grammar and syntax, so that certain kinds of behavioral 'statements' have high probability, and others are either impossible or highly improbable.

2.4 Cognitive behavior

A broad class of cognitive organizational phenomena – necessarily occurring on a relatively short timescale compared with the development and transmission of a corporate culture – can be characterized in terms of a dual information source that can interact with other such sources. The argument is straightforward. Atlan and Cohen (1998) argue that the essence of cognition is comparison of a perceived external signal with an internal, learned picture of the world, and then, upon that comparison, the choice of one response from a much larger repertoire of possible responses. Such reduction in uncertainty inherently carries information, and it is possible to make a very general model of this process as an information source (Wallace 2005).

Cognitive pattern recognition-and-selected response as conceived here, proceeds by convoluting an incoming external 'sensory' signal with an internal 'ongoing activity' – which includes, but is not limited to, a learned picture of the world – and, at some point, triggering an appropriate action based on a decision that the pattern of sensory activity requires a response. It is not necessary to specify how the pattern recognition system is trained, and hence possible to adopt a weak model, regardless of learning paradigm, that can itself be more formally described by the asymptotic limit theorems of information theory. Fulfilling Atlan and Cohen's (1998) criterion of meaning-from-response, it is possible to define a language's contextual meaning entirely in terms of system output.

The model is as follows.

A pattern of 'sensory' input, say an ordered sequence $y_0, y_1, \ldots$, is mixed in a systematic (but unspecified) algorithmic manner with internal 'ongoing' activity, a sequence $w_0, w_1, \ldots$, to create a path of composite signals $x = a_0, a_1, \ldots, a_n, \ldots$, where $a_j = f(y_j, w_j)$ for some function f. This path is then fed into a highly nonlinear, but otherwise similarly unspecified, decision function generating an output $h(x)$ that is an element of one of two (presumably) disjoint sets B_0 and B_1. We take $B_0 \equiv \{b_0, \ldots, b_k\}, B_1 \equiv \{b_{k+1}, \ldots, b_m\}$.

Thus the structure permits a graded response, supposing that if $h(x) \in B_0$ the pattern is not recognized, and if $h(x) \in B_1$ the pattern is recognized and some action $b_j, k+1 \leq j \leq m$ takes place.

The principal focus of interest is those composite paths x triggering the pattern recognition-and-response. That is, given a fixed initial state a_0, such that $h(a_0) \in B_0$, one examines all possible subsequent paths x beginning with a_0 and leading to the event $h(x) \in B_1$. Thus $h(a_0, \ldots, a_j) \in B_0$ for all $0 \leq j < m$, but $h(a_0, \ldots, a_m) \in B_1$.

For each positive integer n let $N(n)$ be the number of grammatical and syntactic high probability paths of length n which begin with some particular a_0 having $h(a_0) \in B_0$ and lead to the condition $h(x) \in B_1$. Call such paths meaningful and assume $N(n)$ to be considerably less than the number of all possible paths of length n – pattern recognition-and-response is comparatively rare. Again assume that the longitudinal finite limit $H \equiv \lim_{n \to \infty} \log[N(n)]/n$ both exists and is independent of the path x. Call such a cognitive process *ergodic*.

Disjoint partition of state space may be possible according to sets of states which can be connected by meaningful paths from a particular base point, leading to a natural coset algebra of the system, a groupoid. This is a matter of some importance pursued at more length in the next chapter. See the Mathematical Appendix for summary material on groupoids.

It is thus possible to define an ergodic information source **X** associated with stochastic variates X_j having joint and conditional probabilities $P(a_0, ..., a_n)$ and $P(a_n|a_0, ..., a_{n-1})$ such that appropriate joint and conditional Shannon uncertainties may be defined which satisfy the relations above.

This information source is taken as *dual* to the ergodic cognitive process.

Again, the Shannon-McMillan Theorem and its variants provide 'laws of large numbers' permitting definition of the Shannon uncertainties in terms of cross-sectional sums of the form $H = -\Sigma P_k \log[P_k]$, where the P_k constitute a probability distribution.

Different quasi-languages will be defined by different divisions of the total universe of possible responses into various pairs of sets B_0 and B_1. Like the use of different distortion measures in the Rate Distortion Theorem, however, it seems obvious that the underlying dynamics will all be qualitatively similar.

Nonetheless, dividing the full set of possible responses into the sets B_0 and B_1 may itself require higher order cognitive decisions by another module or modules, suggesting the necessity of choice within a more or less broad set of possible quasi-languages. This would directly reflect the need to shift gears according to the different challenges faced by the organization or a subsystem. A critical problem then becomes the choice of a normal zero-mode language among a very large set of possible languages representing accessible excited states. This is a fundamental matter which mirrors, for isolated cognitive systems, the resilience arguments applicable to more conventional ecosystems, that is, the possibility of more than one zero state to a cognitive system. Identification of an excited state as the zero mode becomes, then, a kind of generalized autoimmune disorder that can be triggered by linkage with external ecological information sources that might represent various kinds of structured stress.

In sum, meaningful paths – creating an inherent grammar and syntax – have been defined entirely in terms of system response, as Atlan and Cohen (1998) propose, a formalism that can easily be applied to the stochastic neuron in a neural network (Wallace 2005).

Ultimately, it becomes necessary to parameterize the information source uncertainty of the dual information source to a cognitive pattern recognition-and-response with respect to one or more variates, writing $H[\mathbf{K}]$, where $\mathbf{K} \equiv (K_1, ... , K_s)$ represents a vector in a parameter space. Let the vector **K** follow some path in time, that is, trace out a generalized line or surface $\mathbf{K}(t)$. We assume that the probabilities defining H, for the most part, closely track changes in $\mathbf{K}(t)$, so that along a particular piece of a path in parameter space the information source remains as close to stationary – the probabilities are fixed in time – and ergodic as is needed for the mathematics to work. Such a system is characterized as 'adiabatic' in the physics literature. Between pieces it is possible to impose phase transition characterized by a renormalization symmetry, as described in the Mathematical Appendix. Such an information source will be termed 'adiabatically piecewise stationary ergodic' (APSE).

Again, the ergodic nature of the information sources is a generalization of the law of large numbers and implies that the long-time averages we will need to calculate can, in fact, be closely approximated by averages across the probability spaces of those sources. For non-ergodic information sources, a function, $\mathcal{J}(x_n)$, of each path $x_n \rightarrow x$, may be defined, such that $\lim_{n \rightarrow \infty} \mathcal{J}(x_n) = \mathcal{J}(x)$, but $\mathcal{J}$ will not in general be given by the simple cross-sectional laws-of-large numbers analogs above (Khinchin 1957). More details are given in Wallace et al. (2009).

The essential argument is that the long-term corporate heritage information source that changes slowly with experience or diffusion is the 'genotype' that constrains the cognitive behavior of the firm in the context of rapidly changing patterns of threat and opportunity. That is, the cognitive behavior of the firm is the 'phenotype,' and selection, as is well known, acts on phenotypes.

2.5 Interacting sources

Here the three basic interacting information sources – embedding socioeconomic environment, slowly changing corporate heritage, and rapid cognitive organizational response – are modeled using a formalism similar to that invoked both for nonequilibrium thermodynamics and traditional coevolution (e.g., Diekmann and Law 1996).

Consider a set of information sources representing these three phenomena.

Use the $H_j, j \neq m$ as *parameters for each of the others* writing $H_m = H_m(K_1 \ldots K_s, \ldots H_j), j \neq m$, where the K_s represent other relevant parameters.

Now segregate the H_j according to their relative rates of change. Cognitive process would be among the most rapid, followed by ecosystem dynamics and corporate heritage.

The dynamics of such a system becomes a recursive network of stochastic differential equations, similar to those used to study many other highly parallel dynamic structures (Wymer 1997).

Letting the K_j and H_m all be represented as parameters Q_j, (with the caveat that H_m not depend on itself), one can define a 'disorder' measure analogous to entropy in nonequilibrium thermodynamics. Following the arguments of Wallace and Wallace (2008b, 2009) and Wallace et al. (2009), this can be done via the Legendre transform (Pettini 2007) $S^m_H \equiv H_m - \Sigma_i Q_i \partial H_m / \partial Q_i$, giving a complicated recursive system of phenomenological 'Onsager relations' stochastic differential equations:

$$dQ_t^j = \sum_i \left[L_{j,i}\left(t, \ldots \partial S_H^m / \partial Q^i \ldots\right)dt + \sigma_{j,i}\left(t, \ldots \partial S_H^m / \partial Q^i \ldots\right)dB_t^i \right]$$
$$= L_j\left(t, Q^1, \ldots, Q^n\right)dt + \sum_i \sigma\left(t, Q^1, \ldots, Q^n\right)dB_t^i \tag{2.4}$$

Terms have been collected, expressing both the Hs and the external Ks as 'Q_j'.

The index m ranges over the crosstalk and it is possible to allow different kinds of 'noise' dB_t^i, having particular forms of quadratic variation that may, in fact, represent a projection of environmental factors under something like a rate distortion manifold (Glazebrook and Wallace 2009a, b).

One approach to this result hinges on the homology between information source uncertainty and free energy density, following the example of Feynman (2000). Then the S^m are analogous to entropies in nonequilibrium thermodynamics, and Equation (2.4) is simply an empirical Onsager equation in the gradient of the entropies, recognizing that there are no 'reciprocal Onsager relations' possible for this system, since there is not local reversibility. For example the sequence 'eht' does not have the same probability as 'the' in English.

The basis of the general argument lies in the formal similarity between the expression for free energy density and information source uncertainty, explored in more detail in Wallace and Wallace (2008b, 2009).

Let $F(K)$ be the free energy density of a physical system, K the normalized temperature, V the volume and $Z(K,V)$ the partition function defined from the Hamiltonian characterizing energy states E_i. Then

$$Z(V,K) = \Sigma_i \exp[-E_i(V)/K],$$

and

$$F(K) = \lim_{V \to \infty} -K \frac{\log[Z(V,K))}{V} \equiv \frac{\log[\hat{Z}(K,V)]}{V}$$

similar to the first part of Equation (2.3).

If a nonequilibrium physical system is parameterized by a set of variables $\{Q_i\}$, then the empirical Onsager equations are defined in terms of the gradient of the entropy S as

$$dQ_j/dt = \Sigma_i L_{i,j} \partial S/\partial Q_i$$

where the $L_{i,j}$ are empirical constants. The stochastic version is just Equation (2.4). There are several obvious possible dynamic patterns that will repeatedly recur in this work:

1   Setting the expectation of Equation (2.4) equal to zero and solving for stationary points gives attractor states since the noise terms preclude unstable equilibria.
2   This system may converge to limit cycle or pseudorandom 'strange attractor' behaviors in which the system seems to chase its tail endlessly within a limited venue – the traditional Red Queen.
3   What is converged to in both cases is not a simple state or limit cycle of states. Rather it is an equivalence class, or set of them, of highly dynamic information sources coupled by mutual interaction through crosstalk. Thus 'stability' in this structure represents particular patterns of ongoing dynamics rather than some identifiable static configuration, what physicists call 'nonequilibrium steady states' (e.g., Derrida 2007).

4 Application of the Ito chain rule to $(Q'_t)^2$ permits estimation of variable variances, which may lead to parameter-driven instabilities.

Here we are indeed deeply enmeshed in a highly recursive phenomenological stochastic differential equations (e.g., Zhu et al. 2007), but in a dynamic rather than static manner. The objects of this dynamical system are equivalence classes of information sources, rather than simple 'stationary states' of a dynamical or reactive chemical system. The necessary conditions of the asymptotic limit theorems of communication theory have beaten the mathematical thicket back one layer.

This general line of argument will subsequently recur in a number of different contexts, and is the dynamic systems equivalent to '$y = mx + b$' regression models based on the Central Limit Theorem.

It is of some interest to compare these results to those of Diekmann and Law (1996), who invoke evolutionary game dynamics to obtain a first order canonical equation for coevolutionary systems having the form

$$ds_i \, / \, dt = K_i(s)\partial W_i(s'_i, s)\big|_{s'_i = s_i} \tag{2.5}$$

The s_i, with $i = 1, \dots, N$ denote adaptive trait values in a community comprising N species. The $W_i(s'_i, s)$ are measures of fitness of individuals with trait values s'_i in the environment determined by the resident trait values s, and the $K_i(s)$ are non-negative coefficients, possibly distinct for each species, that scale the rate of evolutionary change. Adaptive dynamics of this kind have frequently been postulated, based either on the notion of a hill-climbing process on an adaptive landscape or some other sort of plausibility argument.

When this equation is set equal to zero, so there is no time dependence, one obtains what are characterized as 'evolutionary singularities' or stationary points.

Diekmann and Law contend that their formal derivation of this equation satisfies four critical requirements:

1 The evolutionary process needs to be considered in a coevolutionary context.
2 A proper mathematical theory of evolution should be dynamical.
3 The coevolutionary dynamics ought to be underpinned by a microscopic theory.
4 The evolutionary process has important stochastic elements.

Equation (2.4) above is similar, although reached by a much different route, one giving elaborate patterns of phase transition punctuation in a highly natural manner (Wallace et al. 2009). Champagnat et al. (2006), in fact, derive a higher order canonical approximation extending Equation (2.5) that is closer to Equation (2.4), that is, a stochastic differential equation describing evolutionary dynamics. Champagnat et al. (2006) go even further, using a large deviations argument to analyze dynamical coevolutionary paths, not merely evolutionary singularities. They contend that in general, the issue of evolutionary dynamics drifting away from trajectories predicted by the canonical equation can be investigated by considering the asymptotic of the probability of 'rare events' for the sample paths of the diffusion.

By 'rare events' they mean diffusion paths drifting far away from the canonical equation. The probability of such rare events is governed by a large deviation principle: when a critical parameter (designated ε) goes to zero, the probability that the sample path of the diffusion is close to a given rare path ϕ decreases exponentially to 0 with rate $\mathcal{I}(\phi)$, where the 'rate function' $\mathcal{I}$ can be expressed in terms of the parameters of the diffusion. This result, in their view, can be used to study long-time behavior of the diffusion process when there are multiple attractive evolutionary singularities. Under proper conditions the most likely path followed by the diffusion when exiting a basin of attraction is the one minimizing the rate function $\mathcal{I}$ over all the appropriate trajectories. The time needed to exit the basin is of the order $\exp(H/\varepsilon)$ where H is a quasi-potential representing the minimum of the rate function $\mathcal{I}$ over all possible trajectories.

An essential fact of large deviations theory is that the rate function $\mathcal{I}$ which Champagnat et al. (2006) invoke can almost always be expressed as a kind of entropy, that is, in the form

$$\mathcal{I}=-\Sigma_j P_j \log(P_j)$$

for some probability distribution. This result goes under a number of names; Sanov's Theorem, Cramer's Theorem, the Gartner-Ellis Theorem, the Shannon-McMillan Theorem, and so forth (Dembo and Zeitouni 1998). A more detailed exploration will take place later. Again, this is an argument that will recur repeatedly.

These considerations lead very much in the direction of Equation (2.4) above, now seen as subject to internally driven large deviations that are themselves described in terms of information sources providing another H parameter that can trigger punctuated shifts between quasi-stable modes, in addition to resilience transitions driven by 'catastrophic' external events that may well include the exchange of heritage information between different classes of organization or at different organizational scales.

Equation (2.4) provides a very general statistical model indeed.

2.6 Punctuated change

The model reexpresses external socioeconomic ecosystem dynamics, corporate cultural heritage, and corporate cognitive behavior generating 'behavioral phenotypes,' in terms of interacting information sources. This instantiates Principle (5) of the Introduction, producing a system of stochastic differential equations closely analogous to those used to describe more traditional coevolutionary biological phenomena, and subject to punctuated resilience shifts driven by internal large deviations or by external perturbations.

We have used the formalism of an expanded Modern Synthesis (Wallace 2010a) to characterize something of a generalized Darwinism appropriate to the study of economic pattern and process, generating, in Equation (2.4), what amount to dynamic regression models that can be fitted to real data. Like simple static regression models, these empirical Onsager equations can be used to compare behaviors of a single system under different, or different systems under the same, conditions. Like simple regression models, these do not do the hard business of scientific inference: the asymptotic limit theorems of probability theory, from the Central Limit to the Rate Distortion Theorem provide necessary, but not sufficient, structure.

Socioeconomic environments affect firms, and firms affect embedding environments. Organizations can, locally, engage in niche construction to protect themselves from environmental vagaries. Thus environments select phenotypes that, in a sense, select environments. Corporate culture records the result, as does the embedding socioeconomic landscape, and the system coevolves as a unit, with sudden, complicated transitions between the nonequilibrium quasi-steady states of Equation (2.4).

This is a slightly different picture than envisioned by Aldrich et al. (2008) or by Hodgson and Knudsen (2010), but one that is, perhaps, more consonant with evolving evolutionary theory.

In contrast with Haldane and May (2011), and in agreement with Johnson (2011), we do not see simple models as providing a basis for policy decisions. Generalized Darwinism, and the related statistical models developed here, provide necessary conditions for many social system behaviors, but the hard work of science lies in using these constraints to analyze data, and proper data analysis alone, in an ideal world, supplies the primary rational basis for policy decisions. Mathematical models of complex ecosystem phenomena, in the sense of Pielou (1977, p.106), serve only to suggest directions for that analysis.

Most centrally, a cognitive paradigm for 'gene expression,' in the largest sense, implies there is no deterministic 'mapping' as such between genotype and phenotype. Thus the distinction between them dissolves into a complex regulatory system profoundly affected by signals from the embedding world which that system, in turn, affects through a kind of niche construction. Again, see Wallace (2010a) for further discussion.

Chapter 3 examines Knightian 'Black Swan' events from these perspectives, and Chapter 4 outlines a theory of lies and deception – the relation between niche construction, in the sense of Odling-Smee et al. (2003), and a measure of fitness in the disjunction between the phenotype of the firm and the demands of the embedding environment. Chapter 5 will introduce the 'farming' paradigm and Chapter 6 further extends the theory. Chapters 7, 8, and 9 will explore interrelated case histories of catastrophic economic farming in the USA and elsewhere that was carried out under the mask of free market ideology.

3   Black Swans and Red Queens

3.1 Introduction

Taleb's 2007 book *The Black Swan: The Impact of the Highly Improbable* made popular the notion of unexpected extreme events (Gumbel 1958) or Knightian uncertainty (Knight 1921) in large-scale social enterprise, particularly a business environment. Here, we examine such events from an ecosystem perspective, viewing system-and-environment as a unit that may undergo path-dependent punctuated dynamics, much in the spirit of 'punctuated equilibrium' treatments of evolutionary process (Gould 2002) or ecosystem resilience shifts (Gunderson 2000; Holling 1973, 1992).

Cognitive behaviors of complex systems have long been explored under the label 'distributed cognition.' To paraphrase Hollan et al. (2000), the theory of distributed cognition, like any cognitive theory, seeks to understand the organization of cognitive systems. Unlike traditional theories, however, it extends the reach of what is considered cognitive beyond the individual to encompass interactions between people and with resources and materials in the environment. It is important from the outset to understand that distributed cognition refers to a perspective on all of cognition, rather than a particular kind of cognition. Distributed cognition looks for cognitive processes, wherever they may occur, on the basis of the functional relationships of elements that participate together in the process. A process is not cognitive simply because it happens in a brain, nor is a process noncognitive simply because it happens in the interactions between many brains. In distributed cognition one expects to find a system that can dynamically configure itself to bring subsystems into coordination to accomplish various functions.

Here, we extend recent models of individual animal consciousness to a hierarchy of 'global broadcasts' that engage cognitive institutional, machine, or hybrid submodules into dynamic collectives to address changing patterns of threat and affordance. Unlike animal consciousness, which is limited to a single global broadcast, institutions, machines, or their cockpit hybrids, must 'consciously' address multiple simultaneous challenges via multiple broadcasts. This presents mathematical difficulties that transcend the description of individual consciousness, considered by some a 'scientific mystery' akin to dark matter and dark energy. Social scientists, however, might well recognize that that the 'mystery' of consciousness is a social construct, more in the realm of the religious than the scientific. The reality is more mundane (e.g., Baars 1988; Wallace 2012).

The dynamic statistical models that result – interweaving analytic and topological properties via index theorem methods – will show clearly how alterations in the exchange of information between functional elements can trigger punctuated changes in the cognitive capacity of the entire system, and parallel punctuation in its modes of interaction with an embedding and highly dynamic environment.

The first step involves expressing inherent environmental dynamics as the product of an information source, a counterintuitive perspective for some.

Recall the arguments of Chapter 2. Firms and institutions, cognitive machines, or their cockpit hybrids, interact with, affect, and are affected by, embedding environments. It is possible to reexpress environmental dynamics in terms of symbolic dynamics having a 'grammar' and 'syntax' that represent the output of an information source – a generalized language.

Again, rather than taking symbolic dynamics as a simplification of more exact analytic or stochastic approaches it is possible to generalize to a more comprehensive structure. Social, economic, or biological ecosystems may not have identifiable sets of stochastic dynamic equations like noisy, nonlinear mechanical clocks, but, under appropriate coarse-graining, they may still have recognizable sets of grammar and syntax over the long-term.

The next stage of the argument involves recent developments in animal consciousness theory that will serve as the basis for characterization of more complicated – organizational, machine, hybrid – cognitive process as an information source.

Following Sergent and Dehaene (2004), a growing body of empirical work shows large all-or-none changes in neural activity when a stimulus fails to be consciously reported as compared to when it is reported. A qualitative difference between unconscious and conscious processing is generally expected by theories that view recurrent interactions between distant brain areas as a necessary condition for conscious perception. One of these theories – that of Bernard Baars – has proposed that consciousness is associated with the interconnection of multiple areas processing a stimulus by a dynamic 'neuronal workspace' within which recurrent connections allow long-distance communication and auto-amplification of the activation. Neuronal network simulations suggest the existence of a fluctuating dynamic threshold. If the primary activation evoked by a stimulus exceeds this threshold, reverberation takes place and stimulus information gains access, through the workspace, to a broad range of other brain areas allowing, among other processes, verbal report, voluntary manipulation, voluntary action, and long-term memorization. Below this threshold, however, stimulus information remains unavailable to these processes. Thus the global neuronal workspace theory predicts an all-or-nothing transition between conscious and unconscious perception. More generally, many non-linear dynamical systems with self-amplification are characterized by the presence of discontinuous transitions in internal state.

Thus Baars' global workspace model of animal consciousness sees the phenomenon as a dynamic array of unconscious cognitive modules that unite to become a global broadcast having a tunable perception threshold not unlike a theater spotlight, but whose range of attention is constrained by embedding contexts (Baars 1988, 2005). Baars and Franklin (2003) describe these matters as follows:

1   The brain can be viewed as a collection of distributed specialized networks (processors).
2   Consciousness is associated with a global workspace in the brain – a fleeting memory capacity whose focal contents are widely distributed – 'broadcast' – to many unconscious specialized networks.
3   Conversely, a global workspace can also serve to integrate many competing and cooperating input networks.
4   Some unconscious networks, called contexts, shape conscious contents, for example unconscious parietal maps modulate visual feature cells that underlie the perception of color in the ventral stream.
5   Such contexts work together jointly to constrain conscious events.
6   Motives and emotions can be viewed as goal contexts.
7   Executive functions work as hierarchies of goal contexts.

The basic mechanism emerges from a relatively simple application of the asymptotic limit theorems of information theory, once a broad range of unconscious cognitive processes is recognized as inherently characterized by information sources – generalized languages (Wallace 2000, 2005, 2007, 2012). This permits mapping physiological unconscious cognitive modules onto an abstract network of interacting information sources, allowing a simplified mathematical attack that, in the presence of sufficient linkage – crosstalk – permits rapid, shifting, global broadcasts in response to sufficiently large impinging signals. The topology of that broadcast is tunable, limited, however, by contextual constraints.

While the mathematical description of animal consciousness is surprisingly straightforward, the evolutionary trajectories leading to its emergence seem otherwise. By contrast, Wallace (2012) concludes that physical restrictions on the availability of metabolic free energy provide sufficient conditions for the emergence, not only of consciousness, but of a spectrum of analogous 'global' broadcast phenomena acting across a variety of biological scales of space, time, and levels of organization.

That argument is in the spirit of Gould and Lewontin's (1979) famous essay "The Spandrels of San Marco and the Panglossian Paradigm: A Critique of the Adaptationist Programme." Spandrels are the triangular sectors of the intersecting arches that support a cathedral roof – simple byproducts of the need for arches – and their occurrence is in no way fundamental to the construction of a cathedral. Crosstalk between 'low level' cognitive modules is a similar inessential byproduct that evolutionary process has exapted to construct the dynamic global broadcasts of consciousness and a spectrum of roughly analogous physiological phenomena: evolution built many new arches from a single spandrel (Wallace 2012).

Here we take a roughly analogous approach to institutional, machine, or hybrid, distributed cognition. A '$y = mx+b$' statistical argument much like Section 2.5 again leads to dynamic 'regression equations' useful for data analysis, and to Kadanoff models of the punctuated phase transitions that must characterize – indeed, inevitably haunt – all institutional hierarchies and their embedding environments.

Recall, now, the arguments of Section 2.4. Atlan and Cohen (1998) argue, in the context of the immune system, that cognitive function involves comparison of a perceived signal with an internal, learned or inherited picture of the world, and then choice of one response from a much larger repertoire of possible responses. That is, cognitive pattern recognition-and-response proceeds by an algorithmic combination of an incoming external sensory signal with an internal ongoing activity – incorporating the internalized picture of the world – and triggering an appropriate action based on a decision that the pattern of sensory activity requires a response.

For each positive integer n, let $N(n)$ be the number of high probability paths of length n that begin with some particular base state and lead to an action. Call such paths 'meaningful,' assuming that $N(n)$ will be considerably less than the number of all possible paths of length n leading from the base state to the action.

Note that identification of the 'alphabet' of states and actions may depend on the proper system 'coarse graining' in the sense of symbolic dynamics (Beck and Schlogl 1993).

Again, the assumption permitting inference on necessary conditions constrained by the asymptotic limit theorems of information theory is that the finite limit $H \equiv \lim_{n \to \infty} \log[N(n)]/n$ both exists and is independent of the path x.

Call such a pattern recognition-and-response cognitive process *ergodic*. Not all cognitive processes are likely to be ergodic, implying that H, if it indeed exists at all, is path dependent, although extension to nearly ergodic processes in a certain sense, seems possible (e.g., Wallace 2005, pp. 31–32).

Invoking the spirit of the Shannon-McMillan Theorem, it is possible to define an adiabatically, piecewise stationary, ergodic information source **X** associated with stochastic variates X_j such that appropriate joint and conditional Shannon uncertainties satisfy the classic relations of Equation (2.3). This information source is defined as *dual* to the underlying ergodic cognitive process, in the sense of Wallace (2000, 2005, 2007).

To reiterate the argument of Chapter 2, 'adiabatic' means that, when the information source is parameterized according to some appropriate scheme, within continuous 'pieces,' changes in parameter values take place slowly enough so that the information source remains as close to stationary and ergodic as needed to make the fundamental limit theorems work. 'Stationary' means that probabilities do not change in time, and 'ergodic' (roughly) that cross-sectional means converge to long-time averages. Between 'pieces' one invokes various kinds of phase change formalism, for example renormalization theory in cases where a mean field approximation holds, as in the Mathematical Appendix, or variants of random network theory where a mean number approximation is applied.

3.2 The cognitive groupoid

Extending the argument of Section 2.4, note that an equivalence class algebra can be constructed by choosing different origin points a_0, and defining the equivalence of two states a_m, a_n by the existence of high probability meaningful paths connecting them to the same origin point. Disjoint partition by equivalence class, analogous to orbit equivalence classes for a dynamical system, defines the vertices of a network of cognitive dual languages. Each vertex then represents a different information source dual to a cognitive process. This is not a representation of a cognitive network as such. It is, rather, an abstract set of 'languages' dual to the set of cognitive processes of interest, that may become linked into higher order structures. Characterization via equivalence classes defines a groupoid, an extension of the idea of a symmetry group, as summarized by Brown (1987) and Weinstein (1996). Linkages across this set of 'languages' occur via the groupoid generalization of Landau's spontaneous symmetry breaking arguments that will be used below (Landau and Lifshitz 2007; Pettini 2007). See the Mathematical Appendix for summary material on groupoids.

3.3 No free lunch

Given a set of cognitive modules that become linked to solve a problem, the famous 'no free lunch' theorem of Wolpert and Macready (1995, 1997) illuminates the next step in the argument. To paraphrase English (1996), there can be no generally superior computational function optimizer. There is no 'free lunch' in the sense that superior performance on some functions implies inferior performance on others so that gains and losses balance precisely, and all optimizers have identical average performance. That is, an optimizer has to 'pay' for its optimality on one subset of functions with suboptimality on the complementary subset. This is analogous to the famous Bode Integral Theorem whose generalization is the Data Rate Theorem.

Another way of stating this conundrum is to say that a computed solution is simply the product of the information processing of a problem, and, by a very famous argument, information can never be gained simply by processing. Thus a problem X is transmitted as a message by an information processing channel, Y, a computing device, and recoded as an answer. By the 'tuning theorem' argument of the Mathematical Appendix, there will be a channel coding of Y which, when properly tuned, is *itself* most efficiently 'transmitted,' in a sense, by the problem – the 'message' X. In general, then, the most efficient coding of the transmission channel, that is, the best algorithm turning a problem into a solution, will necessarily be highly problem-specific. Thus there can be no best algorithm for all sets of problems, although there will likely be an optimal algorithm for any given set.

Indeed, something much like this result is well-known, using another description. Following Chiang and Boyd (2004), Shannon (1959) found that there is a curious and provocative duality between the properties of an information source with a distortion measure and those of a channel. This duality is enhanced if we consider channels in which there is a cost associated with the different letters. Solving this problem corresponds, in a sense, to finding a source that is right for the channel and the desired cost. In a somewhat dual way, evaluating the rate distortion function for a source corresponds to finding a channel that is just right for the source and allowed distortion level.

Evolutionary exaptation of these constraints is represented by various forms of cognitive 'tuning': different challenges facing any cognitive entity must be met by different arrangements of cooperating 'low level' cognitive modules. It is possible to make a very abstract picture of this phenomenon based on the network of linkages between the information sources dual to the 'unconscious' cognitive modules (UCM). That is, the remapped network of lower level cognitive modules is reexpressed in terms of the information sources dual to the UCM. Given two distinct problems classes, there must be two different 'wirings' of the information sources dual to the available UCM, as in Figure 3.1, with the network graph edges measured by the amount of information crosstalk between sets of nodes representing the dual information sources. A different treatment of such coupling can be given in terms of network information theory (Cover and Thomas 2006), particularly incorporating the effects of embedding contexts, implied by the 'external' information source Z – signals from the environment.

The possible expansion of a closely linked set of information sources dual to the UCM into a global broadcast depends, in this model, on the underlying network topology of the dual information sources and on the strength of the couplings between the individual components of that network, in the context of an interaction with an embedding environment.

For random networks the results are well known (Erdos and Renyi 1960). Following the review by Spenser (2010) closely (see, e.g., Boccaletti et al. 2006, for more detail), assume there are n network nodes and e edges connecting the nodes, distributed with uniform probability – no nonrandom clustering. Let $G[n,e]$ be the state when there are e edges. The central question is the typical behavior of $G[n,e]$ as e changes from 0 to $(n-2)!/2$. The latter expression is the number of possible pair contacts in a population having n individuals. Another way to say this is to let $G(n,p)$ be the probability space over graphs on n vertices where each pair is adjacent with independent probability p. The behaviors of $G[n,e]$ and $G(n,p)$ where $e=p(n-2)!/2$ are asymptotically the same.

For the simple random case, parameterize as $p=c/n$. The graph with $n/2$ edges then corresponds to $c=1$. The essential finding is that the behavior of the random network has three sections:

1   If $c < 1$, all the linked subnetworks are very small, *and no global broadcast can take place*
2   If $c = 1$, there is a single large interlinked component of a size $\approx n^{2/3}$.
3   If $c > 1$, then there is a single large component of size yn – a global broadcast – where y is the positive solution to the equation

$$\exp(-cy)=1-y \qquad (3.1)$$

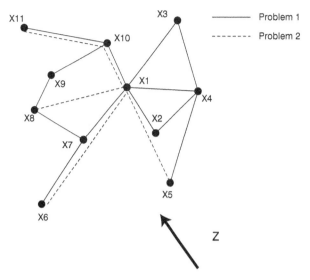

Figure 3.1 By the no free lunch theorem, two markedly different problems facing a cognitive entity must be optimally solved by two different linkages of available lower level cognitive modules – characterized now by their dual information sources X_j – into different temporary networks of working structures, here represented by crosstalk among those sources rather than by the UCM themselves. The embedding information source Z represents the influence of external signals whose effects can be accounted for more completely using network information theory. For an institution or complex real-time machine, these processes will often be simultaneous, as more than one challenge/ affordance may occur at any instant.

Then

$$y = \frac{W(-c/\exp(c)) + c}{c} \tag{3.2}$$

where W is the Lambert W function.

The solid line in Figure 3.2 shows y as a function of c, representing the fraction of network nodes that are incorporated into the interlinked giant component – a de-facto global broadcast for interacting UCM. To the left of $c=1$ there is no giant component, and large scale cognitive process is not possible.

The dashed line, however, represents the fraction of nodes in the giant component for a highly nonrandom network, a star-of-stars-of-stars (SoS) in which every node is directly or indirectly connected with every other one. For such a topology there is no threshold, only a single giant component, showing that the emergence of a giant component in a network of information sources dual to the UCM is dependent on a network topology that may itself be tunable. A generalization of this result follows from an index theorem argument below.

Note that c in Figure 3.2 can be identified as an intensity index analogous to a generalized temperature. Identifiable cognitive submodules within or across the organization define equivalence classes leading to a groupoid symmetry as

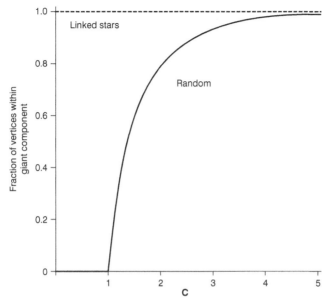

Figure 3.2 Fraction of network nodes in the giant component as a function of the crosstalk coupling parameter c. The solid line represents a random graph, the dashed line a star-of-stars-of-stars network in which all nodes are interconnected, showing that the dynamics of giant component emergence are highly dependent on an underlying network topology that, for UCM, may itself be tunable. For the random graph, a strength of $c<1$ precludes emergence of a larger-scale 'global' broadcast.

described. To reiterate, groupoids can be understood as a generalization of the group symmetry concept, the simplest groupoid being a disjoint union of different groups. This leads toward something much like Landau's perspective on phase transition (e.g., Pettini 2007; Landau and Lifshitz 2007). The essential idea is that certain phase transitions take place in the context of a significant symmetry change, with one phase, at higher temperature, being more symmetric than the other. A symmetry is lost in the transition, what is called spontaneous symmetry breaking. The transition is usually highly punctuated. In this context, Equation (3.2) can be interpreted as defining the 'temperature' c at which a complex network of interacting cognitive submodules requires establishment of a Baars-like global broadcast, representing accession to 'consciousness' of the perturbing signal.

For a physical system, such a transition is usually indexed by the collapse of an 'order parameter' existing under broken symmetries that occurs when the temperature reaches a critical value where higher symmetry becomes manifest, for example magnitization, crystal structure, and the like (Landau and Lifshitz 2007; Pettini 2007). Here, the order parameter would be the number of independently active 'unconscious' cognitive modules minus one. When c reaches a critical value, the system converges on the single, large-scale, correlated global broadcast.

Again, this is a paradigmatic argument that will frequently recur.

3.4 Multiple broadcasts

The random network development above is predicated on there being a variable average number of fixed-strength linkages between components. Clearly, the mutual information measure of crosstalk is not inherently fixed, but can continuously vary in magnitude. This suggests a parameterized renormalization. In essence, the modular network structure linked by mutual information interactions has a topology depending on the degree of interaction of interest.

Define an interaction parameter ω, a real positive number, and look at geometric structures defined in terms of linkages set to zero if mutual information is less than, and 'renormalized' to unity if greater than, ω. Any given ω will define a regime of giant components of network elements linked by mutual information greater than or equal to it.

Now invert the argument: a given topology for the giant component will, in turn, define some critical value, ω_C, so that network elements interacting by mutual information less than that value will be unable to participate, i.e., will be locked out and not be 'consciously' perceived. Thus ω is a tunable, syntactically dependent, detection limit that depends critically on the instantaneous topology of the giant component of linked cognitive modules defining the global broadcast. That topology is the basic tunable syntactic filter across the underlying modular structure, and variation in ω is only one aspect of a much more general topological shift. Further analysis can be given in terms of a topological rate distortion manifold (Glazebrook and Wallace 2009a, b).

There is considerable empirical evidence from fMRI brain imaging and many other experiments to show that individual consciousness – restricted by necessity of a time constant near 100ms – involves a single, shifting and tunable, global broadcast, a matter leading to the phenomenon of inattentional blindness. Multiple cognitive submodules within systems not constrained to the 100ms time range, for example institutions – individuals, departments, formal and informal workgroups – by contrast, can do more than one thing, and indeed, are usually required to multitask. Clearly, then, multiple global broadcasts – indexed by a vector $\Omega = (\omega_1, ..., \omega_n)$ – lessen the probability of inattentional blindness (Wallace 2007), if there is time to support them, but do not eliminate it, and introduce critical failure modes related to the degradation of information transmitted between global broadcasts, a central matter addressed below.

Thus, Ω represents a vector of crosstalk information measures between cognitive submodules, each associated with its own tunable giant component having its own special topology.

Again, although consciousness, with its 100ms time constant, seems restricted to a single tunable global broadcast, it is clear that slower institutional global broadcast analogs would permit individual subsystems, or localized sets of such subsystems, to engage in more than one global broadcast at a time, to multitask, so that workgroups within an institution will usually be given more than one task at a time. In a physiological setting, the immune system can be expected to simultaneously engage in wound healing, attack on invading microorganisms, neuroimmuno dialog, and routine tissue maintenance tasks (Cohen 2000). In an institutional setting, a firm might simultaneously engage in research, product development, manufacturing, marketing, price fixing, industrial espionage, and lobbying or bribing regulators.

3.5 Cost constraints

The information sources dual to the linked lower-level cognitive modules represented in Figure 3.1 are not independent, but are correlated, so that a joint information source can be defined having the properties

$$H(X_1, ..., X_n) \leq \Sigma_{j=1}^{n} H(X_j) \tag{3.3}$$

This is the information chain rule (e.g., Cover and Thomas 2006), and has implications for energy consumption (in a broad sense that may include cost) that may impose limits on institutional success. Feynman (2000) describes in great detail how information and free energy have an inherent duality. Feynman, in fact, defines information precisely as the free energy needed to erase a message. The argument is surprisingly direct (e.g., Bennett 1988), and for very simple systems it is easy to design a small (idealized) machine that turns the information within a message directly into usable work – free energy. Information is a form of free energy and the construction and transmission of information within living things – the physical instantiation of information – consumes considerable free energy, with inevitable – indeed, massive – losses via the second law of thermodynamics.

Suppose an intensity of available free energy (basically a cost index) is associated with each information source $H(X,Y)$, $H(X)$, $H(Y)$, e.g., rates $M_{X,Y}, M_X, M_Y$.

Although information is a form of free energy, in the sense of Feynman (2000) and Bennett (1988), there is massive entropic loss in its actual expression, so that the probability distribution of a source uncertainty H might be written in Gibbs form as

$$P[H] = \frac{\exp[-H/\kappa M]}{\int \exp[-H/\kappa M] dH} \tag{3.4}$$

assuming κ is very, very small.

To first order, then,

$$\hat{H} = \int H P[H] \, dH \approx \kappa M \tag{3.5}$$

and, using Equation (3.3),

$$\hat{H}(X,Y) \leq \hat{H}(X) + \hat{H}(Y)$$
$$M_{X,Y} \leq M_X + M_Y \tag{3.6}$$

Thus, as a consequence of the information chain rule, allowing crosstalk consumes a lower rate of free energy than isolating information sources. A more detailed calculation is given in the Mathematical Appendix. That is, in general, it takes more free energy – higher total cost – to isolate a set of cognitive phenomena than it does to allow them to engage in crosstalk, a signal interaction that, under typical circumstances, grows as the inverse square of the separation between circuits. This is a well-known problem in electrical engineering that can consume considerable attention and other resources for proper address.

Again, this argument will recur.

3.6 External signals

Lower level cognitive modules operate within larger, highly structured, impinging external signals and other constraints whose regularities may, from the arguments of Section 3.4, also have a recognizable grammar and syntax. This is represented in Figure 3.1 by an embedding information source Z. Under such a circumstance, the splitting criterion for three jointly typical sequences is given by the classic relation of network information theory (Cover and Thomas 2006, Theorem 15.2.3)

$$I(X_1,X_2|Z)=H(Z)+H(X_1|Z)+H(X_2|Z)-H(X_1,X_2,Z) \tag{3.7}$$

that generalizes as

$$I(X_1, ..., X_n|Z)=H(Z)+\Sigma_{j=1}{}^{n}H(X_j|Z)-H(X_1, ..., X_n, Z) \tag{3.8}$$

More complicated multivariate typical sequences are treated much the same (e.g., El Gamal and Kim 2010, p.2–26). Given a basic set of interacting information sources $(X_1, ..., X_k)$ that one partitions into two ordered sets $X(\mathcal{J})$ and $X(\mathcal{J})$, then the splitting criterion becomes $H[X(\mathcal{J}|\mathcal{J})]$. Extension to a greater number of ordered sets is straightforward.

Then the joint splitting criterion – I, H above – however it may be expressed as a composite of the underlying information sources and their interactions, satisfies a relation like the first expression in Equation (2.3), where $N(n)$ is the number of high probability jointly typical paths of length n, and the theory carries through, now incorporating the effects of external signals as the information source Z.

3.7 Dynamic 'regression models' reconsidered

Recall the arguments of Section 2.5. Given the splitting criteria $I(X_1, ..., X_n|Z)$ or $H[X(\mathcal{J}|\mathcal{J}')]$ as above, the essential point is that these are the limit, for large n, of the expression $\log[N(n)]/n$, where $N(n)$ is the number of jointly typical high probability paths of the interacting information sources of length n. Again, as Feynman (2000) argues at great length, information is simply another form of free energy, and its dynamics can be expressed using a mathematical approach similar to Onsager's nonequilbrium thermodynamics (de Groot and Mazur 1984). This is particularly apt in view of the enormous levels of free energy needed to physically instantiate information transmission.

First, the physical model. Recall from Section 2.5 that, if a nonequilibrium physical system is parameterized by a set of variables $\mathbf{K}=(K_1, ..., K_n)$, then the *empirical Onsager equations* are defined in terms of the gradient of the physical system's entropy S as

$$dK_i/dt = \Sigma_r L_{i,j} \partial S/\partial K_i \tag{3.9}$$

where the $L_{i,j}$ are empirical constants. For a physical system having microreversibility, $L_{i,j}=L_{j,i}$. For an information source where, for example, 'the' has a much different probability than 'eht,' no such microreversibility is possible, and no 'reciprocity relations' can apply.

For stochastic systems, this generalizes to a set of stochastic differential equations

$$dK_t^j = L_j(t, \mathbf{K})dt + \Sigma_i \sigma_{j,i}(t, \mathbf{K})dB_t^i \tag{3.10}$$

where terms have been collected and expressed in the driving parameters. The dB_t^i represent different kinds of 'noise' whose characteristics are usually expressed by their quadratic variation. See any standard text for definitions, examples, and details (e.g., Protter 1990).

For the splitting criteria $I(X_1, ..., X_n|Z)$ or $H[X(\mathcal{J}|\mathcal{J}')]$, the role of information as a form of free energy make it possible to define entropy-analogs as the *Legendre transforms* in the temperature-analogs Ω (Landau and Lifshitz 2007; Pettini 2007):

$$S \equiv I(\Omega, \mathbf{K}) - \Omega \cdot \nabla_\Omega I(\Omega, \mathbf{K})$$
$$S \equiv H[\Omega, \mathbf{K}] - \Omega \cdot \nabla_\Omega H[\Omega, \mathbf{K}] \tag{3.11}$$
$$S \propto M(\Omega, \mathbf{K}) - \Omega \cdot \nabla_\Omega M(\Omega, \mathbf{K})$$

The last relation invokes the embedding free energies (cost-analogs) that instantiate the actual mechanisms by which information is transmitted within and across the institution, machine system, or hybrid. Note that, for real-time machines or hybrid systems, response time delay may index cost: recent examples abound.

The basic dynamic 'regression equations' for the system of Figures 3.1 and 3.2, driven by a set of external 'sensory' and other, internal, signal parameters $\mathbf{K}=(K^1, ..., K^n)$ that may be measured by the information source uncertainty of other information sources, is then precisely the set of equations (3.10) above.

That is, the underlying picture becomes reversed, and the actual driving free energy measures M_X are now seen as indexed by the source uncertainties $H[X]$. The different M_X become each others' embedding environments in an analog to coevolutionary dynamics, very much in the sense of Champagnat et al. (2006).

As described in Section 2.5, several features emerge directly from invoking such a coevolutionary approach:

1 Setting the expectation of Equation (3.10) equal to zero and solving for stationary points gives attractor states since the noise terms preclude unstable equilibria.
2 This system may converge to limit cycle or pseudorandom 'strange attractor' behaviors in which the system seems to chase its tail endlessly within a limited venue – a kind of 'Red Queen' pathology.

3   What is converged to in both cases is not a simple state or limit cycle of states. Rather it is an equivalence class, or set of them, of highly dynamic information sources coupled by mutual interaction through crosstalk. Thus 'stability' in this structure represents particular patterns of ongoing dynamics rather than some identifiable static configuration. Again, in physical theory this is characterized as a nonequilibrium steady state (e.g., Derrida 2007).

4   Use of the Ito chain rule permits estimation of variate varineces driven by critical parameters.

Again, this represents a highly recursive phenomenological set of stochastic differential equations, but operates in a dynamic rather than static manner. The objects of this dynamical system are equivalence classes of information sources, rather than simple 'stationary states' of a dynamical or reactive chemical system.

3.8   The butcher, the turkey, and the Red Queen

Taleb's (2007) fable of the butcher and the turkey – what is a Black Swan for the turkey at Christmas is not for the butcher – can be made more precise: as Champagnat et al. (2006) note, shifts between the quasi-steady states of a coevolutionary system can be addressed by a large deviations approach. Again, the issue of dynamics drifting away from trajectories predicted by the canonical equations (3.10) can be investigated by considering the asymptotic of the probability of 'rare events' for the sample paths of the diffusion.

'Rare events' are the diffusion paths drifting far away from the direct solutions of the canonical equation. Following again Section 2.5, the probability of such rare events is governed by a large deviation principle: the probability that the sample path of the diffusion is close to a given rare path ϕ decreases exponentially with rate $\mathcal{I}(\phi)$, where the 'rate function' $\mathcal{I}$ can be expressed in terms of the parameters of the diffusion.

Recall again that the rate function $\mathcal{I}$ can be expressed as a kind of entropy measure, that is, having the canonical form

$$\mathcal{I} = -\Sigma_j P_j \log(P_j) \tag{3.12}$$

for some probability distribution (Dembo and Zeitouni 1998).

Equation (3.10) can now seen as *subject to internally driven large deviations that can themselves be described by an information source* say L_D, providing parameters that can trigger punctuated shifts between quasi-stable modes. Thus both external signals, characterized by the information source Z, and internal 'ruminations,' characterized by an information source L_D, can provide K-parameters that serve to drive the system to different quasi-equilibrium 'conscious attention states' in a highly punctuated manner.

A schematic of these ideas has become something of a common currency in systems biology (e.g., Kitano 2004).

The focus of Chapter 7, in fact, will be on how the draconian planned economy of Pentagon capitalism – very much an L_D – drove the US from a conventional market economy Red Queen into a state of deindustrialized collapse.

3.9 Index theorems

More generally, however, following the topological arguments of Section 3.4, setting the expectation of Equation (3.10) to zero generates an index theorem (Hazewinkel 2002), in the sense of Atiyah and Singer (1963). An index theorem relates analytic results – the solutions to the equations – to an underlying set of topological structures that are eigenmodes of a complicated Ω–network geometric operator whose spectrum represents the possible multiple global broadcast states of the system. This structure, and its dynamics, do not really have simple mechanical or electrical system analogs.

Index theorems, in this context, instantiate relations between 'conserved' quantities – here, the quasi-steady states of basins of attraction in parameter space – and underlying topological form – here, the cognitive network conformations of Figure 3.1. Section 3.2, however, described how that network was itself defined in terms of equivalence classes of meaningful paths that, in turn, defined groupoids, a significant generalization of the group symmetries more familiar to physicists.

The approach, then, in a sense – via the groupoid construction – generalizes the famous relation between group symmetries and conservation laws uncovered by E. Noether that has become the central foundation of modern physics (Byers 1999). Thus this work proposes a kind of Noetherian (NER-terian) statistical dynamics of institutional cognition. The saving grace of the method is that it represents the fitting of dynamic regression-like statistical models based on the asymptotic limit theorems of information theory to data, and does not presume to be a 'real' picture of the underlying systems and their time behaviors.

As with simple fitted regression equations, actual scientific inference is done most often by comparing the same systems under different, and different systems under the same, conditions. Statistics is not science, and one can easily imagine the necessity of 'nonparametric' or 'non-Noetherian' models.

3.10 Phase transitions reconsidered

It is possible to refine the topological 'renormalization' arguments of Section 3.4 in terms of the joint uncertainty measure driven by changes in the coupling parameter ω, taken here as a kind of temperature analog. Joint dynamic trajectories are assumed constrained by crosstalk, as indexed by ω that in turn defines a joint source uncertainty of the linked submodules, H, a free energy analog. Following the arguments of Pettini (2007), this is to be taken as a Morse Function, in the sense of the Mathematical Appendix.

Argument is now by abduction from statistical physics (Landau and Lifshitz 2007; Pettini 2007). H is seen as constrained by the crosstalk linkage parameter ω in a manner that allows application of Landau's theory of punctuated phase transition in terms of groupoid, rather than group, symmetries.

Recall, again, Landau's perspective on phase transition (Pettini 2007). The essence of his insight was that certain physical phase transitions took place in the context of a significant symmetry change, with one phase being more symmetric than the other. A symmetry is lost in the transition, i.e., spontaneous symmetry breaking. The greatest possible set of symmetries being that of the Hamiltonian describing the energy states. Usually, states accessible at lower temperatures will lack the symmetries available at higher temperatures, so that the lower temperature state is less symmetric, and transitions can be highly punctuated.

Here, dynamic process is characterized in terms of groupoid, rather than group, symmetries, and the argument by abduction is essentially similar: Increasing crosstalk – rising ω – will allow richer interactions between the interacting information sources, and will do so in a highly punctuated manner.

Given H as a free energy analog, a mathematical treatment of transitions between adiabatic realms is of interest. Define a characteristic 'length,' r, on the network of interacting information sources, as more fully described below. It is then possible to apply renormalization symmetries in terms of the 'clumping' transformation, so that, for clumps of size R, in an external 'field' of strength J (that can be set to 0 in the limit), in the usual manner (e.g., Wilson 1971),

$$H[\omega(R), J(R)] = f(R)H[\omega(1), J(1)],$$
$$\chi(\omega(R), J(R)) = \frac{\chi(\omega(1), J(1))}{R} \tag{3.13}$$

where χ is a characteristic correlation length.

Many 'biological' renormalizations, $f(R)$, are possible that lead to a number of quite different universality classes for phase transition. A version of these methods will be applied in Section 7.4.

In order to define the metric r, impose a topology on the system of interacting information sources, so that, near a particular 'language' A defining some uncertainty measure H there is (in an appropriate sense) an open set U of closely similar languages $\hat{A}$, such that $A, \hat{A} \subset U$.

Since the information sources are 'similar,' for all pairs of languages $A, \hat{A}$ in U, it is possible to:

1   Create an embedding alphabet which includes all symbols allowed to both of them.
2   Define an information-theoretic distortion measure in that extended, joint alphabet between any high probability (grammatical and syntactical) paths in A and $\hat{A}$, which we write as $d(Ax, \hat{A}x)$ (Cover and Thomas 2006). Note that these languages do not interact, in this approximation.
3   Define a metric on U, for example

$$r(A, \hat{A}) = | \lim \frac{\int_{A, \hat{A}} d(Ax, \hat{A}x)}{\int_{A, A} d(Ax, A\hat{x})} - 1 | \tag{3.14}$$

using an appropriate integration limit argument over the high probability paths. Note that the integration in the denominator is over different paths within A itself, while in the numerator it is between different paths in A and $\hat{A}$. Consideration suggests r is indeed a metric.

Note that, while Wilson's (1971) calculation necessarily had a volume functional dependence, $f(R) = R^3$, source uncertainty is likely to 'top out' and not increase without limit, or at least not so rapidly, and Wallace (2005) explores the influence of different forms of $f(R)$: R^δ, $m\log(R)+1$, $\exp[m(R-1)/R]$. Surprisingly, the Kadanoff /Wilson renormalization argument carries through for a variety of functional forms for $f(R)$. Details are in the Mathematical Appendix.

3.11 Expanding the model

The phase transitions inherent to global broadcasts, as indexed by the ω_i of Section 3.4, must be iterated when multiple, simultaneous broadcasts occur: renormalize the interlinking information sources constituting a single broadcast down onto a single 'point' each representing a joint information source, and now examine the crosstalk between individual global broadcasts in terms of a 'higher' $\hat{\omega}$–measure. That is, $\hat{\omega}$ represents crosstalk between global broadcasts in which individual submodules are multitasking, engaging in more than one broadcast at a time. For example, in a physiological context, the immune system simultaneously engages in routine tissue maintenance, pathogen surveillance and attack, and neuroimmuno dialog. This global broadcast of global broadcasts represents, in this model, the integrity of the firm. If the $\hat{\omega}$ of this larger structure falls below some critical value, the firm/machine/cockpit hybrid cannot function.

Iterating this model further generates patterns of 'social' interaction between the system of interest and its embedding environment.

The index theorem approach in ω, $\hat{\omega}$, or larger structures, however, makes clear that ω–measures are only part of the story. The networks, and networks-of-networks linking internal subsystems by crosstalk are topologically structured, not at all random, and seldom similar. The internal topology of a firm – the de-facto power relations between subgroups – may critically determine the ability to respond to environmental changes in a timely and effective manner.

3.12 A rate distortion simplification

A different perspective emerges through an index theorem attack based on an Onsager-like nonequilibrium treatment of the disjunction between a system's intent and its's actual impact. This is done via the Rate Distortion Theorem, leading to a condensation of the previous arguments.

Many real time problems are inherently rate distortion problems, in the same sense that the retina is a tool for projection of complex visual stimuli down onto a 'simpler' neural substrate, and it is possible to reformulate the underlying theory from that perspective. The implementation of a complex cognitive structure, say a sequence of control orders generated by some regulatory dual information source Y, having output $y^n = y_1, y_2, \ldots$ is 'digitized' in terms of the observed behavior of the regulated system, say the sequence $b^n = b_1, b_2, \ldots$. The b_i are thus what happens in real time, the actual impact of the cognitive structure on its embedding environment. Assume each b^n is then deterministically retranslated back into a reproduction of the original control signal, $b^n \rightarrow \hat{y}^n = \hat{y}_1, \hat{y}_2, \ldots$.

Define a distortion measure $d(y, \hat{y})$ that compares the original to the retranslated path. See Cover and Thomas (2006) for examples. Suppose that with each path y^n- and b^n-path retranslation into the y–language, denoted $\hat{y}^n$, there are associated individual, joint, and conditional probability distributions.

The average distortion is given as

$$D \equiv \sum_{y^n} p(y^n) d(y^n, \hat{y}^n) \tag{3.15}$$

It is possible, using the distributions given above, to define the information transmitted from the incoming Y to the outgoing $\hat{y}$ process using the Shannon source uncertainty of the strings:

$$I(Y, \hat{Y}) \equiv H(Y) - H(Y|\hat{Y}) = H(Y) + H(\hat{Y}) - H(Y, \hat{Y}) \tag{3.16}$$

If there is no uncertainty in Y, given the retranslation $\hat{y}$, then no information is lost, and the regulated system is perfectly under control. In general, this will not be true.

The rate distortion function $R(D)$ for a source Y with a distortion measure $d(y, \hat{y})$ is defined as

$$R(D) = \min_{p(y,\hat{y}); \sum_{(y,\hat{y})} p(y)p(y|\hat{y})d(y,\hat{y}) \leq D} I(Y, \hat{Y}) \tag{3.17}$$

Cover and Thomas (2006) provide more detail.

The minimization is over all conditional distributions $p(y|\hat{y})$ for which the joint distribution $p(y, \hat{y}) = p(y)p(y|\hat{y})$ satisfies the average distortion constraint (i.e., average distortion $\leq D$) .

The Rate Distortion Theorem states that $R(D)$ is the minimum necessary rate of information transmission – essentially minimum channel capacity – that ensures the transmission does not exceed average distortion D. The rate distortion function has been calculated for a number of systems, using Lagrange multiplier methods. Cover and Thomas (2006) show that $R(D)$ is necessarily a decreasing convex function of D, that is, always a reverse J-shaped curve. This is a critical observation, since convexity is an exceptionally powerful mathematical condition (Ellis 1985; Rockafellar 1970).

Recall, now, the classic relation between information source uncertainty and channel capacity. First, $H[\mathbf{X}] \leq C$, where H is the uncertainty of the source X and C the channel capacity. Recall also that C is defined according to the relation $C \equiv \max_{P(X)} I(X|Y)$, where $P(X)$ is the probability distribution of the message chosen so as to maximize the rate of information transmission along a channel Y.

3.13 The first iteration

The rate distortion function places limits on information source uncertainty. Thus distortion measures can drive information system dynamics. That is, the rate distortion function itself has a homological relation to free energy density.

The motivation for this approach is the observation that a Gaussian channel with noise variance σ^2 and zero mean has a Rate Distortion Function $R(D)=1/2$ $\log[\sigma^2/D]$ using the squared distortion measure. Defining a 'Rate Distortion entropy' as the Legendre transform

$$S_R = R(D) - D\, dR(D)/dD = 1/2\ \log[\sigma^2/D] + 1/2 \tag{3.18}$$

the simplest possible nonequilibrium Onsager equation (de Groot and Mazur 1984) is just

$$dD/dt = -\mu\, dS_R/dD = \mu/2D \tag{3.19}$$

where t is the time and μ is a diffusion coefficient. By inspection, the solution is

$$D(t) = \sqrt{\mu t} \tag{3.20}$$

This is very precisely the classic solution to the diffusion equation. This 'correspondence reduction' to well-known results is of singular importance, and serves as a base to argue upward in both scale and complexity.

Suppose the relation between system challenge and system response – the manner in which activities of the cognitive systems of interest more-or-less accurately reflect what is called for by environmental demands – is characterized by another Gaussian channel. Again, defining a rate distortion entropy as the Legendre transform $S_R = R(D) - DdR/dD$ permits definition of a more complicated nonequilibrium Onsager equation in the presence of an incoming system perturbation δK as

$$dD_t = (\frac{\mu}{2D_t} - 1/\delta K)dt + bD_t dW_t \tag{3.21}$$

where dW_t represents ordinary white noise.

Volatility – the term $bD_t dW_t$ – can introduce critical instability. Letting $Y_t = D_t^2$, applyng the Ito chain rule gives

$$dY_t = [2\sqrt{Y_t}(\frac{\mu}{\sqrt{Y_t}} - 1/\delta K) + b^2 Y_t]dt + 2bY_t dW_t \tag{3.22}$$

where $b^2 Y_t$ is the Ito correction to the time term of the SDE.

At equilibrium, no real number solution for the expectation of $Y_t = D_t^2$ can exist unless

$$\delta K \le \frac{1}{b\sqrt{\mu}} \equiv \delta K^{max} \tag{3.23}$$

Volatility, even in the context of simple white noise and external perturbation, may introduce extraordinary instability. As recent spectacular failures of complex financial derivatives based on Black–Scholes models show (Derman and Taleb 2005; Haug and Taleb 2011), neither regulation nor 'hedging' strategies suffice if noise itself is sufficiently unstable, typically characterized as 'fat tailed.'

This might, in fact, be viewed as something of a converse to the Data Rate Theorem, as described in Section 5.6.

3.14 The second iteration

Consider individual responses of the interacting cognitive submodules, for the moment, to be a set of m independent but not identically distributed normal random variates having zero mean and variance σ^2_i, $i=1\ m$. Following the argument of Section 10.3.3 of Cover and Thomas (2006), assume a fixed channel capacity R available with which to represent this random vector. How should we allot signal to the various components to minimize the total distortion D? A brief argument shows it necessary to optimize

$$R(D) = \min_{\sum D_i = D} \sum_{i=1}^{m} \max\{1/2\log[\sigma_i^2/D_i], 0\} \tag{3.24}$$

subject to the inequality restraint $\Sigma_i D_i \leq D$.

Using the Kuhn-Tucker generalization of the Lagrange multiplier method necessary under inequality conditions (e.g., Nocedal and Wright 1999) gives

$$R(D) = \sum_{i=1}^{m} 1/2\log[\sigma_i^2/D_i] \tag{3.25}$$

where $D_i = \lambda$ if $\lambda < \sigma_i^2$ or $D = \sigma_i^2$ if $\lambda \geq \sigma_i^2$, and λ is chosen so that $\Sigma_i D_i = D$.

Thus, even under conditions of 'independence,' there is a complex 'reverse water-filling' relation for Gaussian variables.

In the real world, the different subcomponents will engage in complicated crosstalk.

Assume m different subsystems that are not independent. Again, define a Rate Distortion function $R(D_1, ..., D_m) = R(\mathbf{D})$ and an associated 'rate distortion entropy,' S_R, as a Legendre transform of the rate distortion function

$$S_R \equiv R(\mathbf{D}) - \Sigma_j D_j \partial S_R / \partial D_j \tag{3.26}$$

The most direct generalization of Equation (3.21) is

$$dD_i/dt = -\Sigma_j L_{i,j} \partial S_R / \partial D_j - 1/\delta K_i \tag{3.27}$$

At nonequilibrium steady state, all $dD_i/dt \equiv 0$, so that it becomes necessary to minimize *each* D_i under the joint constraints

$$[\sum_j L_{i,j} \partial S_R / \partial D_j] + 1/\delta K_i = 0 \tag{3.28}$$

$$\sum_i D_i \leq D, D_i \leq D_i^{max} \, \forall i$$

remembering that $R(\mathbf{D})$ must always be a convex function.

The D_i^{max} represent limits on both internal and external distortion measures as needed for survival.

This is a complicated problem in Kuhn-Tucker optimization for which the exact form of the crosstalk-dominated $R(\mathbf{D})$ is quite unknown, in the context that even the independent Gaussian channel example involves constraints of mutual influence via reverse water-filling. In sum, changing a single perturbation δK_i will inevitably reverberate across the entire system, necessarily affecting – sometimes markedly – each distortion measure that characterizes the difference between needed and observed subsystem response to challenge.

Most importantly, there may, in fact, be no general solution having $D_i \leq D_i^{max}$ $\forall i$, that is, no possible Pareto surface defining the limits of optimality. Such failure of solution is precisely the onset of a Knightian uncertainty or a Black Swan event. The setting of the variates D_i^{max} represents the tuning of the system of interacting cognitive modules. More subtle tuning, in the presence of noise, leads to the final model.

3.15 Another index theorem

Equation (3.28) admits unstable equilibria. Their elimination, and the imposition of more general tuning criteria, can be met by an appropriate system of stochastic Onsager differential equations, having the form

$$dD_t^i = [L_i(t,\mathbf{D}) - 1/f_i(\mathbf{K})]dt + \sigma_i(t,\mathbf{D},\mathbf{K})dB_t^i,$$
$$\sum_i D_i \leq D, D_i \leq D_i^{max}, \forall i \tag{3.29}$$

where, again, the dB_t^i represent noise terms having characteristic quadratic variations (Protter 1990) and the $f_i(\mathbf{K})$ are monotonic increasing functions of the perturbation vector $\mathbf{K} = (\delta K_1, ..., \delta K_n)$. As above, noise precludes unstable nonequilibrium steady states, and is thus quite important as a kind of crosstalk, neglecting estimates of the variances in the D^i.

Thus both the vectors $\mathbf{D} \equiv (D_1, ..., D_n)$ and $\mathbf{K}$ provide tuning criteria under the stochastic Kuhn-Tucker optimization conditions that would generalize Equation (3.29).

That is, $\mathbf{D}$ establishes thresholds for perturbation detection, and the $f_i(\mathbf{K})$ tune the sensitivity of the system across the perturbation vector $\mathbf{K}$, determining what will be 'looked for' under nominal circumstances. Amplified perturbations that resonate across the system, and cause some D_i to exceed its D_i^{max}, represent one kind of Black Swan event.

Note that Equation (3.29) can be more simply expressed as

$$dD_t^i = \mathcal{L}_i(t,\mathbf{D},\mathbf{K})dt + \sigma_i(t,\mathbf{D},\mathbf{K})dB_t^i$$
$$\sum_i D_i \leq D, D_i \leq D_i^{max} \forall i \tag{3.30}$$

Then the stochastic Kuhn-Tucker optimization for the mean expectation is across the system of equations

$$E[\mathcal{L}_i(t,\mathbf{D},\mathbf{K})dt + \sigma_i(t,\mathbf{D},\mathbf{K})dB_t^i] = 0$$
$$\sum_i D_i \leq D, D_i \leq D_i^{max} \forall i \tag{3.31}$$

at a fixed perturbation setting **K**, dependent on the noise spectra of the dB^i_t.

By the network linkages inherent in the functions $\mathcal{L}_j(t, \mathbf{D}, \mathbf{K})$, a perturbation δK_j can influence more than just the distortion measure $\hat{D}_j$. That is, a perturbation δK_j that does not trigger a particular $D_j > D_j^{max}$ may still resonate across the system's crosstalk connections, violating an apparently distant D_i constraint, $i \neq j$ or causing a variance instability as in Equation (3.23), another kind of Black Swan event.

Equations (3.29–3.31) represent generalized index theorems, in the sense discussed above, in that – underlying the analytic conditions – there are particular topologies of interconnected dual information sources linked by crosstalk, as described earlier. The details, however, can become mathematically complicated (e.g., Glazebrook and Wallace 2009a, b).

This argument provides another approach, via necessary conditions imposed by the asymptotic limits of information theory, to empirical models for a broad spectrum of global broadcast phenomena that recruit individual cognitive modules into shifting cooperative arrays that have both tunable detection thresholds for perturbation, and tunable sensitivities to perturbation. These dynamic rate distortion models are, again, analogous to empirical regression models based on the Central Limit Theorem. The failure of optimization by the cognitive system – there is no Pareto surface – can be interpreted as a Knightian uncertainty or a Black Swan event. Sufficient perturbation may also cause a variance instability event.

3.16 Summary

The purpose of this extended meditation is not simply to show that institutional, machine, or hybrid, distributed cognition can be explored using models that generalize those now popular in consciousness studies. That argument has been made elsewhere at greater length (e.g., Wallace and Fullilove 2008). The central idea here is that a cognitive system of interest and its environment form a joint, mutually influential, ecosystem. This composite is inherently subject to dynamics much in the spirit of the path-dependent punctuated equilibrium of evolutionary theory (Gould 2002), or ecological resilience theory (Holling 1973; Gunderson 2000). Within the system, in addition, the phase transitions inherent to individual global broadcasts, in terms of the topologically defined coupling parameters ω, must be iterated in the case of multiple, simultaneous, global broadcasts representing the interaction of different workgroups, divisions, key personnel, machine network components, and their extended cockpit hybrids.

Several points: First, for a firm, it costs more to isolate workgroups than it does to allow them to interact. How does one combat the informal information exchange within an organization? How well does secrecy work when an institution faces evolutionary selection pressures? How can managers shut down the rumor mill? Transparency may require fewer resources. A firm working close to the bone may well suffer markedly increased costs from systematic attempts to limit transparency, particularly those associated with inattentional blindness (Wallace 2007).

Second, the global broadcast of global broadcasts represents the functional integrity of the system. If the information exchange index $\hat{\omega}$ of this larger structure falls below a critical value – if 'interservice rivalry' becomes rampant under resource constraint or other pathologies – the system, in effect, falls apart into fragments and cannot respond effectively to changing patterns of threat and opportunity.

Third, the index theorem arguments make particularly clear that ω or $\hat{\omega}$ measures are only part of the story. The networks, and the networks-of-networks, linking internal information sources by crosstalk are topologically structured, not at all random. From an institutional perspective, a socialist commune will not have the same communication topology as a Wall Street investment bank, even though it may be possible to characterize the strength of crosstalk 'temperature' linking interacting components. Strongly hierarchical institutions will have different dynamic patterns of growth and failure from those that are more egalitarian. That is, changing an ω or $\hat{\omega}$ measure may not be enough to change cognitive capacity, in the absence of significant alterations of the underlying power relations within an organization that sculpt network topologies.

Fourth, it is possible to further iterate the model, constructing an ecosystem-analog: the cognitive system is linked by crosstalk to an embedding 'environment.' Again, the index theorem approach implies that, for this larger ecosystem, the topology defined by power relations between subcomponents and subgroups will determine critical levels of crosstalk for the spectrum of structural punctuations characterizing different degrees of function or pathology: the frequency of, and the the ability to, detect, avoid or ride-out, Black Swans or Knightian uncertainties.

Fifth, machine-dominated real-time 'cockpits' like millisecond trading firms, or complex real-time cognitive machines themselves – traffic control systems, network management, process regulation, weapons systems etc. – will be subject to similar ecosystem-wide phase transitions, as the 'firm' and the 'environment' affect each other through crosstalk.

Finally, other statistical strategies are possible. The second part of this chapter used a nonequilibrium rate distortion function methodology that can also be iterated. Under particular patterns of multifactorial constraints, there may be no Pareto surface characterizing optimal solutions for a set of 'unconscious' cognitive modules: a Black Swan, a Knightian uncertainty. Similarly, sufficient perturbation may trigger a variance castrophe.

Much of this should, in a qualitative sense, be familiar from current theories of management or military strategy, but the statistical models developed here may provide analogs to empirical regression equations that can be used to track system performance and estimate the likelihood of failure under stress.

4   Lies and deceit

'Niche construction'

4.1 Introduction

There circulates an apocryphal story involving a meeting between a number of physicists and social scientists interested in economic structure and process. At the conclusion of a particularly egregious 'econophysics' presentation, a sociologist is reported to have asked 'and how does your model propose to account for deceit in economic interaction?' The answer is not on record.

Here, we will attempt to model deceit.

Expanding the Modern Evolutionary Synthesis requires elevating the role of interaction within and across various biological scales to the status of an evolutionary principle. One way to do this is to characterize genes, gene expression, and embedding environment as information sources linked by crosstalk, constrained by the asymptotic limit theorems of information theory (Wallace 2010a). This produces an inherently interactive structure that escapes the constraints of mathematical population genetics and other replicator dynamics.

The second chapter makes application of this perspective to economic process, viewing the heritage system of the firm, the cognitive process by which the firm responds to patterns of threat and opportunity in a way that must be consistent with that heritage, and the embedding economic environment, as interacting information sources. The third chapter restricted the venue to short time scales so as to examine Black Swan events.

It is possible to examine the fitness of a firm, institution, machine, or composite, from similar perspectives, finding it to be intimately intertwined with niche construction – the process by which the firm adapts the immediate environment to its needs. Two complementary models are explored: niche construction as mediating the connection between environmental signals and the cognitive functioning of the firm, and as a means of tuning the channel for the transmission of heritage and other information in a noisy environment. These are different views of the same elephant, in a sense, seen as simplified projections down from the larger dynamic system of the second chapter.

That is, we restrict the theory to recover a closer analog to conventional selection and fitness theory, inherently modified, however, by processes of niche construction (e.g., Odling-Smee et al. 2003) analogous to biofilms, multicellularity, burrows, eusocial nests, and larger social formations that mediate between individual development and environmental signals. This perspective recovers something much like the fitness concept of traditional evolutionary theory.

Processes of niche construction, in economic terms, might include the establishment of, and active participation in, trade associations and 'standards' bodies, whose lobbying and regulatory activities smooth the path for firms in a particular industry. Advertising is clearly another such mode. Similar activities could involve special discounts to favored clients, the use of social networks for marketing, the payment of bribes, the suborning of trade unions, the enlistment of de-facto goon squads against competitors or reluctant clients, insider trading, consumer fraud, and so on. Empirical indices of these latter activities might include legal fees and records of prosecution.

Lies, then, may be an essential component of economic niche construction.

4.2 Niche construction 1

The basic schema is that of Figure 4.1. A multifactorial environmental signal, a 'message,' $y^n = \{y_1, y_1, ..., y_n\}$, representing the systematic output of the embedding economic ecosystem information source, is reexpressed by an information source

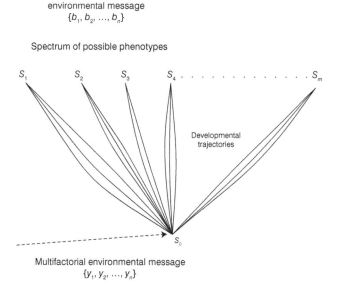

Figure 4.1 An environmental 'message' $y = \{y_1, y_2, ..., y_n\}$ is expressed as a response 'message' $b = \{b_1, b_2, ..., b_n\}$ in terms of the possible 'phenotypes' from the underlying set $\{S_1, ..., S_m\}$, that is deterministically translated into a reconstruction of the environmental message written as $\hat{y}$. A distortion measure $d(y, \hat{y})$ characterizes the difference between what was sent and what was received, allowing construction of an average distortion D, inversely measuring fitness, and a rate distortion function $R(D)$ that permits analysis in terms of an index of available free energy.

representing the cognitive response of the firm to that embedding ecosystem in terms of a multifactorial pattern of behavioral phenotypes chosen from some set $\{S_1, ..., S_m\}$ that becomes the serial 'message' $b^n = \{b_1, b_2, ..., b_n\}$. We deterministically retranslate, 'decode,' the phenotype message b^n to produce a new version of the original environmental message, i.e., the environment inferred from the firm's phenotype expressions. Write that inferred picture as $\hat{y}^n = \{\hat{y}_1, \hat{y}_2, ... \hat{y}_n\}$. Next, introduce a numerical distortion measure that compares y_i with $\hat{y}_i$, writing it as $d(y_i, \hat{y}_i)$. As Cover and Thomas (2006) indicate, as summarized in the Mathematical Appendix, many such measures are possible and have been used, and the essential dynamics are, remarkably, independent of the precise measure chosen.

Suppose that with each path y^n and b^n-path retranslation into the y language, $\hat{y}^n$, there are associated individual, joint, and conditional probability distributions $p(y^n)$, $p(\hat{y}^n)$, $p(y^n, \hat{y}^n)$, $p(y^n|\hat{p}^n)$.

Recall that the average distortion is defined as

$$D = \sum_{y^n} p(y^n) d(y^n, \hat{y}^n) \tag{4.1}$$

Clearly, D *is an inverse fitness measure* phenotypes that match environments produce higher rates of successful persistence of the firm, in this model.

A first model

$R(D)$ is, by the arguments of the earlier chapters, a dimensionless free energy measure, constrained by the availability of 'metabolic' free energy, in a large sense. We therefore, as a first approximation, write a probability density function for the average distortion D – an inverse fitness measure – as driven by the classic Gibbs relation

$$\exp[-R/Q(\kappa M)]$$

where M is a measure of available free energy, κ an inverse energy scaling constant, and $Q(\kappa M)$ is monotonic increasing with $Q(0)=0$. Then

$$P[D] = \frac{\exp[-R(D)/Q(\kappa M)]dR(D)/dD}{\int_0^{max} \exp[-R(D)/Q(\kappa M)][dR(D)/dD]dD} \tag{4.2}$$

Higher M, in this model, permits lower average distortion, and we can find the mean of the average distortion – again, an inverse index of fitness – as a function of M.

For the Gaussian channel under the squared distortion measure direct calculation gives

$$<D_G> = \int DP[D]dD = \frac{\sigma^2}{2Q(\kappa M)+1} \tag{4.3}$$

Note here that, if, for example, $Q(\kappa M) = \sqrt[n]{\kappa M}$, then

$$\kappa M = [\frac{1}{2}(\frac{\sigma^2}{<D>} - 1)]^n,$$

and high fitness – small $<D>$ – can require enormous rates of 'metabolic' free energy, if σ^2 is not very small.

According to this model, $<D>$, representing an inverse fitness measure, that is, how well a dynamical structure can represent environmental signals, depends on both critical internal parameters such as σ^2, and on the exact form of $Q(\kappa M)$.

This result has significant implications for understanding niche construction: in the sense of a recent treatment of intrinsically disordered proteins in a rough folding funnel (Wallace 2010b), niche construction 'self-lubricates' or impedance-matches the relation between cognitive corporate functioning and environmental demands, decreasing σ^2, thus reducing the expenditure of analogs to metabolic free energy that are needed to lower D, and hence to increase fitness.

The analysis has been based on the Gibbs relation, defining probabilities in terms of $\exp[-R(D)/Q(\kappa M)]$, where R is the rate distortion function and Q an index of available 'metabolic free energy,' in a large sense. A more general model emerges from viewing $R(D)$ itself as a free energy measure, generating an empirical Onsager equation something like the development in Sections 2.5 and 3.13.

Recall the arguments of equations (3.18–3.20).

In the presence of 'free energy' resources, the Onsager equation of Equation (3.19) becomes

$$dD/dt = -\mu \, dS_R/dD - F(\kappa M) \tag{4.4}$$

so that, for the Gaussian channel at equilibrium, when $dD/dt=0$,

$$0 = \mu / 2D_{equilib} - F(\kappa M),$$

$$D_{equilib} = \frac{\mu}{2F(\kappa M)} \tag{4.5}$$

Choosing $F \equiv \mu(2Q(\kappa M)+1)/2\sigma^2$ gives Equation (4.3),

$$D_{equilib} = \frac{\sigma^2}{2Q(\kappa M)+1} \tag{4.6}$$

Using the Ito chain rule for D^2, the stochastic differential equation version of this expression leads to an estimate of the standard deviation of the average distortion as a function of driving parameters.

Spontaneous symmetry breaking

Taking $R(D)$ as a free energy measure constrained by the availability of 'metabolic' free energy, in a large sense, that is itself a temperature analog, we have shown that one can invoke something much like empirical Onsager equations that are not restricted to the Gibbs format based on $\exp[-R/Q]$. More results in this direction are possible.

Suppose that, in response to environmental clues, adaptive phenotypes – behaviors of the firm – can occur in recognizable equivalence classes. For example, tracking, say, a decline in average demand, a coordinated set of responses emerges: cutbacks, searches for greater efficiency, cheaper sources of raw materials, and so on. Equivalence classes, by standard arguments (e.g., Brown 1987; Weinstein 1996), generate groupoids, and groupoids permit adoption of Pettini's (2007) topological hypothesis, a variant of Landau's perspective on phase transition. Recall, first, that the simplest groupoid is just a disjoint union of groups, and the generalization to equivalence classes is direct. Second, under these circumstances, R can itself be taken as a Morse Function (e.g., Pettini 2007; Matsumoto 2002). Thus Pettini's arguments are directly applicable, so that fundamental topological changes in phenotype structure are a necessary, but not sufficient, index of phase transition. The outline is as follows.

Recall, yet again, the essence of Landau's insight on phase transitions (e.g., Landau and Lifshitz 2007): certain of them take place in the context of symmetry change, with one phase, at higher temperature, being more symmetric than the other. A symmetry is lost in the transition. The highest possible set of symmetries is that of the Hamiltonian describing the energy states. States accessible at lower temperatures will not have the symmetries available at higher temperatures, and the transitions will be highly punctuated. Pettini (2007) expands this argument in a formal Morse-theoretic framework.

Taking R itself as the 'free energy' Morse Function, and $Q(\kappa M)$ as the 'temperature'-analog, in the context of a groupoid structure for equivalence classes of phenotype responses, gives the result.

Further exploration of this kind of argument is given in the next chapter.

4.3 Niche construction 2

Another picture of niche construction emerges from application of the 'tuning' version of Shannon's Coding Theorem, as described in the Mathematical Appendix, to instantiate a Rate Distortion Manifold (Glazebrook and Wallace 2009a, b). The basic argument follows that of Wallace et al. (2009, Section 2.10). The focus is now on the successful transmission of information within a noisy environmental channel, and the role of niche construction in tuning that channel. For a Gaussian channel characterized by a simple environmental parameter, the added noise σ^2, this becomes another form of impedance-matching lubrication, in the sense of the previous sections.

Messages from an information source, seen as symbols x_j from some alphabet, each having probabilities P_j associated with a random variable X, are encoded into the language of some transmission channel, a random variable Y with symbols y_k, having probabilities P_k, possibly with error. The received symbol y_k is then retranslated – decoded – (without error) into some x_k, which may or may not be the same as the x_j that was sent.

Recall that the capacity of the channel is defined as

$$C \equiv \max_{P(X)} I(X|Y)$$

subject to the subsidiary condition that $\Sigma P(X)=1$, where $I(X|Y)$ is the information transfer along the channel Y.

Recall also that the critical trick of the Shannon Coding Theorem for sending a message with arbitrarily small error along the channel Y at any rate $R < C$ is to encode it in longer and longer 'typical' sequences of the variable X: that is, those sequences whose distribution of symbols approximates the probability distribution $P(X)$ above which maximizes C.

If $S(n)$ is the number of such 'typical' sequences of length n, then $\log[S(n)] \approx n H(X)$, where $H(X)$ is the uncertainty of the stochastic variable defined above. Some consideration shows that $S(n)$ is much less than the total number of possible messages of length n. Thus, as $n \to \infty$, only a vanishingly small fraction of all possible messages is meaningful in this sense. This observation, after some considerable development, is what allows the Coding Theorem to work so well. In sum, the prescription is to encode messages in typical sequences, that are sent at very nearly the capacity of the channel. As the encoded messages become longer and longer, their maximum possible rate of transmission without error approaches channel capacity as a limit. Again, Ash (1990), Khinchin (1957), and Cover and Thomas (2006) provide details.

This approach can be, in a sense, inverted to give a tuning theorem that parsimoniously describes the essence of the Rate Distortion Manifold. As the Mathematical Appendix demonstrates, in a purely formal mathematical sense, the message transmits the channel, and there will indeed be, according to the Shannon Coding Theorem, a channel distribution $P(Y)$ which maximizes C^*.

One may, as described previously, do better than this, however, by modifying the channel matrix $P(Y|X)$, in our case, via niche construction. Since $P(y_j) = \Sigma_{i=1}^{M} P(x_i) P(y_j|x_i)$, $P(Y)$ is entirely defined by the channel matrix $P(Y|X)$ for fixed $P(X)$ and

$$C^* = \max_{P(Y),P(Y|X)} I(Y|X) = \max_{P(Y|X)} I(Y|X) \tag{4.7}$$

The essential point is that, *for the transmission of information in a noisy environment, niche construction provides a means to tune the transmitting channel around the message.*

Some further insight to this process can be found by examining a Gaussian channel, now focusing on the channel capacity rather than on the distortion, as in the previous sections. Channel capacity is, here, a direct measure of fitness. The analysis for a Poisson channel is similar, but more algebraically involved.

We assume a real number coarse graining for the index of interest, represented by a stochastic variate X, acting under a 'power constraint' such that the expectation of X^2 is limited: $E(X^2) \leq \mathcal{P} > 0$. If σ^2 is the variance in the (zero-mean) noise affecting the channel, then the channel capacity, the maximum rate at which information can be transmitted, is given by the relation (Cover and Thomas 2006)

$$C = \frac{1}{2}\log[1+\frac{\mathcal{P}}{\sigma^2}] \tag{4.8}$$

Here, again, C is a direct fitness measure, in contrast to the average distortion D of the previous section, and we would expect $P=Q(\kappa M)$ as above, so that

$$C = \frac{1}{2}\log[1 + \frac{Q(\kappa M)}{\sigma^2}]$$ (4.9)

Tuning the channel – impedance matching lubrication by niche construction, in this model – is equivalent to *decreasing* the noise σ^2, increasing the effectiveness of a given level of available free energy, M.

Indeed, earlier arguments might well be reformulated from this perspective.

4.4 Available free energy

Equations (4.3) and (4.5) relate a monotonic increasing function of available free energy to the ability of a firm to adapt to environmental signals and to faithfully transmit internal heritage information in a noisy environment. Consideration suggests that such a concept involves three interacting phenomena:

1   the quality of information received from the embedding environment (external or internal),
2   the quality of resources accessible to respond to the signals sent by the embedding environment(s), and
3   the efficiency with which information or resources can be applied within the culture of the firm.

This implies a synergistic relation of the form:

$M \propto$ Corporate Efficiency $\times$ Information Quality $\times$ Resource Availability.

All three factors are profoundly affected by the cognitive functioning of the firm that may, as described in Chapter 3, depend on the ability of multiple global workspace broadcasts within the firm to engage with each other. This represents a kind of slow-speed multiple personality collective consciousness that requires considerable mathematical overhead for adequate description. The essential points revolve around the ability of the multiple workspace broadcasts to both interact efficiently and have enough diversity to avoid the trap of inattentional blindness (e.g., Wallace 2007). Details of the pathologies of cognitive process within the firm can be found in Wallace and Fullilove (2008). A summary of the basic ideas was given earlier.

4.5 Deceit and the fitness of the firm

Taking a corporate cognition/environment perspective, a firm whose ability to respond to environmental signals, to match corporate behavioral or structural phenotypes to the demands of an embedding economic ecosystem, is constrained by channel capacity, faces a serious challenge. High noise in the channel, represented by large σ^2, must inevitably cause diminished fitness, requiring considerable free energy resources to adapt the corporate developmental trajectory to selection pressures.

But what of a firm that can interact, in a hierarchical manner, with the embedding economic environment, in the sense of Principle (5) of Chapter 2? In a purely biological context, biofilms, multicellularity, burrows, eusocial nests, herds, and the more structured social assemblages of the hominids and their cultures, all provide means to limit noise or increase signal strength, by, essentially, impedance matching environment to development. That is, examining the fitness of the firm in terms of its constructed niche decreases an 'effective' σ^2 in equations (4.8) and (4.9), representing increased fitness in terms of decreased distortion in the channel between the firm and an embedding environment now primarily represented by the constructed niche.

Another way of looking at this is to say that it is the hierarchical structure of firm-in-niche that interacts with the environment, now via impedance-matching effective parameters.

Looking at the transmission of information in a noisy environment – a quite different view – Section 4.3 suggests that niche construction can also be viewed as a means of tuning the heritage information transmission channel so as to maximize the fidelity of the heritage message. For a simple Gaussian channel, Equation (4.8) shows such tuning can sometimes be viewed as another form of impedance-matching lubrication.

These are, then, complementary perspectives that characterize aspects of the same process via added epicycles to the limited machinery of the first four principles of the Modern Evolutionary Synthesis, as described in the second chapter. Introduction of Principle (5), incorporating environmental interaction, collapses the argument, and subsumes both models, providing a more complete picture of the entire elephant, in a manner of speaking, at the expense of the considerable mathematical machinery inherent to Equation (2.4).

Introducing higher order embedding culture directly into the model is most simply done by invoking a fourth information source – the larger culture as a generalized language – into Equation (2.4). The argument is direct, although the effects are likely to be most subtle.

Clearly, then, Principle (5) of Chapter 2 permits introduction into formal theory of at least some of the immense amount of social and cultural process – like lying and deceit – that is missing from current mathematical treatments of economics but is inherent in all economic interaction. Most critically, ideas of fitness and niche construction must become intimately intertwined in any such expanded formulation.

5   Farming an economy

5.1 Introduction

Black Swans, systematic deceit, financial derivatives based on unrealistic mathematical models, deindustrialization, the relentless cycle of collapsing houses-of-cards, and on and on, the litany is all too familiar. Haldane and May (2011), taking the 'econophysics' perspective of Caccioli et al. (2009), explored risk in banking ecosystems, adopting tools from network theory to study the effects of interaction between individual subcomponents leading to the propagation of shocks within large-scale financial structures. But other approaches to the origin and propagation of such 'shocks' arise more naturally from the generalized Darwinian perspectives of Aldrich et al. (2008) and Hodgson and Knudsen (2010), based on a necessary-conditions application of the Modern Evolutionary Synthesis to economic phenomena that we have explored.

Wallace (2010a) has proposed expanding the Modern Synthesis itself by introducing 'The principle of environmental interaction,' i.e., that individuals and groups engage in powerful, often punctuated, dynamic mutual relations with their embedding environments that may include the exchange of heritage material between markedly different organisms. Others have taken a similar perspective, without using the constraints available from information theory (e.g., Gabora and Aerts 2005, 2007).

The previous chapters apply the expanded model to the generalized Darwinism of Hodgson and Knudsen (2010). The approach characterizes the heritage system of the firm, the cognitive process by which the firm responds to patterns of threat and opportunity, and embedding socioeconomic environment, as interacting information sources constrained by the asymptotic limit theorems of information theory. This leads to a statistical model of an inherently coevolutionary system described in terms of a formalism quite similar to that of Onsager's nonequilibrium thermodynamics, having quasi-stable 'coevolutionary' states coupled by highly structured large deviations all much in the sense of Champagnat et al. (2006).

The possibility arises that such structured large deviations, rather than merely expressing the self-dynamic processes of a language that speaks itself, can be harnessed by an external 'farmer,' that is, regulated to produce a directed socioeconomic ecosystem akin to the primitive neolithic agriculture that enabled the construction of richer social and cultural milieus. In a sense, this is already done through 'niche construction' that involves matching the needs of a firm to its embedding environment through a variety of strategies that range from simple advertising through formation of cartels, consumer fraud, bribery, and the like.

The previous chapters introduce powerful methods from the statistical physics of phase transitions into generalized Darwinian evolutionary theory, much in the spirit of Goldenfeld and Woese (2010) as quoted in Section 1.3, who focus on evolution 'as a problem in nonequilibrium statistical mechanics, where the key dynamical modes are collective.' Again, others have repeatedly commented on the self-referential character of biological and evolutionary phenomena (e.g., Langton 1992; Sereno 1991; Von Neumann 1966).

Here, we will first review such self-referential dynamics explicitly from the perspectives of the previous chapters. We recognize that the representation of fundamental biological and socioeconomic processes in terms of information sources restrains their inherent nonequilibrium nature. That is, although the operation of information sources is both nonequilibrium and irreversible in the most fundamental sense (e.g., few and short palindromes) the asymptotic limit theorems of information theory beat back, somewhat, the mathematical thicket surrounding such phenomena. The theorems permit something of a formal regularization of inherently nonequilibrium processes under proper circumstances that may lead to the development of new statistical tools for the study of empirical data beyond the narrow confines of network theory.

5.2 Extending the basic formalism

The evolutionary process of generalized Darwinism, in the sense of Aldrich et al. (2008) and Hodgson and Knudsen (2010), as envisioned in the earlier chapters, involves dynamic interplay between (at least) three information sources representing transmission of corporate heritage, the cognitive response of a corporation to patterns of threat and opportunity, and embedding environment, given that both corporation and environment 'remember,' producing serial correlations in time.

Recall, again, the arguments of Section 2.5. The basic idea is to write each information source as a function of those with which it interacts:

$$H_m = H_m(Q_1, ..., Q_s, ... H_j ...), j \neq m$$

where the Q_k represent other relevant parameters. The dynamics of such a system is defined by the usual recursive network of stochastic differential equations, using gradients in a 'disorder' construct as analogs to the more usual gradients in entropy, the 'thermodynamic forces,' where 'entropy' is taken as the Legendre transform of the information source uncertainty:

$$S_m \equiv H_m - \Sigma_j \partial H_m / \partial K_j \tag{5.1}$$

Both the H_j and Q_j have been themselves written as driving parameters $\mathbf{K} = (... K_j ...)$, again with the proviso that one not express H_m directly as a function of itself.

Then, via the homology between information and free energy, the dynamics become driven by the usual empirical Onsager set of stochastic differential equations,

$$dK_t^j = \sum_i \left[L_{i,j}\left(t,...\partial S_m / \partial K^i ...\right)dt + \sigma_{i,j}\left(t,...\partial S_m / \partial K^i ...\right)dB_t^i \right]$$

$$= L_j\left(t,\mathbf{K}\right)dt + \sum_i \sigma_{i,j}\left(t,\mathbf{K}\right)dB_t^i$$

(5.2)

where we have collected and simplified terms. L_j and the $\sigma_{i,j}$ are functions, and the terms dB_t^j represent different kinds of 'noise' constrained by particular forms of quadratic variation, in the usual manner (e.g., Protter 1990).

Again, since information sources are not locally time-reversible, there are no 'Onsager reciprocal relations.'

Reiterating the ' $y=mx+b$ ' arguments of Sections 2.5 and 3.7, several patterns are obvious:

1   Setting the expectations of this system of equations to zero and solving for stationary points gives nonequilibrium quasi-stable attractor states since the noise terms preclude unstable points. The system then undergoes diffusive drift about the quasi-stable configuration.
2   The system may converge to a Red Queen limit cycle or a pseudorandom strange attractor.
3   What is converged to, however, is not a simple state or set of such states. Rather, this system, via the constraints imposed by the asymptotic limit theorems of information theory, converges to an equivalence class of highly dynamic information sources coupled by mutual crosstalk, and equivalence classes define groupoids, as above.
4   Again, use of the Ito chain rule permits variance estimates, which may characterize critical instabilities.

Via the Shannon-McMillan Theorem, we have expressed a complex dynamical system in terms of a relatively simple 'regression equation' statistical model abducted from nonequilibrium statistical mechanics.

Again, shifts between the quasi-equilibria of this system of equations can be addressed by the large deviations formalism: the evolutionary dynamics drifting away from trajectories predicted by the canonical equation can be investigated by considering the asymptotic of the probability of 'rare events' for the sample paths of the diffusion.

Recall from Section 2.5 that the most likely path followed by the diffusion when exiting a basin of attraction is the one minimizing a rate function $\mathcal{I}$ over all the appropriate trajectories that can be expressed as

$$\mathcal{I} = -\Sigma_j P_j \log(P_j)$$

(5.3)

for some probability distribution (Dembo and Zeitouni 1998). A more complete treatment of large deviations theory is provided in the Mathematical Appendix.

Equation (5.2) can again be seen as subject to internally driven large deviations *that are themselves described in terms of information sources* providing 'coevolutionary' parameters that can trigger punctuated shifts between quasi-stable modes or Red Queen systems, in addition to resilience transitions driven by 'catastrophic' external events or the exchange of heritage information between different classes of 'organisms,' in a large sense.

The model of Equation (5.2) can be reexpressed using the formalism of Equation (3.14).

We have not made explicit the parameters K_j, and can incorporate them into the $r(A, \hat{A})$ of Equation (3.14) to produce a simple-appearing stochastic Onsager equation of the form

$$dr/dt = LdS/dr + \sigma W(t) \tag{5.4}$$

representing the dynamics of the 'flow' from A to $\hat{A}$, where L and σ are constants and $W(t)$ represents noise. This generalizes to the stochastic differential equation

$$dr_t = L(t, r)dt + \sigma(t, r)dB_t \tag{5.5}$$

where L and σ are appropriately regular functions of t and r and dB_t represents the noise structure, characterized by its quadratic variation.

This 'simplification,' however, leads directly to deep realms of stochastic differential geometry, in the sense of Emery (1989), most easily seen by reintroducing an explicit parameterization for $r(A, \hat{A})$.

Letting the parameters be a vector $\mathbf{K}$ having components K_j, we assume it is possible to write $r(A,\hat{A})$ in terms of a metric tensor $g_{i,j}(\mathbf{K})$ as

$$r(A, \hat{A}) = \int_A^{\hat{A}} \left[\sum_{i,j} g_{i,j}(\mathbf{K}) \frac{dK_i}{dt} \frac{dK_j}{dt} \right]^{1/2} dt \tag{5.6}$$

where the integral is taken over some parameterized curve from A to $\hat{A}$. Substituting this result into the two equations above produces very complicated expressions in the parameters K_j. Some simplification is possible using a standard hand-waving argument. Various semi-plausible resource-limitation considerations suggest that a minimal $r(A, \hat{A})$ will be more probable than one using more 'energy.' Application of the calculus of variations to minimize Equation (5.6) produces a classical geodesic equation having the traditional component-by-component form

$$d^2 K_i / dt^2 + \sum_{j,m} \Gamma^i_{j,m} \frac{dK_j}{dt} \frac{dK_m}{dt} = 0 \tag{5.7}$$

where the Γ terms are the famous Christoffel symbols involving sums and products of $g_{i,j}$ and $\partial g_{i,j}/\partial K_m$. This must be extended by the introduction of noise terms dB_t to produce Emery's stochastic differential geometry. Although we do not explore the development further, it is clear that this formalism provides a 'highly natural' means of introducing complications such as geographic and other social structure in the underlying populations of interest, albeit only in a necessary conditions regression model-like format that provides limiting riverbanks for, but does not otherwise determine, the flow of a self-dynamic evolutionary process.

5.3 Regulation by information catalysis

Incorporating the influence of a regulatory context – the 'epigenetic' effects of the farmer in Equation (5.3) – can be viewed from another perspective by invoking the Joint Asymptotic Equipartition Theorem (JAEPT) (Cover and Thomas 2006). For example, given an embedding contextual information source, the influence, Y, of the farming entity, that affects system development, then the dual cognitive source uncertainty of the firm, for example, say H_{Di}, is replaced by a joint uncertainty $H(X_{Di}, Y)$. The objects of interest then become the jointly typical dual sequences $z^n = (x^n, y^n)$, where x is associated with the cognitive functioning of the firm and y with the embedding contextual regulating agent or agency. Restricting consideration of x and y to those sequences that are in fact jointly typical allows use of the information transmitted from Y to X as the splitting criterion.

One important inference is that, from the information theory 'chain rule' (Cover and Thomas 2006), $H(X,Y) = H(X) + H(Y|X) \leq H(X) + H(Y)$, so that, by the Feynman/Bennett arguments, the effect of the embedding regulatory context, in this model, is to lower the *relative* free energy of a particular developmental channel for the firm, as described in Section 3.5.

Extending the argument by induction to larger scales, the effect of the epigenetic regulation of the farmer is to channel development of the overall system into pathways that might otherwise be inhibited by an energy barrier, in a broad sense. Hence the epigenetic information source Y acts as a *tunable catalyst*, a kind of second order cognitive enzyme, to enable and direct developmental pathways at various scales. This result permits hierarchical models in a natural way.

It critical to note that this is analogous to a relative energy argument, since two systems must now be supported, i.e., that of the 'farmed' economy itself, and that of its catalytic regulator. 'Programming' and stabilizing inevitably intertwined, as it were.

West-Eberhard (2003) argues, in a purely biological context, that any new input, whether it comes from the genome, like a mutation, or from the external environment, like a temperature change, a pathogen, or a parental opinion, has a developmental effect only if the preexisting phenotype is responsive to it. A new input causes a reorganization of the phenotype, or 'developmental recombination.' In developmental recombination phenotypic traits are expressed in new or distinctive combinations during ontogeny, or undergo correlated quantitative change in dimensions. Developmental recombination can result in evolutionary divergence at all levels of organization.

Individual development can be visualized as a series of branching pathways. Each branch point, according to West-Eberhard, is a developmental decision, or switch point, governed by some regulatory apparatus, and each switch point defines a modular trait. Developmental recombination implies the origin or deletion of a branch and a new or lost modular trait. It is important to realize that the novel regulatory response and the novel trait originate simultaneously. Their origins are, in fact, inseparable events. There cannot, West-Eberhard concludes, be a change in the phenotype, a novel phenotypic state, without an altered developmental pathway.

These mechanisms, at the level of the firm, are accomplished in our formulation by allowing the set B_1 in Section 2.4 to span a distribution of possible 'final' states. Then the associated groupoid arguments expand to permit traverse of both initial states and possible final sets, recognizing that there can now be a possible overlap in the latter, and the farmer's epigenetic effects are realized through the joint uncertainties $H(X_{Di}, Y)$, so that the epigenetic information source of the farmer, Y, serves to direct as well the possible final states. Argument by induction to the full hierarchical structure of the economic ecosystem is direct.

These considerations can be made more precise, applying the results of Section 3.5.

Since $H(X,Y) < H(X) + H(Y)$ if $H(Y|X) < H(Y)$, at the expense of adding the considerable energy burden of the regulatory apparatus Y, it becomes possible to canalize the reaction paths of Figure 4.1, so as to make one set of pathways beginning with S_0 far more probable than another.

That is, by raising the entire reaction free energy landscape corresponding to $H(X)$ by the amount $H(Y)$ it becomes possible to deepen the energy channel leading from S_0 to some desired outcome. Complicated internal reaction mechanisms have been subsumed by the Shannon-McMillan Theorem, in the same sense that the Central Limit Theorem subsumes the behavior of long sums of stochastic variates into the normal distribution.

Within systems of interest, however, there will be ensembles of possible developmental states and pathways, driven by available 'metabolic' free energy, so that, taking $<..>$ as representing an average,

$$[<H(X,Y)>] < [<H(X)> + <H(Y)>].$$

Typically, letting M represent an index of the intensity of available free energy, a rate measure, one expects, following the arguments of Section 3.5,

$$< H > \approx \frac{\int H \exp[-H/\kappa M]dH}{\int \exp[-H/\kappa M]dH} \approx \kappa M \qquad (5.8)$$

where κ, an inverse energy rate scaling constant, may be quite small indeed, a consequence of entropic translation losses between available free energy and the expression of information.

Again, the resulting relation, $M_{X,Y} < M_X + M_Y$, suggests an explicit free energy mechanism for developmental canalization.

In reality, there will be a large, nested, set of appropriately coarse-grained regulatory and/or signaling processes expressed as information sources – $Y_1, ..., Y_m$ – in which the systems of interest will be embedded, ranging from sets of 'firms,' in the largest sense, to patterns of social and cultural interaction, mediated by historical inheritance and processes of niche construction that may include deceit. Then

$$[<H(X,Y_1,...,Y_m)>]<[<H(X)>+\sum_j<H(Y_j)>]$$

$$M_{X,Y_1,...,Y_m}<M_X+\sum_j M_{Y_j}$$

(5.9)

and the resource consumption of the desired developmental trajectory – what the farmer desires – becomes, in a stationary model, a relative minimum for the system as a whole.

Crudely, this all depends on establishing an embedding regulatory structure that, of itself, consumes much free energy, both directly and as opportunity cost. Later chapters will examine examples of excessive regulatory overhead and opportunity cost that triggered a devastating economic ratchet and a social catastrophe.

The next two sections examine in more detail the costs of regulation, and the character of regulatory failure.

5.4 Estimating the cost of management

Although the Black–Scholes formalism for financial options trading fails in practice for fundamental reasons (e.g., Derman and Taleb 2005; Haug and Taleb 2011), the methodology is of interest as a conceptual model. The central purpose of the approach is to eliminate or mitigate the effects of unpredictability – noise – in relations like Equation (5.2) or, more to the point, a regulated or managed system like Equation (3.31).

Consider the example of a stock price S, determined by the stochastic differential equation

$$dS_t=\mu\,S_t dt + b\,S_t dW_t$$

(5.10)

where dW_t is now ordinary white noise.

Given a known payoff function $V(S,t)$, one uses the Ito formula to define another SDE, in the usual manner. Now define a 'portfolio function' as the Legendre transform of V;

$$\Pi = -V + S\,\partial V/\partial S$$

(5.11)

Manipulation, using the derived SDE for V, gives the result that

$$\Delta\Pi = (-\partial V/\partial t - \frac{1}{2}b^2S^2\partial^2V/\partial S^2)\Delta t$$

(5.12)

which 'eliminates' the noise term by incorporating b into the final, non-stochastic, partial differential equation. Setting $\Delta\Pi/\Delta t \propto \Pi$, and a little more algebra, leads to the classic Black–Scholes equation for V.

The question arises whether a culturally sculpted, farmed economic ecosystem can apply similar hedging strategies to mitigate the effects of noise. This will ultimately provide an estimate of management costs in the presence of noise.

The change in average distortion between regulatory intent and effect with time can be seen as representing the dynamics of the Rate Distortion Function (RDF) characterizing the disjunction between the intent of a managing farmer and the actual responses of the farmed economic ecosystem or, indeed, of a relatively isolated subcomponent. Let R_t be the RDF at time t. The relation can, under conditions of both white noise and volatility, be expressed as

$$dR_t = f(t, R_t) dt + \beta R_t dW_t \tag{5.13}$$

where β represents added, internal 'regulatory noise' in addition to the channel noise σ^2. This is a consequence of the fact that regulation takes place across the entire firm, adding another level of organization through which signals must be transmitted.

Let $M(R_t, t)$ represent the rate of free energy cost, by some measure that may include opportunity cost, associated with R_t and expand using the Ito chain rule:

$$dM_t = [\partial M / \partial t + f(R_t, t) \partial M / \partial R + \frac{1}{2} \beta^2 R_t^2 \partial^2 M / \partial R^2] dt$$
$$+ [\beta R_t \partial M / \partial R] dW_t \tag{5.14}$$

Again, define Π as the Legendre transform of the free energy consumption rate M, an entropy index, having the form

$$\Pi = -M + R \partial M / \partial R \tag{5.15}$$

Using the heuristic of replacing dX with ΔX in these expressions, and applying the results of Equation (5.14), produces an exact analog to Equation (5.12):

$$\Delta \Pi = (-\partial M / \partial t - \frac{1}{2} \beta^2 R^2 \partial^2 M / \partial R^2) \Delta t \tag{5.16}$$

Again, precisely as in the Black–Scholes calculation, the terms in f and dW_t cancel out, giving a noiseless relation, or rather, one in which the effects of noise are subsumed in the Ito correction involving β. Clearly, however, the approach invokes powerful regularity assumptions on noise structure that may often be violated. Matters then revolve about model robustness in the face of such violation.

Π, as the Legendre transform of the free energy measure M, is a kind of entropy index that can be expected to reach a constant level at nonequilibrium steady state. There, $\Delta \Pi / \Delta t = \partial M / \partial t = 0$, and we obtain the final relation:

$$-\frac{1}{2} \beta^2 R^2 \partial^2 M / \partial R^2 = 0 \tag{5.17}$$

Thus, at nonequilibrium steady state,

$$M_{nss} = \kappa_1 R_{nss} + \kappa_2 \tag{5.18}$$

in first order, and the cost of regulation or management, depending on the scale of observation, can grow very rapidly with increases in channel capacity, or, conversely, decline in the average distortion between regulatory intent and effect: κ_1 can is expected to be very large indeed.

Taking a distortion approach provides a different perspective that, when merged with the results of this section, permits estimate of management or regulatory costs in the presence of noise.

More elaborate models emerge taking $\Delta \Pi / \Delta t = f(\Pi), g(R)$ for appropriate functions.

5.5 The distortion model

The rate distortion function places limits on information source uncertainty. Thus average distortion measures D can drive information system dynamics as well as $R(D)$, via the convexity relation. Recall that the rate distortion function itself has a homological relation to free energy density, in the sense of Feynman (2000) and Bennett (1988), and one can apply Onsager methods using D as a driving parameter.

Again, the motivation for this approach is the argument of equations (3.18–3.20) for a Gaussian channel.

Let $G(M)$ represent a monotonic increasing function of the free energy consumption rate M. Then a plausible generalization of Equation (3.19), in the presence of an internal regulatory noise in addition to the channel noise defined by σ^2, is

$$dD_t = (\frac{\mu}{2D_t} - G(M))dt + \frac{\beta^2}{2} D_t dW_t \qquad (5.19)$$

This has the nonequilibrium steady state expectation

$$D_{nss} = \frac{\mu}{2G(M)} = \sigma^2 \exp[-2R_{nss}] \qquad (5.20)$$

for a Gaussian channel, representing the massive levels of free energy consumption needed to limit distortion between the intent and effect of regulation: M can be expected to increase very sharply with rise in G.

Recapitulating the argument of Section 3.14, and using the Ito chain rule on Equation (5.19), one can calculate the variance in the distortion as $E(D_t^2) - (E(D_t))^2$.

Letting $Y_t = D_t^2$ and applying the Ito relation,

$$dY_t = [2\sqrt{Y_t}(\frac{\mu}{2\sqrt{Y_t}} - G(M)) + \frac{\beta^4}{4} Y_t]dt + \beta^2 Y_t dW_t \qquad (5.21)$$

where $(\beta^4/4)Y_t$ is the Ito correction to the time term of the SDE.

Again, a little algebra shows that no real number solution for the expectation of $Y_t = D_t^2$ can exist unless the discriminant of the resulting quadratic equation is ≥ 0, so that

$$G(M) \geq \frac{\beta^2}{2} \sqrt{\mu} \qquad (5.22)$$

From equations (5.20) and (5.22),

$$G(M) = \frac{\mu}{2\sigma^2} \exp[2R_{nss}] \geq \frac{\beta^2}{2}\sqrt{\mu} \tag{5.23}$$

Solving, using Equation (5.18), gives the necessary conditions

$$R_{nss} \geq (1/2)\log(\sigma^2\beta^2 / \sqrt{\mu})$$

$$M_{nss} \geq \frac{\kappa_1}{2}\log[\frac{\beta^2\sigma^2}{\sqrt{\mu}}] + \kappa_2 \tag{5.24}$$

for there to be a real second moment in D. κ_1 is, again, expected to be very large indeed. Given the context of this analysis, failure to provide adequate rates of free energy, M, necessary for the minimum channel capacity defined by R_{nss}, would represent the onset of a regulatory catastrophe, a massive 'crop failure,' as it were.

Many variants of the model are possible. The most natural, perhaps, is to view M as a free energy measure *per unit external perturbation* That is, $\hat{M} \equiv d\hat{M}/dK$, where $\hat{M}$ is now perceived as the rate of free energy consumption needed to meet an external perturbation of (normalized) magnitude K. Then the condition of Equation (5.24), now on $\hat{M}$, becomes

$$\hat{M} \geq \int[\frac{\kappa_1}{2}\log[\frac{\beta^2\sigma^2}{\sqrt{\mu}}] + \kappa_2]dK \tag{5.25}$$

Under constant conditions, for stability, the system must supply the free energy index at a rate

$$\hat{M} \geq [\frac{\kappa_1}{2}\log[\frac{\beta^2\sigma^2}{\sqrt{\mu}}] + \kappa_2]\Delta K \tag{5.26}$$

where ΔK is the magnitude of the imposed perturbation. Thus the demand on free energy created by imposed perturbations can be greatly amplified, in this model, suggesting that erosion of stability by public policy or other externalities can make the system more sensitive to the impact of 'natural' shocks in accordance, it would seem, with observations on the recent US banking industry collapse, or on the famous earlier failure of a hedge fund run by winners of the Nobel Prize in Economics.

Extension of the argument to other forms of Rate Distortion Function is direct. For example, the relation for the natural channel is $R(D) \approx \sigma^2/D$, giving a condition based on the discriminant of a cubic in Equation (5.22).

Diversion of essential resources from fundamental economic activities can be expected to markedly increase both β and σ, leading to the kind of crop failures that are described in the next chapter: under conditions of increasing imposed noise, it becomes impossible to provide rates of free energy – meet high costs and opportunity costs – needed to manage a complex firm or a large interacting economic ecosystem of firms.

5.6 The data-rate theorem

The recently formalized data-rate theorem a generalization of the classic Bode integral theorem for linear control systems (e.g., Yu and Mehta 2010; Csete and Doyle 2002), describes the stability of linear feedback control under data rate constraints (e.g., Mitter 2001; Tatikonda and Mitter 2004; Sahai 2004; Sahai and Mitter 2006; Minero et al. 2009; Nair et al. 2007; You and Xie 2013). Given a noise-free data link between a discrete linear plant and its controller, unstable modes can be stabilized only if the feedback data rate $\mathcal{H}$ is greater than the rate of 'topological information' generated by the unstable system. For the simplest incarnation, if the linear matrix equation of the plant is of the form $x_{t+1} = \mathbf{A}x_t + ...,$ where x_t is the n-dimensional state vector at time t, then the necessary condition for stabilizability is

$$\mathcal{H} > \log[|det\mathbf{A}^u|] \tag{5.27}$$

where det is the determinant and $\mathbf{A}^u$ is the decoupled unstable component of $\mathbf{A}$, i.e., the part having eigenvalues ≥ 1.

The essential matter is that there is a critical positive data rate for control signals below which there does not exist any quantization and control scheme able to stabilize an unstable (linear) feedback system.

This result, and its variations, are as fundamental as the Shannon Coding and Source Coding Theorems, and the Rate Distortion Theorem (Cover and Thomas 2006; Ash 1990; Khinchin 1957).

Clearly, Equation (5.24) constitutes a version of the DRT, in the particular context of this analysis. Inherently unstable systems can only be stabilized by control signals of sufficient magnitude characterized by the channel capacity defined by R_{nss} from Equation (5.24).

The results for the 'natural' channel, having $R(D) \approx \sigma^2/D$, are analogous, driven by the convexity of R in D, but more complicated. A full calculation is given in the Mathematical Appendix.

Socioeconomic systems are, by virtue of the potential ease of transition between nonequilibrium quasi-steady states, inherently unstable, and must be strongly regulated to prevent unwanted or unexpected transitions.

This is a fundamental result, with deep implications across economics.

5.7 Phase transitions reconsidered

Recall something of the arguments of Section 3.10. Equations (5.24–5.26) have fundamental implications for socal network dynamics, structure, and stability, in a large sense that includes institutions, firms, and criminal enterprise. Granovetter (1973) characterizes network function in terms of 'the strength of weak ties.' 'Strong' ties, to adapt his perspective, disjointly partition a network into indentifiable submodules. 'Weak' ties reach across such disjoint partitioning, i.e., they are linkages that do not disjointly partition a social network, institution, or firm. The average probability of such weak ties, at least in a random network, defines the fraction of network nodes that will be in a 'giant component' that links the vast majority of nodes. It is well known that the occurrence of such a component is a punctuated event. That is, there is a critical value of the average probability of weak ties below which there are only individual fragments. Figure 3.2 and the surrounding arguments provide something of an introduction, in the context of interacting cognitive submodules that, here, represent the distributed cognition of the full enterprise. A more extended discussion can be found in Wallace and Fullilove (2008).

It seems clear that the maintenance of such weak ties, allowing large-scale distributed cognition, depends critically on the investment of regulatory free energy at rates M or $\hat{M}$. That is, keeping the channels of communication open in an enterprise under fire will require greater and greater rates of free energy investment.

M and $\hat{M}$ can, however, also be interpreted as intensity indices analogous to a generalized temperature. Identifiable submodules within the organization define equivalence classes leading to a groupoid symmetry as described in the Mathematical Appendix. This leads toward something much like Landau's perspective on phase transition. In this context, Equations (5.24–5.26) can be interpreted as defining the 'temperature' M or $\hat{M}$ (or the channel capacity driven by R) at which a complex network of interacting cognitive submodules breaks down into a simpler groupoid structure of disjointly partitioned submodules.

5.8 Evolutionary game dynamics

As discussed in Chapter 2, evolutionary game theory by contrast to the approach of this work, is supposed to provide both a necessary and sufficient model for evolutionary process, according the the famous replicator equation of Taylor and Jonker (1978). Here we follow closely the arguments of Roca et al. (2009). Given an evolutionary game with payoff matrix W, the dynamics of the distribution of strategy frequencies, x_i as elements of a vector $\mathbf{x}$, is determined by the relation

$$dx_i/dt = x_i[(W\mathbf{x})_i - \mathbf{x}^T W\mathbf{x}] \tag{5.28}$$

where the term $\mathbf{x}^T W\mathbf{x}$ ensures that $\Sigma x_i = 1$. Dynamical systems theory then derives the consequences, noting that an appropriate change of variables converts this equation into a system of the Lotka-Volterra type.

Several assumptions are implicit to this perspective:

1   The population is infinitely large.
2   Individuals meet randomly or play against each other, such that the payoff strategy is proportional to the payoff averaged over the current population state.
3   There are no mutations, so that strategies increase or decrease in frequency only due to reproduction.
4   The variation of the population is linear in the payoff difference.

Roca et al. (2009) find the approach seriously lacking:

> Evolutionary game dynamics is one of the most fruitful frameworks for studying evolution in different disciplines, from Biology to Economics. Within this context, the approach of choice for many researchers is the so-called replicator equation, that describes mathematically the idea that those individuals performing better have more offspring and thus their frequency in the population grows. While very many interesting results have been obtained with this equation in the three decades elapsed since it was first proposed, it is important to realize the limits of its applicability. One particularly relevant issue in this respect is that of non-mean-field effect, that may arise from temporal fluctuations or from spatial correlations, both neglected in the replicator equation ... [T]hese temporal and spatial effects [introduce] non-trivial modifications when compared to the outcome of replicator dynamics [as do questions of nonlinearity] ...

The necessary conditions, regression model-like, dynamic approach we have introduced here can incorporate both spatial structure and temporal fluctuation in a natural manner, although at the evident expense of assumptions of sufficiency.

5.9 Summary

As remarked in Chapter 2, the inherently self-referential nature of any generalized Darwinian evolutionary process is truly remarkable. While dependent on indices of available free energy and constrained by physical principles and historical trajectory, raw evolution is a language that speaks itself. For example, 'available free energy,' written as M above, can itself be an evolutionary product, as, in biological systems, with the aerobic transition. In socioeconomic terms, the acquisition of fire, domestication of farm animals for plowing, development of road systems enabling transfer, hence increased availability of existing energy and resources, development of steam technology, use of fossil fuels, and so on, provide examples. The formal description of such bootstrapping will require more comprehensive methods than are available by abduction from relatively simple physical theory.

Consideration suggests, however, that changes of indices representing available free energy can be a necessary, but not sufficient, condition for eukaryotic-like transitions to greater complexity, or, inversely for large-scale structural collapse, as described at some length in Chapters 7, 8, and 9.

We find that socioeconomic dynamics are inherently unstable, albeit in the context of local nonequilibrium quasi-stable modes. The Data Rate Theorem implies that a minimal threshold of regulatory control is necessary for stability, formalizing draconian empirical results across the last century.

6 Cambrian explosions and mass extinctions

6.1 Introduction

Evolutionary scientists have explored in detail the 'Cambrian explosion' of half a billion years ago, a punctuated change in the diversity of life (e.g., Erwin and Valentine 2013; Gould 2002; Marshall 2006; Whittington 1985). Elsewhere (Wallace 2014), we demonstrate that a relatively modest exercise in evolutionary theory accounts neatly for such 'explosions' early on, before path-dependent lock-in of essential biochemical, gene regulation, and more generally biological, Bauplans. Analogously, mass extinction events have also received much attention (e.g., Newman 1997; Schinazi 2005). Similar discussions, under the rubric 'punctuated equilibrium,' have, of course, long been in the literature (e.g., Gould 2002, and references therein). Here, taking the formal approach of Chapter 2 to evolutionary process in socioeconomic systems, we apply these ideas to institutional phenomena, a matter of some considerable ongoing interest (e.g., Beinhocker 2006; Bartolozzi et al. 2006).

Chapter 2 proposes a set of necessary conditions statistical models extending evolutionary theory to socioeconomic process via the asymptotic limit theorems of communication theory. The method represents the embedding 'ecosystem,' corporate heritage, and the cognitive behavior of the firm, as interacting information sources. A fundamental insight is that institutional cognitive behavior can be associated with a 'dual' information source, while the embedding environment's systematic regularities 'remember' imposed changes, resulting in a coevolutionary process in the sense of Champagnat et al. (2006) that is recorded jointly in corporate heritage, corporate cognition, and the embedding environment.

The focus here is more particularly on the effect of 'large deviations' representing transitions between the quasi-stable modes of such systems that are analogous to game-theoretic Evolutionary Stable Strategies. Evolutionary path dependence, in general, limits such possible excursions to high probability sequences consistent with, if not originating in, previous evolutionary trajectories. For example, after some three billion years, as most multicellular organisms evolve, they retain their basic Bauplan, with only relatively small non-fatal variations currently allowed.

We are interested in matters under which path dependence is not solidly locked-in against possible large deviations excursions.

In essence, a sufficiently large number of allowed large deviation trajectories leads, consequently, to many available quasi-equilibrium states. These, in turn, can be treated as an ensemble, i.e., in a manner similar to the statistical mechanics perspective on critical phenomena. This allows a new approach to rapid evolutionary change.

That is, while incorporation of long-term path dependence drastically reduces possible evolutionary dynamics, institutional evolutionary trajectories can be driven by a 'noise' defined as much by policy and alteration in socioeconomic structure as by heritage reassortment and generation time.

6.2 Another variant of the basic model

Following Chapter 2, assume there are n 'firms' interacting with an embedding environment represented by an information source Z. The corporate heritage and cognitive institutional processes associated with each firm i are represented as information sources X_i, Y_i respectively. These undergo a 'coevolutionary' interaction in the sense of Champagnat et al. (2006), producing a joint information source uncertainty (Cover and Thomas 2006) for the full system as

$$H(X_1, Y_1, ..., X_n, Y_n, Z) \tag{6.1}$$

Again, Feynman's (2000) insight that information is a form of free energy allows definition of an entropy-analog as

$$S \equiv H - Q_j \, \Sigma_j \partial \, H / \partial \, Q_j \tag{6.2}$$

The Q_j are taken as driving parameters that may include, but are not limited to, the Shannon uncertainties of the underlying information sources.

Again, and in the spirit of Champagnat et al. (2006), we characterize the dynamics of the system in terms of Onsager-like nonequilibrium thermodynamics in the gradients of S as the set of stochastic differential equations (e.g., de Groot and Mazur 1984),

$$dQ_t^i = L_i(\partial S / \partial Q^1 ... \partial S / \partial Q^m, t)dt + \sum_k \sigma_k^i(\partial S / \partial Q^1 ... \partial S / \partial Q^m, t)dB_k \tag{6.3}$$

where the B_k represent noise terms having particular forms of quadratic variation. The relation can be more simply written as

$$dQ_t^i = L_i(\mathbf{Q}, t)dt + \Sigma_k \sigma_k^i(\mathbf{Q}, t)dB_k \tag{6.4}$$

where $\mathbf{Q} \equiv (Q^1, ..., Q^m)$.

Recapitulating earlier arguments, this is a coevolutionary structure, where fundamental dynamics are determined by component interactions:

1   Setting the expectation of equation (6.4) equal to zero and solving for stationary points gives attractor states since the noise terms preclude

unstable equilibria. These are analogous to the evolutionarily stable states of evolutionary game theory.

2   This system may, however, converge to limit cycle or pseudorandom 'strange attractor' behaviors similar to thrashing in which the system seems to chase its tail endlessly within a limited venue – the 'Red Queen.'

3   What is 'converged' to in any case is not a simple state or limit cycle of states. Rather it is an equivalence class, or set of them, of highly dynamic information sources coupled by mutual interaction through crosstalk and other interactions. Thus 'stability' in this structure represents particular patterns of ongoing dynamics rather than some identifiable static configuration, analogous to the nonequilibrium steady state of physical theory.

4   Applying Ito's chain rule for stochastic differential equations to the $(Q_t^j)^2$ and taking expectations allows calculation of variances. These may depend very powerfully on a system's defining structural constants, leading to significant instabilities (Khasminskii 2012), explored more fully below.

Again recapitulating the arguments of Section 5.2, Equation (6.4) is subject to large deviations that can themselves be described as the output of an information source L_D driving or defining Q^j–parameters that can trigger punctuated shifts between quasi-stable system modes.

Not all large deviations are possible: only those consistent with the high probability paths defined by the information source L_D will take place.

Again, from the Shannon-McMillan Theorem (Khinchin 1957), the output streams of an information source can be divided into two sets, one very large that represents nonsense statements of vanishingly small probability, and one very small of high probability representing those statements consistent with the inherent 'grammar' and 'syntax' of the information source. Again, whatever higher-order evolution takes place, some equivalent of the firm's 'backbone' remains.

Thus we could now rewrite Equation (6.1) as

$$H_L(X_1, Y_1, ..., X_n, Y_n, Z, L_D) \qquad\qquad (6.6)$$

where we have explicitly incorporated the 'large deviations' information source L_D that defines high probability evolutionary excursions for this system.

Again carrying out the argument leading to Equation (6.4), we arrive at another set of quasi-stable modes, but possibly very much changed in number; either branched outward in time by a wave of corporate speciation or splitting, or decreased through a wave of extinctions, aquisitions, or mergers. Iterating the models backwards in time constitutes a cladistic or coalescent analysis.

6.3 Simple extinction

Shifting perspective, somewhat, an extinction model leads to significant extension of the theory.

Let $N_t \geq 0$ represent the magnitude of a firm's essential resource (e.g., 'capitalization,' 'sales,' etc.) at time t, for example that of a buggy-whip manufacturer at the dawn of the automobile age. The simplest dynamic model, in this formulation, is then something like

$$dN_t = -\alpha\, N_t |N_t - N_C| dt + \sigma\, N_t dW_t \tag{6.6}$$

where N_C is the equivalent of an ecological carrying capacity, α is a characteristic time constant, σ is a 'noise' index, and dW_t represents white noise.

Taking the expectation of Equation (6.6), the possible steady state values of N_t are either zero or N_C. Applying the Ito chain rule (Protter 1990) to the second moment in N_t, i.e., to N_t^2, a somewhat lengthy calculation finds there can be no real second moment unless

$$\sigma^2 < 2\alpha\, N_C \tag{6.7}$$

That is, unless Equation (6.7) holds – the product of the rate of resource change and carrying capacity is sufficiently large – noise-driven fluctuations will inevitably drive the corporate species to extinction.

A similar SDE approach has been used to model noise-driven criticality in physical systems (Horsthemeke and Lefever 2006; Van den Broeck et al. 1994, 1997), suggesting that a more conventional phase transition methodology may provide particular insight.

6.4 Relaxing path-dependence

In general, under stable conditions, the number of quasi-equilibria available to a system defined by Equation (6.4), or to its generalization via Equation (6.5), will be relatively small, a consequence of long-term lock-in by path dependent evolutionary process. However, under suddenly relaxed conditions – for example the introduction of some new, revolutionary technology, the economic enfranchisement of a previously excluded population, and so on – the speciation/extinction large deviations information source L_D is far less constrained, and there will be very many possible quasi-stable states available for transition, analogous to an ensemble in statistical mechanics.

The noise parameter in Equation (6.6) can, from the arguments of the previous section, then be interpreted as a kind of temperature-analog, and N_t as an order parameter that, like magnetization or ice crystal form, vanishes above a critical value of σ. This leads to a relatively simple statistical mechanics analog built on the H_L of Equation (6.5).

Define a pseudoprobability for quasi-stable mode j as

$$P_j = \frac{\exp[-H_L^j / \kappa\sigma]}{\sum_i \exp[-H_L^i / \kappa\sigma]} \tag{6.8}$$

where κ is a scaling constant and σ is a noise intensity.

Next, define a Morse Function F, in the sense used by Pettini (2007), as

$$\exp[-F/\kappa\,\sigma] \equiv \Sigma_i \exp[-H_L^i/\kappa\,\sigma] \tag{6.9}$$

Apply Pettini's topological hypothesis to F, taking N_j, the number of members of species (or quasi-species) j as a kind of 'order parameter' in Landau's sense (Landau and Lifshitz 2007). Then σ is seen as a very general temperature-like measure whose changes drive punctuated topological alterations in the underlying ecological and coevolutionary structures associated with the Morse Function F.

Such topological changes, following Pettini's arguments, can be far more general than indexed by the simple Landau-type critical point phase transition in an order parameter.

6.5 Implications

The topological changes inherent in a relaxed path-dependence model can represent a great variety of fundamental and highly punctuated coevolutionary alterations, since the underlying 'species' and 'quasi-species' are not so sharply limited by path-dependent evolutionary trajectory in the manner that constrains variation under very stable circumstances.

That is, under an assumption of less lock-in constraint, such a model accounts well for the observed 'Cambrian Bauplan' explosions associated with steam power, the industrial revolution, the development of the automobile, the onset of the various electric and electronics revolutions, and so on.

According to our model, the degree of punctuation in evolutionary punctuated equilibrium (Gould 2002) will depend strongly on the richness of the distribution of nonequilibrium quasi-steady states to be associated with Equation (6.4). 'Cambrian explosions' therefore require a dense statistical ensemble of them, our analog to the 'roughening of the fitness landscape' described as necessary for biological explosions (e.g., Marshall 2006; Kauffman 1996, p. 205).

The 'noise,' in general, may represent a kind of socioeconomic or technological isolation, via separation by geographic or socioecological niche, that can be suddenly lifted. Permitting greater interaction – lowering σ – may then trigger rapid coevolutionary transitions, an inverse, as it were, of the observations of Hanski et al. (2013) on increasing species extinction via habitat fragmentation.

By contrast, raising σ, for example, by economic disenfranchisement of significant population sectors, or by the hyperconcentration of wealth in limited venues, can act to constrain interaction, triggering large-scale, punctuated economic decline, an analog to a biological mass extinction event.

The general inference is that, in the absence of severe path-dependent lock-in, Cambrian explosions and mass extinctions can be common features of socioeconomic evolutionary process, representing expected outliers in the ongoing routine of evolutionary punctuated equilibrium. Their rates and magnitudes, however, appear to be strongly determined by social policy, according to the arguments of the Data Rate Theorem.

6.6 Hierarchies of intermediate scale

The theory presented in this chapter has focused on two asymptotic limits, i.e., individual species, and statistical ensembles, for which mathematical modeling is straightforward. Typically, however, as Holling (1973, 1992) has noted, ecosystems are highly organized at intermediate scales, and he has introduced the idea of a 'keystone' mesoscale level whose dynamics resonate both upward and downward, driving lower and higher levels of organization.

Such structure is difficult to treat mathematically, and may indeed involve complex hierarchical forms of interacting individual keystones that, acting as one or more *keystone systems*, drive smaller and larger dynamics. Identifying and reconstructing such keystone systems – presuming they exist – would probably be the simplest way of farming an economic ecology. This clearly involves a difficult set of empirical questions whose resolution almost certainly varies greatly across both culture and local historical trajectory.

The simplest direct analysis would invoke a standard block-diagonalization of crosstalk correlation matrices, perhaps involving exchanges of commodities, monies, information, travel, or some composite index of these, between different economic sectors. Again, the problem of coarsegraining to appropriate scales becomes central.

Here, however, the idea would be to construct a correlation matrix between quasi-stable modes, parceling them out by block-diagonalization to create a hierarchical picture of the stability structure.

6.7 Summary

The 'Cambrian explosion' 500 million years ago saw a relatively sudden proliferation of organism Bauplan and ecosystem niche structure. Here, adapting standard methods from information theory and statistical mechanics, we model the socioeconomic versions of the phenomenon as noise-driven phase transitions, in the context of deep-time relaxation of path-dependent evolutionary constraints. In the absence of severe path-dependent lock-in, Cambrian explosions can be expected as standard features of socioeconomic and other evolutionary process, representing outliers in an ongoing routine of evolutionary punctuated equilibrium. By contrast, the model also illustrates how rising economic disenfranchisement, or the hyperconcentration of wealth in a limited venue, can trigger widespread, punctuated, economic extinctions. While the two asymptotic limits studied here provide insight, extension of the theory to hierarchies of intermediate scale is urgently needed.

7 Counterexample: the Pentagon ratchet

This chapter includes a condensation of previously unpublished material written in collaboration with John E. Ullmann, Hofstra University.

7.1 A matter of context

In 1989 the MIT Commission on Industrial Productivity published the best-selling book ever produced by the MIT press. Titled *Made in America: Regaining the Productive Edge*, the book, according to the publisher's blurb,

> [F]ocuses on the reorganization and effective integration of human resources and new technologies within the firm as a principal driving force for long term growth in productivity … [It] singles out the most significant productivity weaknesses … These include short-time horizons and a preoccupation with the bottom line, outdated strategies that focus excessively on the domestic market, lack of cooperation within and among U.S. firms, neglect of human resources, technological failures in translating discoveries to products, and a mismatch between governmental actions and the needs of industry.

The book 'became a landmark in public debates about the U.S. economy' (PIE Report 2013).

From 1989 through 2011, however, US manufacturing employment declined from 18 million to less than 12 million, most precipitously after 2000, in the context of supposedly massive computer and internet-related 'innovations.'

Given the continued debacle, in 2010 MIT convened a similar effort, the 'MIT Production in the Innovation Economy' research group, whose report, titled *Production in the Innovation Economy: Making in America*, is profiled by the MIT press as 'Inspired by the MIT *Made in America* project of the 1980s.'

One of the participants (Bonvillian 2013), describing the results, makes a truly remarkable assertion:

> One part of the U.S. innovation system – the defense sector – has worked at both the front and back ends [of industrial production dynamics], undertaking R&D; prototyping; demonstration; test beds; and, through product

procurement, often initial market creation. This system jumpstarted key innovation waves of the 20th century: aviation, electronics, space, computing, and the Internet With the decline in defense procurement and R&D support in the post-Cold War era, this innovation role has become less central

As has been said, those who do not remember the past are condemned to repeat it.

Here, we examine the 800-pound gorilla-in-the-bedroom that both MIT working groups seem deliberately to have ignored: how a Gosplan-like Pentagon Capitalism drove the industrial collapse of the United States.

7.2 Introduction

Adapting the perspective of the previous chapters – in particular of Section 3.10, the 'cost' calculations of Equation (5.24), and the implications of Equation (6.9) – we study the effects of a distinctly counterproductive economic 'farming' strategy, the massive diversion of US technical and financial resources into the Cold War. The case history provides a clearer view of how firms and technology can become closely intertwined in a highly punctuated coevolutionary process. This can, on the one hand, produce a firm-and-technology complex subject to a self-dynamic 'Red Queen' requiring constant development of technology, and the availability of related capital, for the system to persist in the face of competition. The same mechanism, however, enables an inverse, a 'Pentagon Ratchet' as a similarly self-dynamic process for rapid economic decline if significant technical and fiscal resources are diverted from the system.

Establishment of a draconian military-centered planned economy in the US after WWII, the creation of a 'Pentagon Capitalism,' absorbed sufficient capital and technology from civilian enterprise to kill the Red Queen and enable the Ratchet. Relatively sudden, large-scale 'Rust Belt' deindustrialization followed as a punctuated 'ecosystem resilience' transition akin to a phase change. This has triggered a balance of payments catastrophe and related stresses compromising national security.

A considerable body of work in evolutionary economics (e.g., Nelson 1995; Hodgson 1993), suggests that firms and technology are closely integrated 'coevolutionary objects' whose time dynamics are very complicated in comparison with the predictions of equilibrium-based models derived from eighteenth century analogies with mechanical system (Lawson 2006).

Nelson (1995) finds that, to be effective, a firm needs a package of routines, including those concerned with learning and innovation, that are 'coherent,' imposing a certain rigidity on them. Competencies, according to Nelson (1995), tend to come in strongly intercorrelated complementary packages of traits, and successful firms are difficult to imitate effectively because a competitor must adopt a number of different intercorrelated practices at once. This is a reason why firms that do well in one context may have difficulty in adapting to a new one. Firms must, of course, also persist in time, replicating themselves as coherent patterns of human and organizational behavior.

Technology, of course, is an integrated body of knowledge and technique passed on from one time and group to others by processes ranging from direct teaching to sociogeographic diffusion, both of which are forms of (approximate) self-replication.

Nelson's invocation of coevolutionary interaction between firms and technology is similar to recent theorizing in human evolution, that envisions genes and culture as having become a joint coevolutionary object.

Durham (1991) summarizes the current opinion:

> [G]enes and culture constitute two distinct but interacting systems of information inheritance within human populations ... [and] information of both kinds has influence, actual or potential, over behaviors [which] creates a real and unambiguous symmetry between genes and [human] phenotypes on the one hand, and culture and phenotypes on the other ...
>
> [G]enes and culture are best represented as two parallel lines or 'tracks' of hereditary influence on phenotypes

Natural systems subject to coevolutionary interaction may become enmeshed in the 'Red Queen' dilemma of Alice in Wonderland, in that they must undergo constant evolutionary change in order to avoid extinction – they must constantly run just to stay in the same place.

An example would be a competitive arms race between a highly specialized predator and its prey. Each evolutionary advance in predation must be met with a coevolutionary adaptation which allows the prey to avoid the more efficient predation. Otherwise the system will become extinct, since the predator will literally eat itself out of house and home. Similarly, each prey defense must be matched by a predator adaptation for the system to persist.

While natural populations cannot transmit acquired characteristics, human cultures and organizations are well able to do so, and they are able to forget more rapidly than natural systems. Nelson's perspective suggests the possibility of a Red Queen coevolutionary process affecting firms and technology, but also encompasses the possibility of a rapid inverse, a form of economic ratchet we will explore at some length.

The term 'Red Queen' was used to describe economic interaction as early as 1913 (JMC 1913), and Hugh-Jones (1955) made explicit use of it to characterize the US economy:

> The American firm is like the Red Queen, forced to keep running if it is even to remain in the same place in the economic market, and an increase of productivity of from 3 to 3 1/2% a year is necessary to achieve this. A good American executive is one who is divinely discontented with present methods of doing anything and believes that anything he has done, he can do better. It is a state of mind which regards nothing as impossible, but merely taking a little longer than what is only difficult.

Similarly, Krugman (1979) states:

> Northern [US, Canada, W. Europe, Japan] residents depend in part on the rents from their monopoly of newly developed products. This monopoly is continually eroded by technological borrowing and must be maintained by constant innovation of new products. Like Alice and the Red Queen, the developed region must keep running to stay in the same place.

Thus the macroeconomic Red Queen in one form or another, has been recognized for a century.

Previous chapters present a fairly elaborate theory, based on the parameterization of (self-reproducing) ergodic information sources, showing how coevolutionary interactions, their associated dynamic processes, including circular Red Queen processes and related dynamics, can be very highly punctuated, subject to sudden shifts analogous to ecosystem resilience changes.

The context for our analysis is the massive diversion of capital and technological resources from civilian enterprise in the US, the creation of a Pentagon Capitalism (e.g., Melman 1988, 1997; Tirman 1984; Ullmann 1988), that has been the distinguishing hallmark of the postwar economy. The failure to civilianize the economy after World War II caused an essentially finite technological capacity – Guns or Butter – to be split in a zero-sum game, 'Internet' and 'space program' spillovers to the contrary.

Resulting collapse in the competitiveness of US industry has been catastrophic and is well documented (Melman 1961, 1971, 1983, 1988, 1997; Dumas 1986; Ullmann 1985, 1988). The failure to technologically renew heavy manufacturing, consumer electronics, automobile and other industries has cost stable, unionized jobs throughout the Rust Belt and triggered a balance of payments catastrophe as the US became the dumping ground of choice for the output of Asian Tiger economies, themselves entrained by our precipitate and continuing decline, forming an unstable mutualistic complex.

We study the linked interaction of firms and technology in which the richness of the 'internal language' of each affects the other, that is, when firms and technology have become one another's primary environments. This leads directly and naturally to a coevolutionary Red Queen, but, when acquired characteristics are inherited, to a rapid inverse, a highly punctuated 'Pentagon Ratchet,' as well.

7.3 Red Queen and Pentagon ratchet

Taking the perspective of the previous chapters, envision firms and technology as subject to a coevolutionary Red Queen, treating their respective source uncertainties as recursively parameterized by each other. That is, the internal cultures of a firm and its associated technology base are each other's primary environments. These are, respectively, characterized by information sources $\mathbf{X}$ and $\mathbf{Y}$, whose uncertainties, taking $\mathcal{H}_X \equiv 1/H[\mathbf{X}]$ and $\mathcal{H}_Y \equiv 1/H[\mathbf{Y}]$, interact as

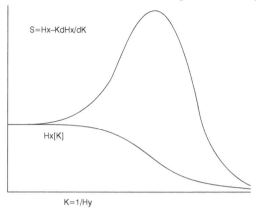

Figure 7.1 A reverse-S-shaped curve for source uncertainty $H[\mathbf{X}]$ – measuring 'language richness' – as a function of the parameter $K=1/H[\mathbf{Y}]$ for some information source $\mathbf{Y}$. Under such conditions, a Red Queen dynamic can become enabled, driving the system strongly to the left. On the other hand, under such circumstances, a policy-driven decline in $H[\mathbf{Y}]$, following the example of equation 3.12, triggers a Pentagon Ratchet, driving the system to an ecosystem resilience transition. The stationary point to the left of the peak in the Legendre transform S is only quasi-stable, representing the Onsager mechanism of the previous chapters.

$$H[\mathbf{X}] = H[\mathcal{H}_Y, \mathbf{X}]$$
$$H[\mathbf{Y}] = H[\mathcal{H}_X, \mathbf{Y}] \tag{7.1}$$

Assume a strongly heritable system for which $H[\mathbf{X}]$ follows a reverse S-shaped curve of Figure 7.1 with $K \equiv \mathcal{H}_Y$, and similarly $H[\mathbf{Y}]$ depends on $\mathcal{H}_X$. That is, increase or decline in the source uncertainty of technology leads to increase or decline in the source uncertainty of the heritable culture of associated firms, and vice versa. The 'richness' of the internal languages of firms and their technologies are closely linked.

Start at the right of Figure 7.1 for $H[\mathbf{X}]$, the source uncertainty of the firm. Assume some improvement in technology is introduced: $H[\mathbf{Y}]$ increases, reflecting the ability to 'say more things' through the increment caused by the new technology, so $\mathcal{H}_Y$ decreases, and thus $H[\mathbf{X}]$ increases, walking up the curve of Figure 7.1 from the right: the richness of the firm's internal language increases. The increase of $H[\mathbf{X}]$ leads, in turn, to an increased capacity of the system to improve its technological base, thus a decline in $\mathcal{H}_X$ triggers an increase of $H[\mathbf{Y}]$, whose increase leads to a further increase of $H[\mathbf{X}]$ and vice versa. This is the Red Queen, taking the system from the right of Figure 7.1 to the left, against the Onsager 'force' generated by the gradient in the Legendre transform S in Figure 7.1.

At the population level, firms undergoing such a dynamic may be expected to become more highly efficient, and thus survive selection by economic competition.

Now enlarge the scale of the argument, and consider the possibility of national-level interactions between the overall structure of civilian firms and technology, i.e., the possibility of national-scale Red Queens. Clearly, the country with the most efficient such coevolutionary structure gains competitive strength in the global marketplace.

Diverting technology and capital from a nation's civilian to military enterprise, however, slows the national-scale Red Queen, via the 'noise' mechanisms characterized by Equations (5.24) or (6.9), giving a significant advantage to less-militarized economies. Competitive exclusion ensues, with the militarized national economy buying cheaper, more sophisticated civilian goods abroad. This further enervates the domestic coevolutionary linkage, leading in turn to even more dynamic mechanisms of national decline: start with an initially strongly linked coevolutionary civilian economy, a national system with $H[\mathbf{X}]$ at the far left of Figure 7.1.

Technological resources are taken from civilian industry, according to a policy reflecting an information source in the sense of Section 3.10 and Equation 3.12, and given to the military, causing declines in global competitiveness. Investment in, and indeed maintenance of, the national civilian technology languishes as imports dominate the domestic market. At some point, $H[\mathbf{Y}]$ actually declines, $\mathcal{H}_Y$ increases and $H[\mathbf{X}]$ decreases as firms lose their 'edge,' causing a further fall in $H[\mathbf{Y}]$. This causes another rapid decline in $H[\mathbf{X}]$, triggering a further decline in $H[\mathbf{Y}]$, and so on, until the system catastrophically collapses. That is, it undergoes a punctuated resilience shift from the quasi-stable region to the left of the peak in the Legendre transform S to another domain to the right of the peak, one that may not, in fact, be quasi-stable.

This is the Pentagon Ratchet leading to very rapid economic extinction under competitive pressures.

The only way to short-circuit such a ratchet mechanism would be to better capitalize the civilian firm-and-technology system, driving the system back to the left: an 'industrial policy' requiring redeployment of capital and technological resources from the military into the civilian sectors. Such reform may, however, face considerable resistance by Onsager mechanisms.

A second perspective is to simply view investment in technology as a form of necessary free energy expenditure under selection pressure, leading directly to the stability conditions of Equations (5.24–5.26). Failure to provide adequate rates of such 'metabolic investment' leads to instability and collapse.

A third perspective, that of Equation (6.9), suggests that increasing 'noise,' here indexed by diversion of resources from civilian industry, can trigger a large-scale phase transition to general economic collapse.

7.4 Fragmentation under ratchet dynamics

What happens on the right hand side of Figure 7.1? How does an economic structure behave during and after the ratchet? Here we address the effect of ratchet rate on the final state of the economic structure. We use the formalism of Section 11.8 of the Mathematical Appendix, following the arguments of Wallace and Fullilove (2008), and expanding on Section 3.10.

Three parameters are taken to describe the relations between an information source and its environment or between different sources. Others might well be chosen, but analogous results follow.

The first, $J \geq 0$, is an inverse measure of the degree to which acquired characteristics are transmitted. For systems without memory, $J=\infty$. $J \approx 0$ thus represents a high degree of inheritance of acquired characteristics.

J will always remain distinguished, a kind of inherent direction or external field strength in the sense of Wilson (1971).

The second parameter, $Q=1/\mathcal{C} \geq 0$, represents the inverse availability of 'capital,' i.e., resources. $Q \approx 0$ thus represents a high ability to renew and maintain a cognitive enterprise.

The third parameter, $K=1/T$, is an inverse index of a 'generalized temperature' T, specified below.

The composite structure of interest is implicitly embedded in, and operates within the context of, a larger manifold stratified by spatial, behavioral or other 'distances.'

Take these as multidimensional vector quantities $\mathbf{A}, \mathbf{B}, \mathbf{C}$. $\mathbf{A}$ may, for example, represent location in space, $\mathbf{B}$ might represent a multivariate analysis of a spectrum of observed behavioral or other factors, in the largest sense, and so on.

It may be possible to reduce the effects of these vectors to a function of their magnitudes $a=|\mathbf{A}|$, $b=|\mathbf{B}|$ and $c=|\mathbf{C}|$, etc. Define a metric R as

$$R^2 = a^2 + b^2 + c^2 + \dots \tag{7.2}$$

Explicitly, an ergodic information source $\mathbf{X}$ is associated with the reproduction and/or persistence of an institution. The source $\mathbf{X}$, its uncertainty $H[J, K, Q, \mathbf{X}]$ and its parameters J, K, Q depend implicitly on the embedding manifold, and in particular on the metric R.

There is a fundamental reason for adding this new layer of complication. Earlier chapters discuss the ubiquity of sudden punctuation in evolutionary process, i.e., relatively rapid, seemingly discontinuous fundamental changes in system structure leading to mass extinctions and/or speciation divergences.

The natural formalism for examination of such punctuation in our context involves application of Wilson's (1971) program of renormalization symmetry – invariance under the renormalization transform – to source uncertainty defined on the R–manifold. The results predict that the transfer of information within an a cognitive enterprise, or between an enterprise and an embedding context, will undergo sudden changes in structure analogous to phase transitions in physical systems.

Much discussion of self-organizing physical phenomena is based on the assumption that at phase transition a system looks the same under renormalization. That is, phase transition represents a stationary point for a renormalization transform in the sense that the transformed quantities are related by simple scaling laws to the original values.

Renormalization is a clustering semigroup transformation in which individual components of a system are combined according to a particular set of rules into a 'clumped' system whose behavior is a simplified average of those components.

Since such clumping is a many-to-one condensation, there can be no unique inverse renormalization, and, as the Mathematical Appendix shows, many possible forms of condensation.

Now define characteristics of the information source **X** and *J, K, Q* as functions of averages across the manifold having metric *R*. That is, 'renormalize' by clustering the entire system in terms of blocks of different sized *R*.

Let $N(K, J, Q, n)$ be the number of high probability meaningful correlated sequences of length *n across the entire community* in the *R*–manifold of Equation (7.2), given parameter values *K, J, Q*. We examine changes in

$$H[K,J,Q,\mathbf{X}] \equiv \lim_{n \to \infty} \frac{\log[N(K,J,Q,n)]}{n}$$

as $K \to K_C$ and/or $Q \to Q_C$ for critical values K_C, Q_C at which the economic system begins to undergo a marked transformation from one kind of structure to another.

Given the metric of Equation (7.2), a correlation length $\chi(K, J, Q)$, can be defined as the average length in *R*– space over which structures involving a particular phase dominate.

Now clump the community into blocks of average size *R* in the multivariate manifold, the 'space' in which the cognitive enterprise is implicitly embedded.

Following the classic argument of Wilson (1971), as in the Mathematical Appendix, it is possible to impose renormalization symmetry on the source uncertainty on *H* and χ by assuming at transition the relations

$$H[K_R, J_R, Q_R, \mathbf{X}] = R^D H[K, J, Q, \mathbf{X}] \tag{7.3}$$

and

$$\chi(K_R, J_R, Q_R) = \frac{\chi(K,J,Q)}{R} \tag{7.4}$$

hold, where K_R, J_R and Q_R are the transformed values of *K, J* and *Q* after the clumping of renormalization. Take $K_I, J_I, Q_I \equiv K, J, Q$, and permit the characteristic exponent *D* to be nonintegral.

Equations (7.3) and (7.4) are assumed to hold in a neighborhood of the transition values K_C and Q_C.

Differentiating these with respect to *R* gives complicated expressions for dK_R/dR, dJ_R/dR and dQ_R/dR depending simply on *R*

$$dK_R / dR = \frac{u(K_R, J_R, Q_R)}{R}$$

$$dQ_R / dR = \frac{w(K_R, J_R, Q_R)}{R} \tag{7.5}$$

$$dJ_R / dR = \frac{v(K_R, J_R, Q_R)}{R} J_R$$

Solving these differential equations represents K_R, J_R and Q_R as functions of *J, K, Q* and *R*.

Substituting back into equations (7.3) an (7.4), and expanding in a first order Taylor series near the critical values K_C and Q_C, gives power laws much like the Widom-Kadanoff relations for physical systems (Wilson 1971). For example, letting $J=Q=0$ and taking $\kappa \equiv (K_C-K)/K_C$ gives, in first order near K_C,

$$H = \kappa^{D/y} H_0$$
$$\chi = \kappa^{-1/y} \chi_0$$

(7.6)

where y is a constant arising from the series expansion.

Note that there are only two fundamental equations – (7.3) and (7.4) – in $n > 2$ unknowns: The critical 'point' is, in this formulation, a complicated implicitly defined critical surface in J, K, Q, ... –space. The 'external field strength' J remains distinguished in this treatment, i.e., the inverse of the degree to which acquired characteristics are inherited, but neither K, Q nor other parameters are, by themselves, fundamental, rather their joint interaction defines critical behavior along this surface.

That surface is a fundamental object, not the particular set of parameters (except for J) used to define it, which may be subject to any set of transformations which leave the surface invariant. Thus 'inverse generalized temperature,' 'resource availability' or whatever other parameters may be identified as affecting the 'richness' of distributed institutional cognition, are inextricably intertwined and mutually interacting, according to the form of this critical evolutionary transition surface. That surface, in turn, is unlikely to remain fixed, and should vary with time or other extrinsic parameters, including, but not likely limited to, J.

At the critical surface, a Taylor expansion of the renormalization Equations (7.3) and (7.4) gives a first order matrix of derivatives whose eigenstructure defines fundamental system behavior. For physical systems the surface is a saddle point (Wilson 1971), but more complicated behavior seems likely in what we study (e.g., Binney et al. 1986).

Taking the simplest formulation, ($J=Q=0$), a well-capitalized structure with memory, as K increases toward a threshold value K_C, the source uncertainty of the reproductive, behavioral or other language common across the community declines and, at K_C, the average regime dominated by the 'other phase' grows. That is, the system begins to freeze into one having a large correlation length for the second phase. The two phenomena are linked at criticality in physical systems by the scaling exponent y.

Assume the rate of change of $\kappa=(K_C-K)/K_C$ remains constant, $|d\kappa/dt|=1/\tau_K$. Analogs with physical theory suggest there is a characteristic time constant for the phase transition, $\tau \equiv \tau_0/\kappa$, such that if changes in κ take place on a timescale longer than τ for any given κ, the correlation length $\chi =\chi_0 \, \kappa^{-s}$, $s=1/y$, will be in equilibrium with internal changes and result in a very large fragment in R–space.

Following Zurek (1985, 1996), the 'critical' freezout time, $\hat{t}$, will occur at a 'system time' $\hat{t}=\chi/|d\chi/dt|$ such that $\hat{t}=\tau$. Taking the derivative $d\chi/dt$, remembering that by definition $d\kappa/dt=1/\tau_K$, gives

$$\frac{\chi}{|d\chi/dt|} = \frac{\kappa\tau_K}{s} = \frac{\tau_0}{\kappa} \tag{7.7}$$

so that

$$\kappa = \sqrt{s\tau_0/\tau_K} \tag{7.8}$$

Substituting this value of κ into the equation for correlation length, the expected size of fragments in R– space, $d(\hat{t})$, becomes

$$d \approx \chi_0 (\frac{\tau_K}{s\tau_0})^{s/2} \tag{7.9}$$

with $s=1/y > 0$.

The more rapidly K approaches K_C, the smaller is τ_K and the smaller and more numerous are the resulting R–space fragments. Thus rapid change – sliding quickly down the the right side of Figure 7.1 – produces small fragments more likely to risk economic extinction in a system dominated by economies of scale.

7.5 The US case history

Instantiating something of the previous section's fragmentation analysis, Bonvillian (2013) writes

> The majority of the U.S. manufacturing sector [presently] consists of small and midsize firms that are risk-averse and thinly capitalized; thus, they are not in a position to perform research or adopt new technologies and processes … Although larger firms once assisted their supply chains in this role, playing a vertical integration function, in an era of intense global competition [sic], they have often cut back to their core competencies. Therefore, they are less able to assist suppliers and have their own competitive problems adapting … [Thus, under current conditions,] manufacturing firms are 'increasingly home alone.'

The precipitate transition of the US economy from the globe's foremost industrial giant in the heady days after World War II to the foremost dump for Asian products is certainly striking. So too is the growing social disintegration caused by sudden widespread 'Rustbelt' deindustrialization which, in synergism with the associated collapse of most US central cities, became a driving force behind the relentless national diffusion of HIV (Wallace et al. 1999).

The argument above suggests that, in terms of our economic system, technology and, of course, capital, fuel the Red Queen, allowing her to run fast enough to stay in place, or even to get a little ahead (remember when real wages were increasing for most workers?). Diversion of technological and capital resources from the requirements of civilian firms serves, then, to diminish the 'richness' of the coupled languages of the principal segments of the modern economy. Our theory suggests that, in taking technology and capital from civilian industry to fuel the Cold War, we enabled the Pentagon Ratchet and rapidly walked down Figure 7.1, a dynamic that was, for much US civilian economic activity, a punctuated extinction event.

What, then, has been the actual burden of Pentagon capitalism for the US economy? Can it be said that technology and capital became so decoupled from the essential needs of civilian firms as to trigger an extinction event? Indeed, would such an event be only the beginning of a more general process of economic and social disintegration for the US? One need only think of current conditions in Detroit, St. Louis, Gary, Camden, North Philadelphia, much of Baltimore, and so on.

Melman (1988) tracks the costs of the arms race to the US economy between 1947 and 1987: in that period the US Pentagon consumed (in 1982 money) nearly $7.6 trillion, as compared to the $7.3 trillion value (1982 money) of the nation's producers' plant, equipment and infrastructure. That is, the US Pentagon used up enough capital to renew the largest part of the nation's industrial and infrastructure plant.

Again, from Melman (1988), in 1965 the numbers of engineers and scientists per 10,000 of the labor force was 64.1 for the US, 24.6 in Japan and 22.6 in West Germany. By 1977 the number of *civilian* engineers per 10,000 workers for those countries was, respectively, 38, 50, 40.

Between 1950 and 1970, manufacturing productivity per worker grew at an annual average rate of 4.1 percent, nearly three times the 1.4 percent rate after 1970 (Dumas 1986). Again from Dumas, for all wage and salary earners, the percent increase in average real income was: 1950s, 3.1; 1960s, 2.5; 1970s, 0.9; 1980–84, 0.0. Declines have continued since.

Melman (1997) shows the continuing nature of the problem, tracking the ratio of military to all civilian asset investment for 1989–90; US 48/100, UK 25/100, France 22/100, Germany 16/100, Japan 4/100. These data imply that for every $100 worth of new civilian assets put in place in the US during 1989–90, the military budget accounted for $48. By 1993, according to Melman (1997), capital/durable goods industries accounted for 45 percent of all US employment in manufacturing but 64 percent of all jobs foregone in manufacturing owing to displacement by imported goods. Melman (1997) gives the accounting by core industry between 1977 and 1992.

Figure 7.2 shows the result: counties in the northeast US which lost more than 1000 manufacturing jobs between 1972 and 1987, the heart of the Rustbelt. The process was rapid, locally concentrated, and socially appalling (e.g., Pappas 1989). Evidence suggests the industrial Red Queen died a punctuated death: as other segments of the US economy suffer a domino-effect feedback, similar punctuated economic extinction events seem likely to occur, a staircase to Hell in which one dying Red Queen kills the next.

It is appropriate to outline in more detail the chain of circumstances which has led to this state of affairs.

A viable industrial system must have certain essential resources, backed by economic and social structures that are able and willing to make ongoing

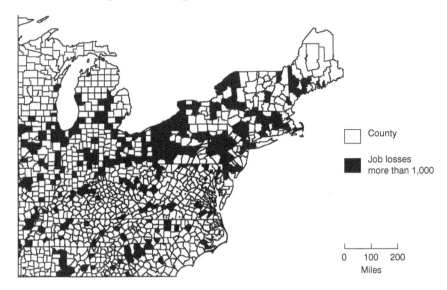

Figure 7.2 The killing of the US industrial Red Queen: counties of the northeastern US 'Rust Belt' losing more than 1000 manufacturing jobs between 1972 and 1987. In the absence of a conscious, long-term, reindustrialization policy diverting significant capital into civilian technology, this is only one catastrophe in a step-wise and highly punctuated deteriorating ratchet that will enmesh both public health and public order in much the same manner as characterizes the present suffering of the former Soviet Union.

contributions to it and maintain it in a state sufficient to meet its needs. This implies that such a resource base is not in a steady state, but rather needs constant attention, investment and innovation. The need for such additions is evident not only from experience or even Red Queen-based coevolutionary arguments, but also represents the energy inputs which, the Second Law of Thermodynamics informs us, are necessary to prevent the decay and ultimate collapse of the system. In turn, the efficient use of these resources, that is, maximizing the benefits to society from them, is paramount in assuring the long-term viability of the system. It is in this respect that the arms race of the Cold War wreaked most of its havoc; the fact that, in many ways, it still goes on, is a profound danger.

Specifically, the following are required to sustain a viable industrial country:

1   *Skills in research, development and production* This implies that it is not enough to come up with scientific discoveries, without the manufacturing resources to turn the most promising among them into viable commercial products that not only satisfy a demand but offer employment to the people who make them. Weapons clearly fail this utility test. In turn, no demand can materialize if people are being systematically impoverished or put to graver risks, as in diminished access to health care.

2   *Enough capital to keep up to date* This means enough for existing plants and new entrants, and enough security for the investment to attract it.

3   *Community resources in education and skills* Technical 'literacy' is the main issue here. Without viable job opportunities, family or community role models and confidence in the future, this vital resource atrophies.

4   *Infrastructure and other support facilities* This includes transportation systems (maintenance and new construction) and the linkages between large factories and the network of support industries, such as tool specialists, plating shops, printers, etc. that serve a major manufacturer. If that dies, so does the support system and its associated communities.

The Cold War arms race fatally compromised every one of the foregoing resources. It was on a gigantic scale: from World War II to 1988 when spending reached its Cold War peak, the US spent $9.6 trillion on the military, in 1982 dollars (Executive Office of the President 1998, p. 289). about $1.5 trillion more than the estimated value of the country's tangible assets in 1988, except for the land itself (US Dept. of Commerce 1991, p. 463). Well over a further $1 trillion has been spent since on the military and an indefinite series of annual appropriations of a $1/4 trillion appears cast in stone. An additional $1.4 trillion is now budgeted over the next ten years in new weapons alone.

The specific industrial effects were drastic indeed: first came the misuse of innovation. In the middle 1950s, the commercial use of solid state technology which had been discovered in the US, was quickly left to others, notably to Japan and later to other East Asian countries. In later major products, such as VCRs, there were no US entries at all, and even in computers, there are no major models wholly made in the US. The Kennedy years saw the beginning of the great and still ongoing increase in the technology content of weaponry. In his time also, there was the first sharp increase in military spending, following such subsequently debunked political gambits as the 'missile gap.' The preemption of technical talent by the military sector was such that about one third of engineers and scientists came to work for it (Dumas 1986, pp. 208–213).

This had two drastic effects. First, it led to ever fewer technological innovations and second, because cost consciousness is generally absent in military industries, it impaired the ability to turn them into commercially viable products. That skill had once been the glory of the American economy. In less industrially dysfunctional times, the US could use superior industrial equipment and product development to enhance the productivity of its manufacturing sector. This in turn justified rising real wages for its workers and generally kept them at a higher level than did its global competitors.

As military industry, with its indifference to costs and ever-open governmental check book, took an ever rising share of the resources, others found it much easier simply to export jobs to places with lower labor costs and worse working conditions, rather than do the work to save the industries at home. Whatever was left had to pass along the higher costs to the customers (Hong 1979; Melman 1983, pp. 12–14, pp. 104–7, p. 137). By 1980, the two trends led to what came to be called 'stagflation.'

The other characteristic of the new weapons also rapidly became significant: because they were so complicated and expensive, they were no longer made in the kind of mass production lines typical of the WW II era, but returned to the extremely expensive 'job shop' or virtual handicraft methods of earlier times. The point here is not that they should (or could) have been mass produced, but rather that this makes their use of technical resources very much more wasteful. A major part of the problem was the explosion of overhead costs largely due to the paperwork load imposed by military procurement. In relation to direct production work it came to be about 5 to 1, compared to 2 to 1 for similar commercial systems (Ullmann 1994).

The danger of all this to the economy had long been clear (Ullmann 1970) but, as military requirements became dominant in the 1980s, these trends accelerated. The patent balance (foreign patents granted to US entities minus US patents to foreign ones) turned negative for the first time in decades (Ullmann 1978; Gamarekian 1986), and even non-military high-tech trade likewise moved into the deficit column (US Congress 1986). None of these trends have been reversed.

To be sure, military spending accounted for an often declining, and what was presented as a relatively small, percentage of the gross national product. However, because of the unprecedented industrial decline, the GNP itself changed. An ever increasing part of it came to consist of often spurious services, rather than making the goods the nation consumed (Ullmann 1985, pp. 116–142). This also means that the long decline of military spending as a proportion of GNP is meaningless in relation to the national future. When the resources it consumes make such inroads on what the nation needs to assure its technical and industrial future, one can but reflect that certain major body parts that one would not wish to do without, also have a small share of body weight.

The resultant decline in manufacturing can be documented in so many ways that is almost appears tautological. The percentage of Americans in the work force who work in manufacturing was 28.2 in 1960, 26.3 in 1970, 22.0 in 1980, 17.9 in 1990 and 16.5 in 1995 (US Dept. of Commerce 1997, p. 415). It is true that the proportion of the GNP contributed by manufacturing has remained roughly the same, but it is its nature and product mix that has changed. Weapons priced at exorbitant cost may increase the GNP and thus maintain its share, but the failure to define security needs realistically in the post-Cold War era means that obsolescent weapons, contributions to overkill, or weapons that no longer serve a rational military purpose are like a company buying machinery that does not work. Yes, they are 'fixed investments' on the balance sheet, but only reduce profits and must eventually and often painfully be written off.

In judging the proportion of the manufacturing work force, much is sometimes made of the fact that farm workers have also steadily declined for even longer than industrial workers. Paralleling the above industrial statistics, they were 4.4 percent of the total in 1970, 3.4 in 1980, 2.6 in 1990 and 2.7 in 1995. The crucial difference, however, is that agriculture has long had a huge favorable export balance (about 10 percent of total exports in 1996) and provides some of the world's cheapest food to the population, whereas US manufacturing has been increasingly unable to produce the goods Americans consume. It must be noted, however, that loss of farmland to debt, soil erosion and development goes on apace, imperiling this absolutely crucial national asset. Farming too is therefore a candidate for the remedial efforts described in the next section.

During the sharp escalation of the arms race between 1980 and 1985, there was a rise in the military share of output of most technically oriented industries, but in the ones most remote from weaponry there also was an overall decline in output. Notable among them were machine-cutting tools, such as lathes and drills (down 60 percent), machine forming tools such as presses (39 percent), turbines (53 percent), industrial trucks (46 percent) and hoists and cranes (49 percent) (Ullmann 1989; Oden 1988). Some of the individual firms that failed were the very first to make the products in question, back in the nineteenth century. Now, what was left of industry showed ever-rising obsolescence (Ullmann 1985, pp. 160–171) and failure to introduce such important innovations as computer-controlled machine tools fast enough (Melman 1983, pp. 1–5, pp. 104–107).

It is most important to note that whatever happened elsewhere in manufacturing, these changes do not mean that the market for these items has declined that drastically. Rather, it has become import-dependent. In a detailed analysis of capital and durable goods manufacturing, Melman (1993) has shown that in 1990, 20 percent of the value of its shipments were imported and that this meant that 1.7 million US jobs had been foregone.

Beyond attempts to defend such depredations by appeals to patriotism of sorts, this decline also came at a time of other rationalizations and slogans such as that of the 'post-industrial' age, the 'knowledge revolution,' the 'information age,' the 'service economy,' and so on. The possible excuses along these lines are legion (Ullmann 1985, pp. 20–24). Suffice it to say here that 'information' or 'knowledge' are not free goods and, if not operationally justified, only create more wasteful spending. Many such expenditures, moreover, are the result of complicating our lives in other ways, such as tax advisors, or make up for deficiencies in other public services, such as paying private guards rather than funding the police adequately, or drinking bottled water, rather than insisting on a good public supply. Spending ever greater proportions of the GNP to fix the damage done elsewhere is thus rapidly emerging as yet another drag on modern economies (Liepert 1989).

The ultimate 'bottom line' of industrial decline is simply what has happened to the goods account in the balance of payments. After showing a positive balance for most of the century, it turned permanently negative in 1976. From then until 1996, the accumulated excess of imports over exports was $1,983.6 billion and estimates since then, reflecting more that $200 billion a year in addition, indicate a total of $2.4 trillion, as of the end of 1998 (Executive Office of the President 1998). To be sure, some of this indebtedness is mitigated by favorable balances in services and income from foreign operations by American business, but it still totals about $1.5 trillion. Moreover, much foreign income derives from foreign manufacturing that turns out imports to the US rather than serving local markets.

In arranging for these foreign sources, American business became a principal actor in a global downward auction in wages and working conditions and downward pressures on whatever safety nets existed. European countries with strong resources of this kind were under particular stress. What should have been progress in repairing the damage wrought by the Cold War and the conservative governments that ran it, expired in an epidemic of 'centrism.' Thus, the governments of President Clinton, British Prime Minister Blair and Gerhard Schröder, the German Chancellor, leaders who replaced regimes further to the right, were unable so to take effective remedial action. The current line of US regimes seem incapable of effective action on any front. At the least, it is high time to recognize the limiting factors in globalization and its implied homogenization of terms of work; for example, workers in tropical countries might mainly be uncomfortable in the heat, but those in temperate climates incur inevitable extra costs because they would freeze to death in the cold.

Returning to the international debt problem, global finance is now in a more precarious state than has been seen for many years. It is therefore well to note that aside from the domestic consequences of exported jobs and stagnant earnings, this is like a huge credit card for which no bill is ever presented. The arrangement is kept together mainly by foreigners holding dollars which have proved to be more reliable than their own currencies. A large proportion of US government bonds is owned by foreign entities; on a smaller scale, it has been estimated that two-thirds of the new $100 bills circulate abroad and, as in the tale of the Flying Dutchman, never return to their home port. Any significant loss of confidence in the dollar would obviously lead to an unprecedented financial meltdown.

Many of these itinerant dollars have made their way to Russia and this draws attention to the collapse of the Soviet Union, after decades as the main US opponent in the Cold War (Ullmann 1997a). It shows, as nothing else can, the further stages of the kind of downward spiral, the Pentagon ratchet, we have described for the American economy. The Soviet Union saw a much more massive diversion of technical and industrial resources to the military sector than that of the US. Its civilian industry was, in effect, living off the table scraps from the military-industrial complex, with Gosplan, the central planning agency, serving as the director of this rationing scheme.

It had been part of the Cold War credo on the American side that the Soviet Union was an 'evil empire' indifferent to the welfare of its citizens, and that therefore the above depletions were irrelevant to estimates of Soviet strength. The resultant exaggerations were central to justifying the huge military budgets and other Cold War excesses (Moynihan 1998). However, eventually, the eternal dysfunctions of the Soviet system took their toll. Whereas the result of military excess in the US turned into industrial decay, wage stagnation and a huge international debt, the Soviet Union had chronic shortages of everything from food to housing to many of the most mundane consumer products. Instead of such shortages, the US imported what it needed, because foreigners took its currency at face value.

The one commodity the US could not import, low-income housing, is now in such short supply as to constitute a housing famine for the poor, leading to widespread homelessness (Wallace 1989, 1990b). Indeed, the industrial decline affects other major projects with a public service component. As also happened in the Soviet Union, rail equipment had to be imported; the need to recreate its once flourishing industry or even manage the adaptation and maintenance of the imports competently, creates serious problems for plans to build a new high speed rail system in the US (Ullmann 1993) or improve public transit.

For many reasons beyond our scope, the Russian recovery effort was botched, but the particularly poor handling of the conversion of military resources was at the center. Not that the job was handled well in the US either (Ullmann 1997b) but the military-industrial complex had been the great tapeworm on the body politic of the Soviet Union; it could not be 'converted' just by not paying soldiers and workers and letting favored panjandrums of the old regime and new 'entrepreneurs' pick up the last viable industrial assets. It is hard to exaggerate the resultant miseries and potentially dangerous destabilization. There comes a time when a society in such turmoil loses its ability to restore itself by its own *human* resources, at which point even the injection of huge new capital is no longer enough, and it reverts to a similar state as the more troubled parts of the developing world.

7.6 Reversing the ratchet: can we raise the dead?

Can the death of the US industrial Red Queen, related subsequent punctuated economic extinction events, and the descent to socioeconomic perdition be halted and, if possible, reversed? One can but stand in awe before such sustained damage as Figure 7.2, its inner-city equivalents and its Russian parallels, which, perhaps, proves most of all that there is nothing, no institution, no economy, no society, no matter how treasured, that cannot be ruined if the job is tackled with sufficient intensity.

The best approach that emerges from the foregoing developments is to focus on the idea of the efficiency with which a country's intellectual and industrial resources are deployed. We have noted the huge waste of them in the military sector, not only in the process of supplying it, but in the very purpose it is supposed to fulfill. The first step must therefore be the drastic reassessment of military and security needs in a post-Cold War world; this sounds almost like a cliché by now, but decades after the Cold War ended, the job still remains to be done. For example, for US military planners to prepare for two conventional wars – meaning mass armies, mass armaments – at the same time is self-serving rather than realistic.

The key to more efficient use would lie in other public initiatives, only some of which would involve direct government activity, rather than incentives and subsidies. Recovery is based on the notion that resources would be applied more efficiently, that is, that more direct public good would be realized per dollar invested. That is still the case in such activity as has survived the public crunch, even though such problems as corruption, rackets and work restrictions would have to be substantially mitigated.

Proponents of a redirection of priorities and industrial recovery in response to the downward spiral, have therefore long focused on proposals for a recasting of energy usage, such as new electric or hybrid automotive drives, high-speed rail, expanded transit systems, development of renewable non-combustion energy sources, such as geothermal, and a multitude of others. Allied to this is the problem of the national water supply and its management; pollution and the rise in climatic extremes and consequent alternations of droughts and floods in critical crop lands, require the most energetic remedial efforts instead of the current piecemeal efforts or simple helplessness or worse still, denial. All these tasks would need new machinery and controls ranging from mass-produced items to sophisticated special machinery.

The market opportunities this would offer to a revived manufacturing sector are correspondingly wide. Nor is anything of this kind mere 'make-work.' The need for maintenance and repair, much of which involves similar kinds of work, is clearly vast. In 1998, the Comptroller of the City of New York estimated that needed repairs to public facilities and systems would cost $90 billion over ten years, while less than half that amount was budgeted (Office of the Controller 1998). We must assume that similar bills could be presented in other cities, let alone in the terminally troubled communities that now exist and are spreading in many parts of the country; East St. Louis, Illinois, and Camden, New Jersey are but two examples. We noted the farm problems earlier; they go to the very heart of national survival. No solutions, however, will materialize until there is a drastic redirection of public funds and related incentives from military to civilian enterprise.

Given the rising level of global economic misery, the time is more than ripe for a Keynesian injection of funds into the economy which would reverse the current trends toward deflation and depression. To assure the effective application of such funds, however, it is essential to cut back on the wholly destructive, wasteful and inefficient ways of the military-industrial excess. The idea, then, is to go back to the beginning, to the process whereby the nation's most crucial intellectual and industrial assets were diverted to essentially wasteful purposes at a faster rate than their possible replenishment. This very diversion also created a host of other problems, from the deindustrialization chronicled above to the decay of communities and resulting health problems that come to affect everyone.

Somewhat heuristically, in our context, the Second Law of Thermodynamics reminds us that a steady energy input to a system is needed to prevent its stagnation and decline. But the First Law also has something to say to us. It states that any energy input to a system is shared between useful work done and 'internal energy,' meaning waste and internal churning about. In a real sense, what the military overemphasis and the post-industrial rationalizations have done to us is to reduce the proportion of 'useful' work done within society. The extent of our success in recovering will be determined by the way we can improve this ratio.

Putting the matter in a more popular vein, the Cold War ended as a classical negative sum game, in which, as in the Peloponnesian War, the Thirty Years War and the Hundred Years War between Britain and France in the Middle Ages, all major participants lost. It is also reminiscent of the Gambler's Ruin model in which anyone who persists in gambling at a casino is mathematically certain to lose everything at the end, the only question being when; that in turn depends on how much the gambler first brings to the table, and when or whether he or she decides to quit while ahead, which is hard once gambling has become compulsive. The reason for the inevitability of ruin is, of course, the 'house handle,' the share taken by the establishment.

In the scenarios of national ruin we have chronicled here for the US and the Soviet Union, what turned out to be an extremely high 'house handle' was exacted by the military and, no matter what the participants brought in at the beginning, greatly accelerated their declines. Some 'house handle' is, of course, inevitable; we may visualize it in this context as what is required of us just to keep going. The job then is to make the 'house handle' less ruinous and thus make solutions to the global problems we face possible, rather than chart new extremes of descent into misery.

Our analysis implies that the effects of an excessive house handle are highly discontinuous, leading to sudden 'resilience transitions' that are de facto extinction events. But the likely punctuated nature of the birth, as well as of the death, of the macroeconomic Red Queen linking firms and technology suggests that a considerable investment of resources will be needed for some time before a renewed productive system can crystallize. The US, like its fallen and fragmented Soviet counterparts, delays at perilous risk.

8 Counterexample: organized hyperviolence

This material was written in collaboration with Robert E. Fullilove, Columbia University.

8.1 Introduction

The current standard economic analysis of crime arose from the famous paper by G.S. Becker (1968), *Crime and punishment: an economic approach* that, in the words of Mochan et al. (2005),

> [C]reated the foundation for the economic analysis of criminal behavior. His model, extended by Ehrlich (1973), postulates that participation in criminal activity is the result of an optimizing individual's response to incentives such as legal and illegal market opportunities. Rational economic agents decide to engage in criminal activity after comparing the financial rewards from crime with those obtained from legal work, taking into account the probabilities [of sanction] ... Empirical observations have generally confirmed the predictions of the original Becker-Ehrlich model, uncovering negative impacts on crime of deterrence variables and improved economic conditions.

Such an inherently atomistic model of criminal behavior is, however, profoundly challenged – not confirmed – by empirical observations of massive Black Swan events like the hyperviolence outbreak currently afflicting much of Mexico, or the Crack Wars that convulsed New York City in the early 1990s (e.g., Halbfinger 1998).

Here, we will adopt the viewpoint of a powerful criminal enterprise that must regulate its stream of commerce – make regulatory investments of resources – under conditions of uncertainty appropriate to a particular scale. We see the enterprise itself as the 'inspector,' while State policy and uncertain events constitute the 'corrupter,' in the sense of Dechenaux and Samuel (2012), but having a scale-dependent mechanism of interaction, in the sense of Wallace (2013a). Thus, we not only study a qualitatively different scale than the Becker–Ehrlich model, but, in a sense, invert the perception of 'rationality.' This evades the error inherent to an atomistic analysis of collective behavior when essential interactions vary, and take place, at and across multiple scales. Here, this involves the dynamics of an institutionally evolved cultural artifact that may have 'emergent' properties different from those expressed at smaller scales. Analogous debate rages in evolutionary theory regarding the 'correct' levels of selection: biology, like social science, is inherently messy, and involves selection pressures that act at all scales and levels (Gould 2002; Wallace 2010a, 2013a).

In fact, a seminal study by Mansour et al. (2006), using game-theoretic methods found that conventional 'deterrence' policies affect the structure of the market for drugs, leading to the counterintuitive result of lower drug prices in the context of fragmented competition. They assume that the production and distribution of illegal drugs is controlled by well-organized criminal organizations. They find that, for a given market structure – a given number of criminal organizations – an increase in deterrence will initially reduce total output and increase the price of drugs. However, this may not be so when the market structure reacts to such deterrence. Using the mathematical theory of coalition-formation, they show how an increase in deterrence can lead to a splintering of the cartel. From there, they simply argue that when more firms operate in an illegal goods market – when the market is more competitive – the output is larger and the price is lower. Thus, by increasing the number of criminal organizations in the market, increased deterrence leads to an increase in output and a fall in prices.

Of course, given the nature of the illegal drug trade, such increasing competition is very likely to lead to high levels of violent conflict.

A number of significant factors, however, limit the usefulness of game-theoretic approaches. First, the rules of the game, the payoff matrix will not likely be well understood by the players in complex real-world situations. Second, the rules of a real-world game are always changing, in ways that players may not, or cannot, recognize. Third, the 'contending actors' may not share sufficient perspective as to have similar value schemes, an agreed-upon idea of utility. Finally, most game theory envisions atomistic interactions, although these may be aggregated into coalitions. Real world systems, by contrast, are highly emergent, i.e., the behavior of collective 'actors' is not simply determined by atomic structure, as it were.

In addition, as Martin (1978) put it, game theory often reifies the values of the game formulator in the study of crime. The application, in his view, takes the expected path, leading to severe limitations. These include ignoring collusion between police and criminals, value change, structural change as the equitable distribution of wealth leading to decreased criminal activity. It defines criminal activity as what is discouraged now by police, and ignores structural violence in society – poverty, war, racism – not to mention crime by other classes or occupations, for example white-collar transgressions. It assumes the continuance of present laws, which may be unnecessary or unjust, and so on. Martin concludes that game theory as applied to crime does not lead to a real elucidation of the problems in a deep way. It serves most importantly, he claims, as a mathematical esoteric way of perpetuating and justifying existing concepts about crime.

Taking a different tack, Garoupa (2007) examined the interaction between law enforcement and criminal organization, arguing (as do we here) that the behaviors of an individual criminal are different from those of a group of criminals. He finds that organization matters, and that it matters in terms of both internal organization and inter firms' relations. He asserts that tougher punishment may actually increase effectiveness of organized crime and make detection less consistent. Following Reuter (1983), he further suggests that, in criminal markets, violence is a substitute for vertical integration, becoming a means of enforcing illegal contracts and resolving disagreements.

Contrasting Becker and Mansour, the central assumption in our work is that what criminal enterprises can recognize, according to their own value systems, is the degree of disjunction between what they want and what they get, under particular strategies and at a particular 'cost,' and this serves as the basis for a far more appropriate formal approach via Rate Distortion Theory.

Our model, nonetheless, reaches conclusions roughly similar to the results of Masour et al. and Garoupa – a good sign – but uses a phase transition-based formalism in a rate distortion context, i.e., applies a statistical model based on the asymptotic limit theorems of probability.

There is similar discussion in the international security and law enforcement literature. For example, Guerrero-Gutierrez (2011), applying a sophisticated social science perspective on the Mexican hyperviolence outbreak, found that a critical misstep leading toward the disaster was a poorly thought-out law enforcement strategy at the organizational scale:

> [State policy of policing and incarceration] contributed to [drug] cartel fragmentation and the emergence of bloody conflicts between organizations.

The consequences threaten to create a failed state on the US border.

Describing the intersection of political disintegration and drug trafficking in the failing states of West Africa, Felbab-Brown and Forest (2012) write:

> It is important to realize that indiscriminate and uniform application of law enforcement – whether external or internal – can generate several undesirable outcomes. For example, the weakest criminal groups can be eliminated ... with law enforcement inadvertently increasing the efficiency, lethality, and coercive and corruption power of the remaining criminal groups ... [L]aw enforcement without prioritization can [also] ... push criminal groups into an alliance with terrorist groups ... Both outcomes have repeatedly emerged in various regions of the world.

Simons and Tucker (2007), in the context of current US security perspectives, write:

> All states consistently fail some portions of their populations ... [F]rom disenfranchised populations can come foot soldiers, from alienated populations can come terrorists. And these exist in pockets everywhere, including our own [USA] backyard ... [Such] problems [are] best handled by means other than ... force.

Skaperdas (2001) concluded that organized crime emerges out of the power vacuum created by the absence of state enforcement. Mafias and gangs are hierarchically organized and can be thought of as providing primitive state functions, with costs much higher than associated with modern governance. Kumar and Skaperdas (2009) infer that, although competition is considered good in economics, in the case of organized crime, predatory competition is likely to be harmful – a scale effect. Capuano and Purificato (2012) likewise infer that organized crime emerges to replace the state where institutions are weak or absent. A roughly analogous perspective can be found in Sung (2004).

Adorno and Salla (2007), describing the Brazilian criminal network known as the Primero Commando du Capital (PCC) write:

> Penitentiary policies that have been implemented by the state government have not been able to interrupt the cycle of expansion and deepening of organized criminality in civil society. To the contrary, there is strong evidence that the mass incarceration associated with the rigorous attack on the leaders of organized criminal groups has produced adverse effects ... it has stimulated sharp perceptions of injustice among the inmates, favoring and legitimating violent reactions orchestrated by the leaders ...
>
> [T]he PCC and its demands for justice [however, do not] constitute the embryo of a social revolution and the construction of a new society based on justice, equality and democracy. What is at play are business interests ... The leaders are not afraid to take punitive measures; they do not hesitate to kill and issue justice with no right to defense. They expect to defeat their enemies although they do not expect to win sympathy, solidarity or support from those who live tormented by their criminal actions. They do not have a political plan for the construction of a democratic society; their conception of society is crude, based on loyalty between 'brothers' and on the conception of the extended family, a constellation of material and moral interests.

Similarly, Arana (2005) explores how

> Ultraviolent youth gangs, spawned in the ghettos of Los Angeles and other U.S. cities, have slowly migrated south to Central America, where they have transformed themselves into powerful cross-border crime networks ...
>
> The solutions attempted so far – largely confined to military and police operations – have only aggravated the problem; prisons act as gangland finishing schools, and military operations have only dispersed the gangs' leadership, making bosses harder than ever to track and capture.

Analogously, Skarbek (2011) finds:

> The illegal narcotics trade in Los Angeles has flourished despite its inability to rely on state-based formal institutions of governance. An alternative system of governance has emerged from an unexpected source – behind bars. The

Mexican Mafia prison gang can extort drug dealers on the street because they wield substantial control over inmates in the county jail system and because drug dealers anticipate future incarceration. The gang's ability to extract resources creates incentives for them to provide governance institutions that mitigate market failure among Hispanic drug-dealing street gangs, including enforcing deals, protecting property rights, and adjudicating disputes ...

The use of terrorism more broadly is a rational and strategic use of threats and violence to influence action from non-group members.

The knee-jerk response of US policymakers, of course, is that 'it can't happen here,' the US is not on a trajectory to becoming a failed state. Overlooked in such a rush-to-judgment, however, is that it is, in fact, already happening here, and that, for many, the US has always been a failed state: a slave was to be counted, for the purposes of representative governance, as 'three-fifths of a man.' More recently, the Report of the National Advisory Commission on Civil Disorders (NACCD 1967), the 'Kerner Report,' put it:

Our nation is moving toward two societies, one black, one white – separate and unequal. What white Americans have never fully understood – but what the Negro can never forget – is that white society is deeply implicated in the ghetto. White institutions created it, white institutions maintain it, and white society condones it.

Forty years later, those ghettos – and others – have collapsed and been 'reborn' in even more degraded form, via policies like 'planned shrinkage,' 'Hope VI' (Wallace and Wallace 1998; Fullilove and Wallace 2011), and, for this work, most centrally, mass incarceration (Christie 1982; Parenti 2000; Garland 2001; Alexander 2010; Thompson 2010). These processes have become synergistic with relentless deindustrialization consequent on the Cold War described in the previous chapter and, since 2008, the foreclosure disaster that, like mass incarceration, has had disproportionate effect on those relatively few African Americans who were able to enter the middle class (Saegert et al. 2011). As Wacquant (2001) describes current conditions,

Along with its economic function of labor pool and the extensive organizational nexus it supported, the ghetto lost its capacity to buffer its residents from external forces. It is no longer Janus-faced, offering a sheltered space for collective sustenance and self-affirmation in the face of hostility and exclusion ... Rather, it has devolved into a one-dimensional machinery for naked relegation, a human warehouse wherein are discarded those segments of urban society deemed disreputable, derelict, and dangerous [becoming] saturated with economic, social and physical insecurity ... Pandemic levels of crime have further depressed the local economy and ruptured the social fabric fear and danger pervade public space; interpersonal relations are riven with suspicion and distrust ...

resort to violence is the prevalent means for upholding respect, regulating encounters, and controlling territory … [R]elations with official authorities are suffused with animosity and diffidence.

In short, all the tokens of a failing state.

We first examine a case history, the outbreak of organized hyperviolence in New York City – the Crack Wars – associated with the 'planned shrinkage' program of the 1970s that saw the targeted withdrawal of firefighting and other essential services from minority voting blocks (Wallace and Wallace 1998; 2011). We then develop a conceptual model based on those observations, and apply it to national patterns. The results imply that mass incarceration serves a critical role in the potential emergence of organized hyperviolence, suggesting a limited window of opportunity for intervention.

8.2 The New York City experience

In the 1970s, New York City withdrew about 50 firefighting units from high fire incidence, high-population-density neighborhoods of older tenement housing – the Black and Hispanic ghettos – using simplistic operations research models that targeted regions having numerous fire companies close together (Wallace and Wallace 1998, 2011). The fire companies had, of course, originally been placed in those neighborhoods precisely because the buildings were crowded fire hazards. Figures 8.1 and 8.2 display some of the results. Figure 8.1 shows the percentage of occupied housing units lost in health areas of the Bronx section of the city between 1970 and 1980 (Wallace 1990b). Health areas are small aggregates of census tracts by which morbidity and mortality statistics are reported.

Figure 8.2 shows an annual index of structural fire number and size from 1959 through 1990, constructed by a principal component analysis of administrative data (Wallace and Wallace 1998; Wallace 1990b). This is the epidemic curve for the contagious urban desertification represented by Figure 8.1. The sharp rise between 1967 and 1968 was met by the opening of some 20 new fire companies as 'second sections' of existing units in high fire incidence areas, the consequence of a labor action by the fire service unions. This stabilized matters through 1972, akin to an immunization program in response to an outbreak of a contagious infection. Beginning in 1972, the city closed some fifty firefighting units, reduced initial response to fires, cut staffing on operating units, and carried out other service reductions.

The fire damage index increase represents the contagious fire and abandonment outbreak that resulted in the housing losses of Figure 8.1. Other badly affected areas included minority communities in Harlem, Bedford-Stuyvesant, Brownsville-East New York, the Lower East Side, South Jamaica, and so on. Forced population displacement into nearby middle class neighborhoods resulted in their social collapse and the evacuation by more affluent residents, bringing the epidemic outbreak to a close by about 1980 as the number of overcrowded housing units declined below threshold (Wallace 1990b).

■	−81 to −55
▨	−55 to −36
▧	−36 to −21
⦀	−21 to 0
☐	0 to 32

Figure 8.1 Percentage of occupied housing units lost between 1970 and 1980 in the Bronx to a process of contagious fire and abandonment triggered by fire service reductions targeting minority voting blocks. See Wallace and Wallace (1998, 2011) for details. Similar maps could be drawn for Detroit, Philadelphia, and many other US cities, although detailed mechanisms vary.

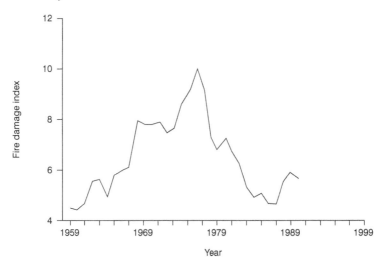

Figure 8.2 NY City structural fire damage index, 1959–1990. This is the epidemic curve for the contagious urban desertification represented by Figure 8.1. The increase between 1967 and 1968 was countered by the opening of some 20 new fire companies as 'second sections' of existing units in high fire incidence areas. This stabilized matters through 1972, like an immunization program against an infection. Beginning in 1972, the city closed some fifty firefighting units, reduced initial response to fires, cut staffing on operating units, and implemented other service reductions.

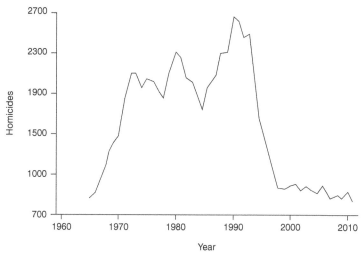

Figure 8.3 NY State homicides between 1965 and 2011, concentrated in or near New York City. The two peaks at 1980 and 1990 represent mechanisms operating at two different levels of organization. The first is the nearly immediate response to the social disintegration caused by the dynamics of Figures 8.1 and 8.2. The second, and larger, peak in 1990 represents the crack wars that engulfed much of the city. Understanding the mechanism of the second peak is one focus of this analysis.

Figure 8.3 shows the number of homicides in New York State between 1965 and 2011, mostly concentrated in New York City and the inner ring of suburbs.

The two peaks at 1980 and 1990 represent, we will argue, qualitatively different mechanisms operating at two different levels of organization. The first is the nearly immediate response to the social disintegration caused by the dynamics represented by Figures 8.1 and 8.2. The second, and larger, peak in 1990 – well after the decline of the fire/abandonment epidemic of Figure 8.2 – is an index of the crack wars that engulfed much of the city (Halbfinger 1998). Understanding the mechanism of that second peak will permit a more precise estimation of the likelihood of widespread organized criminal hyperviolence across the US, and of the role of mass incarceration as a 'keystone' in that likelihood (Holling 1992).

8.3 Individual violence

The political economy of individual violence in New York City has been the subject of commentary for some time. Maxim Gorky (1906), in his classic *The City of the Yellow Devil* writes:

> The youth leaning aganst the lamppost shakes his head from time to time. His hungry teeth are tightly clenched. I believe I understand what he is thinking of, what he wants to possess enormous hands of frightful strength and wings on his back, that is what he wants, I believe. So that, soaring one day over the city, he may reach down with hands like steel levers and reduce the whole

to a heap of rubbish and ashes, mixing bricks and pearls, gold and the flesh of slaves, glass and millionaires, dirt, idiots, temples, the dirt-poisoned trees, and these foolish multi-storeyed skyscrapers, everything, the whole city into one heap, into a dough compounded of dirt and the blood of people – into a loathsome chaos. This frightful wish is as natural in this youth's brain as a sore on the body of a sick man. Where there is much work for slaves, there can be no place for free, creative thought, and only the ideas of destruction, the poisonous flowers of vengeance, the turbulent protest of the brute beast can flourish. This is understandable – if you warp a man's soul you must not expect mercy from him.

The psychiatrist Franz Fanon (1966), in a somewhat different context, described the underlying mechanism in these terms:

The colonized man will first manifest this aggressiveness which has been deposited in his bones against his own people. This is the period when the niggers beat each other up, and the police and magistrates do not know which way to turn when faced with the astonishing waves of crime.

Ninety years after Gorky, thirty years after Fanon, and somewhat less poetically, Wallace et al. (1996) applied an information-theoretic perspective to the onset of individual-level violent behavior under conditions of imposed social disintegration like Figures 8.1 and 8.2. They identified violence as a powerful message of individual efficacy under such conditions, but one that can damage the 'channel' of the embedding sociogeographic network, triggering the need for further violence:

Suppose an optimal behavioral code evolved in a marginalized community in response to externally imposed constraints and pressures, begins itself to damage the social network on which it is transmitted, and thereby to increase the very noise it is designed to circumvent … Suppose that violent behavior, which evolves to encode statements of self-efficacy in disintegrating minority communities subject to public policies [aimed at their dispersal], begins to drive the affected neighborhoods toward further physical and social decay … [A] possible outcome could be to evolve the optimal code so as to raise the 'amplitude' of the very 'signal' which is damaging the channel, causing the noise to reach even higher levels, and initiating a self-destructive positive feedback …

[P]ermanent change in rates of youth violence within devastated ghetto neighborhoods of the United States is unlikely without a widespread regional reform and social reorganization which applies the lessons of the Great Urban Reform Movement of the last century to marginalized subgroups.

It would be possible, in a heuristic sense, to extend this perspective to 'individual' large-scale criminal enterprises driven by particular forms of state policy. For example, analyzing Mexico's outbreak of hyperviolence, or the 1990 drug war peak of Figure 8.3.

Indeed, the approach seems superficially attractive: large criminal enterprises, as all such, engage in distributed cognition, at least in the sense that a thermostat or computer is cognitive, and can carry out sophisticated problem solving (e.g., Wallace and Fullilove 2008). But unlike an individual human embedded in a sociocultural milieu and its historical trajectory, an organization remains a cultural artifact. Like a thermostat, but having a particular scale and particular dynamics. Here, in consonance with the earlier chapters, we will address the behavior of a criminal organization as a cultural artifact at its characteristic scale, without resort to an anthropomorphic or atomistic fallacy that reduces all interaction to a standard model of conflict between chosen actors, regardless of scale or level of organization.

8.4 Managing a criminal enterprise

A criminal organization, unlike a Wall Street investment bank flush with other people's money, cannot simply underwrite political factions to 'deregulate' forbidden activities and emasculate enforcement efforts, although certain parallels are to be found in police corruption and the bribery or sloth of public officials. Hence, organized crime suffers constraints and sanctions not facing legalized forms of economic exploitation, although the recent Wachovia experience suggests a covertly tolerated convergence of the Mexican illegal drug trade with the US banking industry (Vulliamy 2011).

It is possible to examine the problem of managing a criminal enterprise from the point of view of the criminal bureaucracy, under conditions of noise and volatility that may be driven by state policy. The approach takes a rate distortion perspective that is amenable to a simplified variant of conventional Black–Scholes hedging (Black and Scholes 1973). The results suggest the necessity of draconian penalties to ensure stability, providing a rational political economic basis for certain forms of criminal hyperviolence. This seems analogous to the results of Wallace et al. (1996), but actually arises from qualitatively different mechanisms acting on different scales and levels of organization. Policy perspectives abstracted from the study of individual violence may be far off the mark in the context of sophisticated criminal enterprise (Guerrero-Gutierrez 2011).

This is a common problem in population and community ecology and in evolutionary theory. Levin (1989), for example, argues that there is no 'correct' scale of observation. The insights from any investigation are contingent on the choice of scales. Pattern is neither a property of the system alone, nor of the observer, but of an interaction between them. Pattern exists at all levels and scales, and recognition of this multiplicity of scales is fundamental to describing and understanding ecosystems. There can be, then, no 'correct' level of aggregation: we must recognize explicitly the multiplicity of scales within ecosystems, and develop a perspective that looks across scales and that builds on a multiplicity of models rather than seeking the single 'correct' one. Chapter 2 applies this perspective explicitly to economic interaction.

That being said, Holling (1992) makes the point that for many natural ecosystems, in which phenomena are linked across both scale and level of organization, mesoscale structures – what might correspond to the neighborhood in a human community – are ecological keystones in space, time, and population that drive process and pattern at both smaller and larger scales and levels. Here, we will examine dynamics at the level of organization of the criminal enterprise. Linking violent behaviors across the different levels appears to take place via the ecological keystone structures of mass incarceration.

Some heuristics

Recall the arguments from Section 3.12: many regulatory problems are inherently rate distortion problems. The rate distortion function places limits on information source uncertainty. Thus, distortion measures can drive information system dynamics. That is, the rate distortion function itself has a homological relation to free energy in the sense of Feynman (2000), who characterizes information by the free energy needed to erase it, as described in Chapter 2. In general, increasing channel capacity in a regulatory structure requires increased levels of available free energy.

A heuristic approach is fairly simple. Given a rate of available free energy, say M, a system might be expected confront a large number of possible regulatory substructures. For an average distortion D, the channel capacity, a free energy measure, must be at least $R(D)$, a convex function. For a Gaussian channel with noise of mean zero and variance σ^2, this is $R(D)=1/2\log[\sigma^2/D]$.

Using a standard Gibbs model, one can write, for the average of R and some unknown monotonic increasing function $F(M)$, the approximate relation

$$<R>= \frac{\int_0^\infty R \exp[-R/F(M)]dR}{\int_0^\infty \exp[-R/F(M)]dR} = F(M) \tag{8.1}$$

What is the form of $M = F^{-1}(<R>)$? One suspects, in first order, a linear expression, using the first two terms of a Taylor series expansion, i.e., $M \approx \kappa_1<R>+\kappa_2$.

Jensen's inequality for a convex function, here $R(<D>) \leq <R(D)>$, suggests:

$$M \geq \kappa_1 R(<D>)+\kappa_2 \tag{8.2}$$

where κ_1, at least, is quite large as the result of entropic loss, in a general sense. The arguments of Section 5.4 show that, using a formal Black–Scholes approach, to first order,

$$M_{nss}=\kappa_1 R+\kappa_2 \tag{8.3}$$

in accordance with the heuristic argument.

Thus the rate of free energy consumption – that may include both financial and opportunity costs – will, for this model, grow linearly with the channel capacity needed to ensure the average distortion between regulatory intent and regulatory effect is D. The constant κ_1 may, however, be very large indeed, as a consequence of 'entropic' losses in the translation of policy to practice. Under the constraints affecting criminal enterprise, one might expect much higher translation costs than for legitimate (or legitimized) economic activity, even in the context of 'niche construction' by corruption of public officials.

Note, for a Gaussian channel, that the needed channel capacity may grow $\propto \log[\sigma]$ for fixed average distortion D. This suggests that onset of social disintegration, in one form or another, can result in severe demands on regulatory efforts, in this model.

More complicated models, depending on the assumed form of $\Delta\Pi/\Delta t$ in Equation (5.12), are clearly possible. In particular, some models obtained by setting $\Delta\Pi/\Delta t = f(\Pi), g(R)$ are also exactly solvable, albeit with more mathematical overhead.

Regulation can rapidly become prohibitively expensive with increase in σ or κ_1 in this model, suggesting the necessity of increasingly serious penalties for increasingly serious regulatory violations.

Extending this approach involves addressing a coevolutionary set of relations constituting a feedback loop having the general form

$$dR_t = f_1(t,R,M)dt + b_1 g_1(t,R,M)dW_t$$
$$dM_t = f_2(t,R,M)dt + b_2 g_2(t,R,M)dW_t \quad\quad\quad (8.4)$$

Several features emerge from invoking such a coevolutionary approach, as described in Sections 2.5 and 3.7, and as we recapitulate:

1 Setting the expectation of Equations (8.4) equal to zero and solving for stationary points gives attractor states since the noise terms preclude unstable equilibria.

2 Such a system may converge to limit cycle or pseudorandom 'strange attractor' behaviors in which the system seems to chase its tail endlessly within a limited venue – a kind of 'Red Queen' pathology. Another pathology may involve the instability of variance in demand for free energy measures beyond possible bounds. For Gaussian channels, increase in noise indices b_k can markedly increase demand for free energy.

3 The noise terms in Equation (8.4) may not be white, allowing for more subtle behaviors determined by the quadratic variation in the extended version of the Ito chain rule. Indeed, changing the spectrum of noise 'color' may be a signaling modality that carries information.

4 The complete space of quasi-stable modes to which the system can converge – the set of fixed points or strange attractors of the expectation of Equation (8.4) – may itself have a topology allowing definition of 'open sets' within it. These must have the properties (i) that the union of open sets is itself an open set, (ii) the finite intersection of open sets is open, and (iii) the complete space and the zero set are both open.

5 This topological space may have characteristic internal dynamics that are to be mapped onto the structure, providing a kind of change-of-variables that may give a simplified description of the system, much as spherical coordinates can be useful in addressing problems with spherical symmetry.

6 Setting the expectation of Equation (8.4) to zero defines an index theorem in the sense of Atiyah and Singer (1963) and Hazewinkel (2002), relating analytic results to an underlying topological structure. This instantiates relations between 'conserved' quantities – the quasi-equilibria of basins of attraction in parameter space – and underlying topological form. The inherent symmetries, however, are typically those of groupoids defined by equivalence classes of paths rather than by groups (Glazebrook and Wallace 2009a). This suggests the associated 'conserved quantities' will be represented as distinct sets of quasi-stable modes, as described in figures 1 and 2 of Wallace (2010a), leading to the next point.

7 Stationary sets of the system's coevolutionary dynamics are subject to 'ecosystem resilience' transitions between them when driven by increasing noise or by forcing functions of policy that can themselves often be described as the output of information sources, a matter we will explore below.

8 Different quasi-stable points of this system will have widely different levels of associated cost functions M; high values will inevitably be associated with high levels of hyperviolence, in this model.

Stability

Recall the stability arguments of Section 5.5 that apply to the system of equations (8.4) under White noise. This leads to the result that the free energy expenditures must exceed such limits as

$$M \geq \frac{\kappa_1}{2} \log[\frac{\beta^2 \sigma^2}{\sqrt{\mu}}] + \kappa_2 \tag{8.5}$$

for there to be a real second moment in D. β and σ are inherent noise indices, and κ_1 is, again, expected to be very large indeed. Given the context of this analysis, failure to provide adequate rates of free energy expenditure would represent the onset of a regulatory stability catastrophe. The corollary, of course, is that state policies increasing β or σ, or reducing μ, would be expected to overwhelm internal controls, triggering widespread instability.

As the Mexican experience, the New York City crack wars, and so on, indicate, this may not always be a good thing.

Again, taking the approach of Section 5.5, many variants of the model are possible. The most natural, perhaps, is to view M as a free energy measure *per unit external perturbation*. That is, $M \equiv d\hat{M}/d K$, where $\hat{M}$ is now perceived as the rate of free energy consumption needed to meet an external perturbation of (normalized) magnitude K. Then the condition of Equation (8.5), now on $\hat{M}$, becomes

$$\hat{M} \geq \int [\frac{\kappa_1}{2} \log[\frac{\beta^2 \sigma^2}{\sqrt{\mu}}] + \kappa_2] dK \qquad (8.6)$$

Under constant conditions, for stability, the system must supply the free energy measure at a rate

$$\hat{M} \geq [\frac{\kappa_1}{2} \log[\frac{\beta^2 \sigma^2}{\sqrt{\mu}}] + \kappa_2] \Delta K \qquad (8.7)$$

where ΔK is the magnitude of the imposed perturbation. Thus the demand on free energy created by imposed perturbations can be greatly amplified, in this model, suggesting that erosion of stability by public policy or other externalities can make the system more sensitive to the impact of 'natural' shocks.

Punctuated phase change

Equations (8.5–8.7), essentially restating the Data Rate Theorem of Section 5.6, have fundamental implications for social network dynamics, structure, and stability, in a large sense that includes institutions, firms, and criminal enterprise. Granovetter (1973) characterizes network function in terms of 'the strength of weak ties.' 'Strong' ties, to adapt his perspective, disjointly partition a network into indentifiable submodules. 'Weak' ties reach across such disjoint partitioning, i.e., they are linkages that do not disjointly partition a social network, institution, or firm. The average probability of such weak ties, at least in a random network, defines the fraction of network nodes that will be in a 'giant component' that links the vast majority of nodes. It is well known that the occurrence of such a component is a punctuated event. That is, there is a critical value of the average probability of weak ties below which there are only individual fragments. Recall the argument surrounding Figure 3.2 involving interacting cognitive submodules that, here, represent the distributed cognition of the full criminal enterprise. A more extended discussion can be found in Wallace and Fullilove (2008).

It seems clear that the maintenance of such weak ties, allowing large-scale distributed cognition across the enterprise, depends critically on the investment of regulatory free energy at rates M or $\hat{M}$. That is, keeping the channels of communication open in an enterprise under fire will require greater and greater rates of free energy investment.

M and $\hat{M}$ can, however, also be interpreted as intensity indices analogous to a generalized temperature, recalling Section 3.2. Identifiable submodules within the organization define equivalence classes leading to a groupoid symmetry. Groupoids can be understood as a generalization of the group symmetry concept, the simplest groupoid being a disjoint union of different groups. This, again, leads toward Landau's perspective on phase transition (e.g., Pettini 2007; Landau and Lifshitz 2007): certain phase transitions take place in the context of a significant symmetry change, with one phase, at higher temperature, being more symmetric than the other. A symmetry is lost in the transition, what is called spontaneous symmetry breaking. The transition is usually highly punctuated. In this context, Equations (8.5–8.7) can be interpreted as defining the 'temperature' M or $\hat{M}$ at which a complex network of interacting cognitive submodules breaks down into a simpler groupoid structure of disjointly partitioned submodules. Given the nature of criminal enterprise, these may be expected to engage in hyperviolent conflict over remaining resources.

The influence of state policy

Recapitulating Section 2.5, it is possible to examine how the 'external information source' of state policy can influence transitions between quasi-stable nonequilibrium steady states having different levels of inherent violence, or related characteristics.

To reiterate, the rate function $\mathcal{I}$ that Champagnat et al. (2006) invoke to describe large deviations in a coevolutionary system can be expressed as a kind of information free energy measure, that is, having the canonical form

$$\mathcal{I} = -\Sigma_j P_j \log(P_j) \tag{8.8}$$

for some probability distribution. Again, this result goes under a number of names; Sanov's Theorem, Cramer's Theorem, the Gartner–Ellis Theorem, the Shannon–McMillan Theorem, and so forth (Dembo and Zeitouni 1998).

Equations (8.4) and (8.5–8.7) are now seen as subject to large deviations that can themselves be described in terms of information sources, providing a driving parameter that can trigger punctuated shifts between quasi-stable modes, or can represent control mechanisms that can prevent such transitions. Thus external signals – here, state policy – characterized by an information source L_D as in Section 6.3, can provide parameters that serve to drive the system to different nonequilibrium quasi-stable states in a highly punctuated manner.

8.5 Reconsidering the model

According to this approach, the cost of regulation can grow at rates driven by the channel capacity needed to fix the average distortion between regulatory intent and effect at a desired level. System stability may, in addition, require high minimum expenditures driven by the synergism between external and internal noise. This observation suggests that a rational strategy for large-scale criminal enterprise is to apply overwhelming financial and opportunity costs in response to deviations from expected patterns. That is, 'regulatory investment' (RI), under such a climate, becomes 'riskless' if regulators charge violators at a rate M that satisfies essential constraints: let the punishment at least fit the transgression, as it were. If, in addition, RI includes draconian hyperviolent 'opportunity costs,' then RI would not likely be seen as simply another 'cost of doing business' by opponents. All this suggests that large-scale criminal hyperviolence may often have a basis in a rational political economy, and not simply represent the group-level acting out of path-dependent cultural mechanisms, powerful as these may be at the individual level (Wallace et al. 1996).

The arguments above, however, imply that state policy, defining parameters such as σ, β, μ, κ_j, and the 'large deviations' information source characterized by $\mathcal{I}$, can cause phase transitions between various quasi-stable modes of this system, or trigger system-wide instabilities leading to fragmentation. Some modes will have relatively low levels of violence, others, particularly under conditions of instability and fragmentation, will be hyperviolent – the 1990 peak in Figure 8.3.

It would be of interest to expand the observations of Haug and Taleb (2011) on the sophisticated real-world heuristics of options traders to the behaviors of criminal executives who must 'invest' in the management and control of their enterprises.

Pielou (1977, p. 106), as quoted in the Preface, provides an important warning regarding the sort of 'ecosystem' modeling done here, finding that the central usefulness of models consists *not in answering questions but in raising them*. That is, models can be used to inspire new field investigations, and these are the only source of new knowledge as opposed to new speculation.

Several real-world complications also confront the application of Black–Scholes methods here. To reiterate:

1   The noise may not be 'white,' with a uniform spectrum across a frequency domain. That is, it may have a highly complex spectral form, providing an inherent 'color.'

2   In particular, the noise may be 'fat-tailed' so that large disruptive jumps have higher probability than expected from a random walk.

3   In addition to fat-tailed or colored noise complications, the system of Equation (8.4) may be subject to additional resilience transitions driven by structured externalities: as has been said, what is a Black Swan for the turkey at Thanksgiving is not so for the farmer.

4   The calculations here have been based on the Rate Distortion Function for a Gaussian channel. Although all such are convex in the average distortion, exact functional forms may vary greatly with underlying structure. For example many systems follow the 'natural' channel, having a functional form $R(D) \approx \sigma^2/D$, leading to a condition on the discriminant of a cubic, instead of a quadratic.

5   Much hinges on Equation (5.16), and $\Delta \Pi / \Delta t \approx f(\Pi)$, $g(R)$ may take many possible functional forms, giving higher order results.

Modulo these cautions, the Black–Scholes models leading to Equations (8.5–8.7) nonetheless suggest an approach to empirical analysis aimed at identifying keystone scales and level of organization, in the sense of Holling (1992), at which intervention – law enforcement, social reform, etc. – would have most effect in reducing both individual and enterprise hyperviolence. The next section begins such an examination at the national scale for the United States.

8.6 A perfect storm

The shredding of minority voting blocks accomplished through the contagious urban decay and forced migration associated with Figures 8.1 and 8.2 carried with it an immediate burden of a raised rate of individual level violence, through the mechanisms described by Wallace et al. (1996). This resulted in the homicide peak of 1980 in Figure 8.3. In addition to disruption of voting blocks, however, the massive forced migrations also disrupted locally embedded criminal enterprises, fragmenting existing drug cartels, and creating a marketing opportunity for new players (Halbfinger 1998), much as described by Guerrero-Gutierrez (2011). As is now the case in Mexico, this fragmentation, and its associated absence of systematic regulation, triggered deadly conflict between old and newly emerging organizations. Not until the late 1990s did that conflict resolve itself, in the context of recovery of larger-scale regulatory social network structure at the neighborhood scale – grandmothers on the stoops (Halbfinger 1998; Wallace et al. 1996).

Is there a national parallel, albeit on the longer timescales dictated by greater population and more complex geography of the US?

Figure 7.2 showed the counties of the northeast US that lost 1000 or more industrial jobs between 1972 and 1987 – the 'Rust Belt.' It is, in its way, a larger version of Figure 8.1, in that lost industrial jobs tend to stay lost, as does the social, political, and economic capital associated with them and with the stability of union benefits they incorporated.

Figure 8.4 shows the number of industrial jobs in the US between 1980 and 2001. The decline is analogous to Figure 8.2, representing a permanent economic dislocation and forced displacement. As Chapter 7 argues at great length, US deindustrialization is a direct consequence of the massive diversion of engineering and scientific resources from civilian enterprise into what Melman characterizes as 'Pentagon Capitalism,' our grossly mismanaged economy, no less constrained or oppressive than a Soviet Gosplan.

Figure 8.5 suggests something of the cost of deindustrialization. It plots the percent of the voting population convicted of a felony vs. the integral of the industrial job losses of Figure 8.4 between 1980 and 1998. The correlation is very high indeed, suggesting that deindustrialization may, in fact, be driving criminal activity.

The interpretation of Figure 8.5 is, however, complicated by mass incarceration (Thompson 2010). It is not merely that deindustrialization produces or exacerbates poverty, it is that in the US poverty has itself been criminalized: with 5 percent of the world's population we have a quarter of the world's prisoners, disproportionately taken from communities of color. Figure 8.6 shows the US rate of incarceration between 1925 and 2008. The marked increase since 1980 represents the implementation of a policy of mass incarceration.

Although mass incarceration in the United States engaged more than 2.3 million adults in 2009, an often overlooked population involves the 5.1 million individuals who are on parole, on probation, or under the supervision of the courts. This group of ex-prisoners is not behind bars, but they are nonetheless

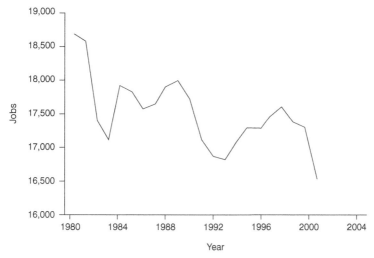

Figure 8.4 US industrial jobs, 1980–2001. The decline is progressive and relentless, a consequence of the diversion of technical resources from civilian enterprise into the Cold War (Ullmann 1988; Melman 1971).

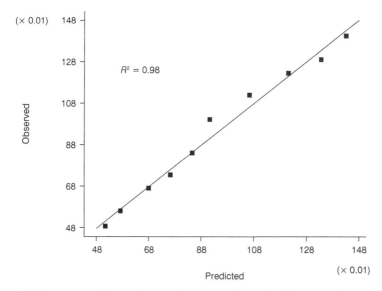

Figure 8.5 Percentage of the voting population convicted of a felony, and thus unable to vote, as a function of the integral of the loss of industrial jobs, 1980–1998.

major contributors to the destabilization of the communities to which they return (Pew Center on the States 2009).

In addition to having lost the right to vote in many states of the US, ex-prisoners have also lost the ability to secure access to public housing, the loss of access to funding for higher education, a loss of access to food stamps, and a loss

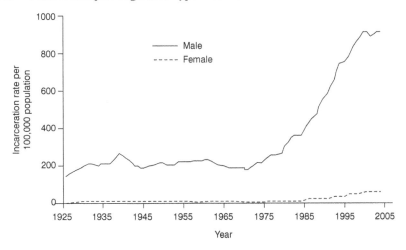

Figure 8.6 Incarceration rate per 100,000 in the US between 1925 and 2008. Mass incarceration began after 1980. Adapted from the Wikipedia entry on mass incarceration.

of access to employment in local, state and federal government jobs. As Michelle Alexander notes in her seminal book, *The New Jim Crow* (p. 93),

> No wonder, then, that most people labeled felons find their way back into prison. According to a Bureau of Justice Statistics study, about 30 percent of released prisoners in its sample were rearrested within six months of release. Within three years, nearly 68 percent were rearrested at least once for a new offense. Only a small minority are rearrested for violent crimes; the vast majority are rearrested for property offenses, drug offenses, and offenses against public order.

The scope of the circulation of ex-prisoners between the community, the prison, and back again to the community cannot be overemphasized. As Alexander points out, a major factor in prison admissions over the course of the period between 1980 and 2009 was the dramatic and significant increase in the number of those who were readmitted for parole violations.

> With respect to parole, in 1980, only 1 percent of all prison admissions were parole violators. Twenty years later, more than one third (35 percent) prison admissions resulted from parole violations. To put the matter more starkly: *About as many people were returned to prison for parole violations in* 2000 *as were admitted to prison in* 1980 *for all reasons.*
>
> [italics from author, Ibid, p. 93]

Mass incarceration is more than just the loss of adult bodies to community life. Convicted felons have no place in a deindustrialized society. They are barred from jobs and from training and educational opportunities that have the potential to reintegrate them back into society. Moreover, these men and women are rapidly becoming an intolerable expense for the states that are increasingly challenged to pay for the costs of their incarceration but do not have the resources to assure their reentry into their communities.

That many of the men who are caught up in this system will ultimately be caught up in the violence of community life only seems inevitable. The tragedy, of course, is that a more efficient system of parole and probation would enable modest investments in job training and education to generate economically productive citizens instead of 'frequent fliers' who are perennially in and out of the system of mass incarceration. Here, the Pew Center for the States (2009) suggests that community corrections not better strategies for policing and incarceration of offenders might be the long sought after solution:

> Better performance in community corrections can cut crime and avert the need not only for new prisons but even for some we already have. And the accrued savings, if used to reinforce probation and parole, support early-intervention strategies, or shore up the high-stakes neighborhoods where prisoners come from and return to, can generate even further reductions in crime and incarceration.

At the national level, then, the urban desertification afflicting many central cities, as represented by Figure 8.1, has been compounded by the economic dislocations indexed by Figure 8.4, and by the relentless depredation of mass incarceration.

Is there more? Unfortunately, yes. Figure 8.7 shows the number of US homes in foreclosure by quarter from first 2007 through first 2010. Much of this loss has also been disproportionately concentrated in communities of color (Saegert et al. 2011), and represents a massive bleeding out of accumulated social and economic capital.

In the background to the current synergism of catastrophes is a 70-year historical trajectory of serial forced displacement affecting minority populations in the US (Fullilove and Wallace 2011). From Redlining to Urban Renewal, to Planned Shrinkage, to Hope VI, minority communities have been subjected to repeated policies and practices that periodically debride them of a generation's accumulation of social, political, and economic capital. This has had a cumulative impact now exacerbated by the dynamics we have explored in this section.

A perfect storm is now upon the United States.

8.7 Summary

Demographic shifts in the US will, by mid-century, make every subpopulation a 'minority.' Increasingly large sectors of that nation's fractured polity are sliding into penury and disorganization, with no 'recovery' in sight. Official policy, established practice, and path-dependent historical trajectory, now dictate a social ecology of continuing fragmentation and disempowerment across the full American

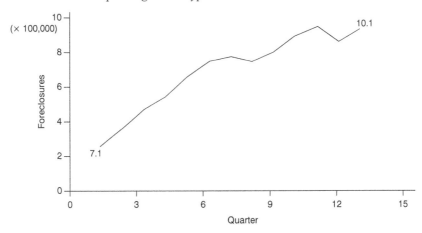

Figure 8.7 Numbers of foreclosed US homes, first quarter 2007 to first 2010. A disproportionate share of this turmoil is centered in communities of color.

subcultural spectrum that is, in its way, analogous to the systematic displacements implied by Figure 8.1. Central to this maelstrom of probabilities and possibilities lies the system of mass incarceration, inextricably linked to deindustrialization. The illegal drug industry is only one likely player now recruiting in that massive training ground and cauldron of socialization. Other failed nations have seen permanent establishment of truly industrial levels of kidnapping, extortion, human trafficking, and the like. The Favelas of South America come to mind, as do Naples, Sardinia, Corsica, and, of course, Sicily. The New York City experience – Figure 8.3 – suggests that the successful management of large-scale criminal enterprise under conditions of comprehensive social decay inevitably invokes hyperviolence as a routine tool, sometimes driving a permanent ecosystem domain shift, analogous to the eutrophication of a pristine lake by sewage runoff.

Thirty years of mass incarceration and its correlates appear to have taken the United States significantly closer to such a collective nightmare. As Wacquant (2001) puts it,

> The convergent changes that have 'prisonized' the ghetto and 'ghettoized' the prison in the aftermath of the Civil Rights revolution suggest that the inordinate and mounting over-representation of blacks behind bars [instantiate] transformations that have interlocked the prison and the (hyper) ghetto via a relation of *function equivalency* (they serve one and the same purpose, the coercive confinement of a stigmatized population) and *structural homology* (they comprise and comfort the same type of social relations and authority pattern) to form a *single institutional mesh* suited to fulfill anew the mission historically imparted to America's 'peculiar institutions.'

Under the impetus of the economic collapse illustrated by Figures 7.2, 8.4, and 8.7, those institutions – traditionally focused on African American communities

– now entrain ever larger sectors of the American populace. As public health scientist Greg Pappas once put it, regarding such dynamic social phenomena, 'concentration is not containment.' Charles Dickens' *Bleak House* (1853) described the social diffusion of the pathologies of the generic urban slum he called Tom-All-Alone's in these terms:

> Even the winds are his messengers, and they serve him in these hours of darkness … There is not an atom of Tom's slime, not a cubic inch of any pestilential gas in which he lives, not one obscenity or degradation about him, not an ignorance, not a wickedness, not a brutality of his committing, but shall work its retribution through every order of society up to the proudest of the proud and to the highest of the high.

Holling (1992) describes ecosystems as driven by 'keystone' scales and levels of organization, subsystems whose dynamics are imposed upon both smaller and larger structures and entities. It seems clear that mass incarceration and its correlated policies causing degradation of civic life are such keystones in the pathological ecology now consuming the US. A prudent ruling elite, for its own protection, would begin working toward the permanent abolition of all such 'peculiar institutions.'

9 Counterexample: farming human pathogens

This chapter was written in collaboration with Robert G. Wallace (Wallace and Wallace 2014).

9.1 Introduction

The formalism introduced in Chapter 6 can, with some modification, be used to explore the synergism between socioeconomic policy, structure, and human pathogen evolution and spread, quite literally, the farming of human pathogens. In essence, such pathogens can be viewed as 'firms' that face both biological and social selection pressures. It is, then, literally possible to 'farm' human pathogens, inadvertantly or otherwise, through economic and other policy decisions, and we provide three case histories.

Population genetics defines evolution by changes in allele frequencies (Hartl and Clark 2006; Ewens 2004). Evolutionary game dynamics track such shifts under natural selection using Taylor and Jonker's (1978) famous replicator model. The system of non-linear first-order differential equations, and variations thereof, are purported a necessary and sufficient definition of evolution across disciplines, from biology to economics, albeit to sometimes scathing criticism (e.g., Roca et al. 2009).

By contrast, Wallace (2010a, 2011a, 2012, 2013a) and Wallace and Wallace (2008b) have proposed a set of necessary conditions statistical models extending evolutionary theory via the asymptotic limit theorems of communication theory. The approach is based upon representing genetic heritage, gene expression, and the environment as interacting information sources. The essential insight the models offer is recognizing gene expression as a cognitive phenomenon associated with a 'dual' information source, while the embedding environment's systematic regularities 'remember' imposed changes, resulting in a coevolutionary process in the sense of Champagnat et al. (2006) recorded in both genes and environment.

Here, as in Chapter 6, we include the effect of 'large deviations' representing transitions between the quasi-stable modes that are analogous to game-theoretic Evolutionary Stable Strategies. The focus will be on incorporating path dependence limiting such possible excursions to high probability paths consistent with, if not originating in, previous evolutionary trajectories: however most multicellular organisms evolve, they retain their basic Bauplan, variations notwithstanding.

While incorporation of such path dependence drastically reduces possible dynamics in higher organisms, viral or viroid evolution can be explored in a far less constrained manner using a statistical mechanics formalism driven by 'noise' defined as much by deliberate economic and other policies and underlying socioeconomic structure as by reassortment and generation time. Changes in policy and economy can, in effect, desterilize a natural or human ecosystem in which pathogen populations had previously been held to low equilibrium values.

The argument is, in a sense, a coevolutionary inverse of species-fragmented area relation studies like those of Hanski et al. (2013). That is, while spatial fragmentation of natural ecosystems can drive wanted species to extinction, proper mosaic design of agricultural systems – fragmentation in time, space, and community structure – can limit the rate of new pathogen evolution and constrain their populations to low endemic levels. In contrast, the inference is that large-scale intensive husbandry, expanding growth and transport of monoculture livestock, is epizootically unsustainable. Increasingly accessed and agroecologically pauperized landscapes should select for pathogens of increasing transmissibility and virulence (Messinger and Ostling 2009).

9.2　The basic model

Following the Bauplan of Chapter 6, we suppose there are n populations interacting with an embedding environment represented by an information source Z. The genetic and (cognitive) gene expression processes associated with each species i are represented as information sources X_i, Y_i respectively. These information sources undergo a 'coevolutionary' interaction, producing a joint information source uncertainty for the full system as

$$H(X_1, Y_1, ..., X_n, Y_n, Z) \tag{9.1}$$

Again, Feynman's (2000) insight that information is a form of free energy allows definition of an entropy-analog as

$$S \equiv H - Q_j \, \Sigma_j \partial \, H / \partial \, Q_j \tag{9.2}$$

The Q_i are taken as driving parameters that may include, but are not limited to, the Shannon uncertainties of the underlying information sources.

Again, in the spirit of earlier developments, we can characterize the dynamics of the system in terms of Onsager-like nonequilibrium thermodynamics in the gradients of S as the set of stochastic differential equations,

$$dQ_t^i = L_i(\partial S / \partial Q^1 ... \partial S / \partial Q^m, t)dt + \sum_k \sigma_k^i(\partial S / \partial Q^1 ... \partial S / \partial Q^m, t)dB_k \tag{9.3}$$

where the B_k represent noise terms having particular forms of quadratic variation. See Protter (1990) or other standard references on stochastic differential equations for details.

This can be more simply written as

$$dQ^i_t = L_i(\mathbf{Q}, t)dt + \Sigma_k \sigma^i_k(\mathbf{Q}, t)dB_k \tag{9.4}$$

where $\mathbf{Q} \equiv (Q^1, ..., Q^m)$.

Again, this is very much a coevolutionary structure, where, if it is sufficiently large, fundamental dynamics are determined by inevitable component feedbacks and other interactions:

1   Setting the expectation of Equations (9.4) equal to zero and solving for stationary points gives attractor states since the noise terms preclude unstable equilibria. These are analogous to the evolutionarily stable states of evolutionary game theory.
2   This system may, however, converge to limit cycle or pseudorandom 'strange attractor' behaviors similar to thrashing in which the system seems to chase its tail endlessly within a limited venue – the 'Red Queen.'
3   What is 'converged' to in any case is not a simple state or limit cycle of states. Rather it is an equivalence class, or set of them, of highly dynamic information sources coupled by mutual interaction through crosstalk and other interactions. Thus 'stability' in this structure represents particular patterns of ongoing dynamics rather than some identifiable static configuration. These are nonequilibrium quasi-steady states.
4   Again, applying Ito's chain rule for stochastic differential equations to the $(Q^i_t)^2$ and taking expectations allows calculation of variances. These may depend very powerfully on a system's defining structural constants, leading to significant instabilities (Khasminskii 2012).

9.3 Large deviations

As has been frequently argued above, shifts between the nonequilibrium quasi-steady states of such a coevolutionary system can be addressed by the large deviations formalism. The dynamics of drift away from trajectories predicted by the canonical equation can be investigated by considering the asymptotic of the probability of 'rare events' for the sample paths of the diffusion.

Recall that 'rare events' are the diffusion paths drifting far away from the direct solutions of the canonical equation. The probability of such rare events is governed by a large deviation principle, driven by a 'rate function' $\mathcal{I}$ that can be expressed in terms of the parameters of the diffusion.

This result can be used to study long-time behavior of the diffusion process when there are multiple attractive singularities. Under proper conditions, the most likely path followed by the diffusion when exiting a basin of attraction is the one minimizing the rate function $\mathcal{I}$ over all the appropriate trajectories.

Recall from large deviations theory that the rate function $\mathcal{I}$ almost always has the canonical form

$$\mathcal{I} = -\Sigma_j P_j \log(P_j) \tag{9.5}$$

for some probability distribution, i.e., the uncertainty of an information source.

These arguments are in the direction of Equation (9.4), now seen as subject to large deviations *that can themselves be described as the output of an information source L_D defining $\mathcal{I}$*, driving or defining Q'-parameters that can trigger punctuated shifts between quasi-stable system modes.

Not all large deviations are possible, only those consistent with the high probability paths defined by the information source L_D.

Recall from the Shannon–McMillan Theorem that all possible utterances of an information source can be divided into two sets, one very large that represents nonsense statements of vanishingly small probability, and one very small of high probability representing those statements consistent with the inherent 'grammar' and 'syntax' of the information source. Again, whatever higher-order multicellular evolution takes place, some equivalent of backbone and blood remains.

Thus we could now rewrite Equation (9.1) as

$$H_L(X_1, Y_1, ..., X_n, Y_n, Z, L_D) \tag{9.6}$$

where we have explicitly incorporated the 'large deviations' information source L_D that defines high probability evolutionary excursions that are possible for this system.

For human ecosystems Z, of course, will include fundamental matters of historically driven socioeconomic structure, itself subject to limitations on large deviations excursions. Any such must be consistent with path-dependent patterns of earlier cultural expression.

Again carrying out the argument leading to Equation (9.4), we arrive at another set of quasi-stable modes, but possibly very much changed in number; either branched outward in time by a wave of speciation, or decreased through a wave of extinction.

This is a central result, and, for virus/human systems, must be seen as including interaction between socioeconomic and viral evolution.

Note that iterating such models backwards in time constitutes a cladistic or coalescent analysis.

Again, social, economic, and cultural structures must be included in examinations of coevolutionary variation and selection, according to this model.

9.4 Extinction

A simple extinction model, using the same approach as Chapter 6, again leads to significant extension of the theory.

Let $N_t \geq 0$ now represent the number of individuals of a particular pathogen species at time t. The simplest dynamic model, in this formulation, is then something like

$$dN_t = -\alpha\, N_t |N_t - N_C| dt + \sigma\, N_t dW_t \tag{9.7}$$

where N_C is the ecological carrying capacity for the species, α is a characteristic time constant, σ is a 'noise' index, and dW_t represents white noise.

Taking the expectation of Equation (9.7), the possible equilibrium values of N_t are either zero or N_C. Again, applying the Ito chain rule to the second moment in N_t i.e., to N_t^2, calculation finds there can be no real second moment unless

$$\sigma^2 < 2\alpha\, N_C \tag{9.8}$$

That is, unless Equation (9.8) holds – the product of the rate of population change and carrying capacity is sufficiently large – noise-driven fluctuations will inevitably drive the species to extinction.

Assuming a very low, but nonzero equilibrium possible – say $N_c \ll N_C$ – then calculation shows N_C in Equation (9.8) is replaced by the difference $\Delta N \equiv N_C - N_c$.

As discussed previously, similar SDE approach has been used to model noise-driven criticality in physical systems, suggesting that a more conventional phase transition methodology may provide particular insight.

The core relationships suggest an epidemiological application.

9.5 Socio-viral evolution

In general, for higher animals, the number of quasi-steady states available to the system defined by Equation (9.4), or to its generalization via Equation (9.6), will be relatively small at any given time. The same cannot be said, however, for virus/viroid species or quasi-species, to which we can apply more general methods. The speciation/extinction large deviations information source L_D is far less constrained.

The noise parameter in Equation (9.7) can be interpreted as a kind of temperature-analog, and N_t as an order parameter that, like magnetization or ice-crystal form, vanishes (or falls to $N_c \ll N_C$) above a critical value of σ. For something as protean as influenza or HIV, this leads to a relatively simple statistical mechanics analog built on the H_L of Equation (9.6).

Define a pseudoprobability for quasi-stable mode j as

$$P_j = \frac{\exp[-H_L^j / \kappa\sigma]}{\sum_i \exp[-H_L^i / \kappa\sigma]} \tag{9.9}$$

where κ is a scaling constant and σ is a noise intensity.

Next, define a Morse Function F, in the sense used by Pettini (2007), as

$$\exp[-F/\kappa\,\sigma] \equiv \Sigma_i \exp[-H_L^i/\kappa\,\sigma] \tag{9.10}$$

Apply Pettini's topological hypothesis to F, taking N_p the number of members of species (or quasi-species) j as a kind of 'order parameter,' in Landau's (2007) sense. Then σ is seen as a very general temperature-like measure whose changes drive punctuated topological alterations in the underlying ecological structures associated with the Morse Function F. In particular, according to the generalization of Equation (9.8), lowering σ below a critical threshold can drive the system from N_c to $N_C \gg N_c$.

However, topological changes, following Pettini's arguments, can be far more general than indexed by the simple Landau-type critical point phase transition in an order parameter. They can represent a great variety of fundamental and highly punctuated ecosystem alterations in microbial or viral populations and their dynamics, since the underlying species and quasi-species are not so sharply constrained by evolutionary trajectory in the manner limiting variation in most higher organisms.

Indeed, one might well use a number of measures of σ. For example neoliberal or colonial exploitation or elimination of traditional farming strategies that previously isolated pathogens from livestock and/or humans, could well induce large-scale ecosystem shifts triggering massive increases in pathogen populations or their rates of speciation, inducing new patterns of transmission and virulence (Leibler et al. 2009). That is, changes in policy or socioeconomic structure can 'desterilize' a natural or human ecosystem in which a pathogen has been traditionally held at a low level equilibrium value N_c, or simply had not previously evolved.

In essence, traditional agriculture can, by its diversity in time, space, and mode, create numerous barriers – counterintuitively, a kind of noise similar to a sterilizing temperature – limiting pathogen evolution and spread. Plantation or factory farming, of course, removes such barriers to improve the 'efficiency' of production in time and space.

The argument suggests that it should be possible to empirically define a 'critical ecosystem sterilizing temperature' incorporating measures of the 'collective roughness' of disease-specific barriers to pathogen evolution and propagation.

It is worth noting that, in deep time, say 500×10^6 years in the past, possible evolutionary trajectories for most species would have, in general, been less locked in by path dependence, and thus more subject to 'viral-like' phase transitions allowing relatively large-scale changes in bauplan or ecological niche. This observation may provide some insight into the Cambrian explosion, the remarkably rapid evolutionary divergence of living organisms that has perplexed evolutionary biologists for some considerable time (Wallace 2014).

9.6 Three case histories

Polio in the UK

Smallman-Raynor and Cliff (2013) examine an abrupt transition to heightened poliomyelitis endemicity and epidemicity in England and Wales between 1947 and 1957 that was found to be associated with a pronounced increase in the geographical rate of disease propagation. Figure 9.1, adapted from their paper, shows the punctuation in disease incidence that is the centerpiece of their analysis. Figure 9.1a examines the UK, 9.1b, the USA. The latter example is more fully explored in Trevelyan et al. (2005).

Using a presence/absence method, Smallman-Raynor and Cliff (2013) define a dimensionless velocity relation, with a value in the range [0–1], measuring the average time from the onset of polio season to the first notified case in a given

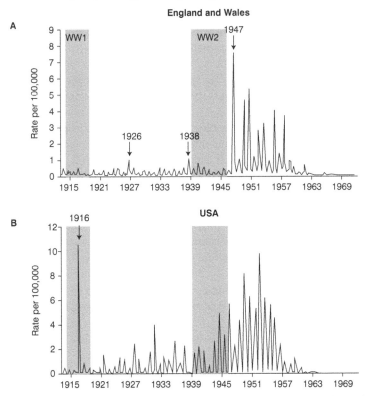

Figure 9.1 Adapted from Smallman-Raynor and Cliff (2013), monthly series of poliomyelitis notification rates per 100,000 population through 1971. (a) England and Wales, (b) the USA.

category of district. Low/high values of *VLE* indicate slow/fast spreading infection waves. See Figure 9.2, and note particularly the increased rate of propagation in the period 1947–1957.

As Smallman-Raynor and Cliff put it, relative to the immediately preceding (1940–1946) and following (1958–1964) years, when vaccine became widely available, the period of heightened endemicity (1947–1957) was associated with a faster rate of spatial advance, a slower rate of spatial retreat, and an extended period of notified activity. The changes were underpinned by a shift in the geographical pattern of disease activity, from small focal outbreaks in the inter-war years to national epidemics in the post-war years. These observations, they conclude, are consistent with the operation of an emergence process that considerably enhanced the efficiency by which poliomyelitis spread from one geographical area to another. The enhancement, however, was not gradual; it occurred abruptly with the onset of heightened epidemicity and involved both urban and rural areas of the country. In particular, the diffusion characteristics of the events of 1947–1957 are analogous to those observed involving the first-time spread of viral diseases such as new pandemic strains of influenza A in a population.

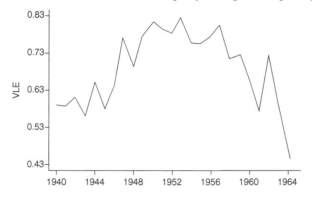

Figure 9.2 Dimensionless reduced traveling wave velocity of polio infection vs. year, 1940–1964, for England and Wales (Smallman-Raynor and Cliff 2013). The period 1947–1957 shows particularly rapid rates of geographic propagation.

Recent work by M.J. Law (2012) suggests a possible mechanism for Figure 9.1: histories of suburban London, in particular, underplay the importance of the car to inter-war mobilities. An emphasis on public transport has, in Law's view, occluded our understanding of the role of motoring in the transformation of suburban life. This is in marked contrast to work on American suburbia that affords the car a prime role in the suburb's formation. A vast array of data shows that, by the end of the 1930s, suburban motoring had highly heterogeneous levels of adoption in the UK, but, where it was popular, it changed mobility in a dramatic manner that prefigured wider developments of the late 1950s.

Figure 9.3, using data from Plowden (1973), shows, for the UK, millions of registered cars vs. year from 1930 through 1957, the last year of severe poliomyelitis outbreaks in the UK. Note the marked decline during the war years. This may, in fact, index a far more general mobility constraint associated with deliberate policies limiting rail and other civilian traffic during the war, carried out under the rubric of 'Is your trip necessary?'

Figure 9.4 shows the dimensionless reduced traveling wave velocity from Smallman-Raynor and Cliff (2013), and Figure 9.5 a plot of poliomyelitis epidemic duration, both as functions of the number of registered cars between 1940 and 1957. A step function phase transition is evident in both cases at about 2 million cars.

Defining a 'normalized characteristic extent' of the epidemics as the dimensionless reduced velocity of the leading edge times the epidemic duration produces an even more distinct step function, representing the shift from isolated foci to a more general national outbreak.

The obvious inference is that the sudden availability of private travel in the UK after World War II was sufficient to breach sterilizing sociogeographic isolation between what would otherwise have been small focal outbreaks, a phase transition triggering the punctuated dynamics of Figures 9.1a and 9.2.

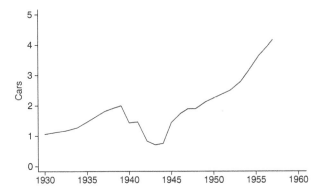

Figure 9.3 Millions of registered cars in the UK between 1930 and 1957, from Plowden (1973). Note the steady increase between 1930 and 1939, the marked decline during the Second World War, and the explosive rise thereafter.

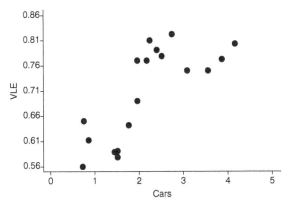

Figure 9.4 Dimensionless reduced leading-edge traveling wave velocity of polio epidemics vs. millions of registered cars, 1940–1957. Note the evident phase transition at about 2 million cars.

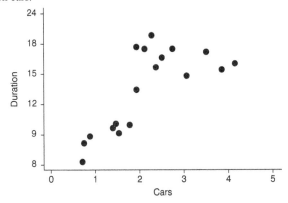

Figure 9.5 Polio epidemic duration in weeks (Smallman-Raynor and Cliff 2013) vs. millions of registered cars, 1940–1957 (Plowden 1973). The phase transition at 2 million is even more clearly displayed.

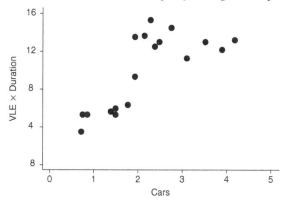

Figure 9.6 VLE × epidemic duration, 1940–1957 vs. millions of registered cars, representing a normalized 'characteristic extent' of the polio epidemics. The failure of constraint to discrete focal centers after 2 million is evident.

In a sense, then, the normalized characteristic extent can be viewed as a classic order parameter, and the number of cars as a smoothing agent, reducing the friction coefficient σ in Equations (9.8), (9.9), and (9.10), eventually driving the coevolutionary socio-viral system across a critical point.

Poliomyelitis, unlike the various influenzas, appears more evolutionarily stable than its embedding social milieu, and successful vaccines continue to include the basic three viral types. This challenges assertions that introduction of a 'new' viral strain to the UK accounts for the explosive post-war outbreaks, as argued by Smallman-Raynor and Cliff (2013). Although a socio-viral coevolution may well have selected type I over less virulent strains, the driving force, as it were, appears to be the shift from travel patterns defined primarily by long-established, and hence epidemiologically stable, public transport to a randomization of contact consequent on increasingly widespread automobile travel. In that regard, the 'signal' epidemiological event of 1938 from Figure 9.1a may well have been a harbinger of things to come, as it took place when car numbers first reached the 2 million mark.

Polio in the US

The United States is, of course, vastly larger than England and Wales, and represents an amalgam of semi-detached geographic regions that would be expected to undergo a qualitatively different pattern of semi-independent polio outbreaks. Nonetheless, Figure 9.1b shows distinct post-WW II spiking.

Unfortunately, VLE statistics for US polio outbreaks are not available, precluding exact comparison with the UK example. What is available, from Trevelyan et al. (2005) and from standard statistical abstracts, is given in Figures 9.7 and 9.8. Figure 9.7 shows the poliomyelitis rate per 100,000 population plotted against billions of motor vehicle miles traveled from 1921 through 1954, the last epidemic year before widespread introduction of the vaccine. Figure 9.8 shows billions of vehicle miles traveled (VMT) between 1940 and 1955, focusing on the critical explosion after World War II.

While a simple linear regression, adjusted for degrees of freedom, accounts for about 63 percent of variance, the upper-right cluster of points, representing the post-WW II outbreaks in Figure 9.1b, is detached from the earlier system, and indicates a phase transiton in the US at about 350 billion VMT.

The phase change is illustrated by Figure 9.9, a simple cluster analysis using a centroid, squared Euclidean distance method. The lower cluster is centered at (5.3, 214.5), the higher at (22.1, 466.6), and transition between the two systems is characteristically unstable.

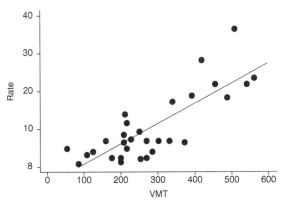

Figure 9.7 Poliomyelitis rate per 100,000 vs. billions of motor vehicle miles traveled for the US, 1921–1955. The fitted linear regression accounts for 63.2 percent of the variance, adjusted for degrees of freedom. Note, however, the upper-right cluster, that appears to represent a national phase transition at about 350 billion VMT.

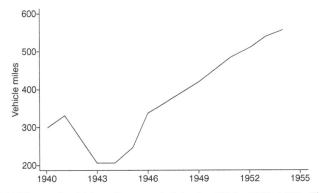

Figure 9.8 Billions of vehicle miles traveled in the USA, 1940–1955. The postwar explosion is evident.

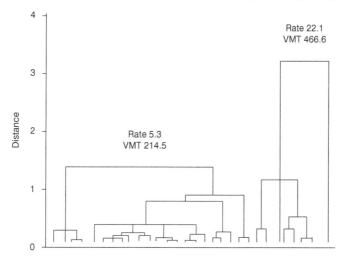

Figure 9.9 Cluster analysis for US polio outbreaks, 1921–1955, centroid method, squared Eculidian distance. Two groups are evident, centered at (5.3, 214.5) and (22.1, 466.6), respectively.

Human-origin swine flu in the US

Less evolutionarily stable pathogens than poliomyelitis present a qualitatively different challenge, since no one vaccine will fit all outbreaks. Unlike for polio, socioeconomic structure and government policy can initiate a synergism of disease spread and evolution, moving the dynamic beyond simply amplifying geographic diffusion.

With the globalization of the livestock filiere the distances over which food animal populations are transported have expanded to continental and even intercontinental scales. Figure 9.10 shows a surge in worldwide hog exports post-1990.

The upswing in livestock miles goes hand in hand with the global spread of a corporate model of vertically integrated husbandry associated with farm consolidation and increases in head count per farm (Wallace 2009b). By way of structural adjustment programs and free trade agreements large-scale agribusinesses are moving company operations to the global South and eastern Europe to take advantage of cheap labor, cheap land, weak regulation, and domestic production hobbled in favor of heavily subsidized agro-exporting. As a result, livestock and poultry monocultures of limited diversity and inherently dubious immunity are being raised right up against what have been long documented as reservoirs of multiple endemic pathogens, including year-round circulating strains of influenza.

But as Burch (2005) explains, companies are also engaging in sophisticated corporate strategy. Agribusinesses are spreading their production line across much of the world. The CP Group, for one, now the world's fourth largest poultry producer, has poultry facilities in Turkey, China, Malaysia, Indonesia, and the

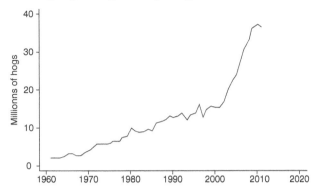

Figure 9.10 FAO data. International hog exports, 1961–2011.

United States. It has feed operations across India, China, Indonesia, and Vietnam. It owns a number of fast-food chain restaurants throughout southeast Asia. A supply chain arrayed across multiple countries allows companies the means by which to compensate for any interruptions in business, including of their own making. CP operates joint-venture poultry facilities across China, producing 600 million of China's 2.2 billion chickens annually sold. When an outbreak of deadly bird flu H5N1 occurred in a farm operated by the CP Group in Heilongjiang province, Japan banned poultry from China. CP factories in Thailand filled the market gap by increasing exports to Japan.

The extent to which agroeconomic pressures on production margins are lengthening animal commodity chains is unprecedented. Genuses, a Manitoba company, flies thousands of specially bred pigs to Germany before a truck trip to Russia: Winnipeg to Krasandor on the other side of the world in four days (Rollason 2009). The implications for influenza are fundamental. First, the scale of transport increases the likelihood previously isolated influenza subtypes can trade genomic segments, as occurred for swine flu's transcontinentally recombinant H1N1 (Wallace 2009b; Vijaykrishna et al. 2011). Second, increasing the virus's geographic scope likely selects for deadlier strains (Messinger and Ostling 2009). A renewable supply of susceptibles is thought to serve as a primary fuel for the evolution of virulence. The cost of killing off one's host declines if another population of susceptibles is easily accessible in the next port of call.

Myers et al. (2006) describe the US context,

> During the past 60 years, the US swine industry has changed in composition from primarily small herds on family farms to include immense herds in large, corporate facilities [our figure 9.11]. The US pork industry now generates $11 billion annually and employs an estimated 575,000 persons (2002 figures). Although pork production facilities today are larger, fewer, and more efficient and require fewer workers, it is estimated that, nationwide, at least 100,000 workers work in swine barns with live pigs …

The potential for animal-to-animal transmission among pigs in a swine confinement operation will be much greater than on a traditional farm because of the pigs' crowding (resulting in prolonged and more frequent contact). In addition, virus-laden secretions from pigs may be more concentrated, and reductions in ventilation and sunshine exposure may prolong viral viability. Thus, a confinement worker's probability of acquiring influenza virus infection may be increased.

The reverse is also documented, that is, the transmission of human influenza to swine, raising the probability that a novel strain can emerge via reassortment. Livestock pigs had long hosted their own version of seasonal H1N1, evolutionarily related to our own, indeed originating in the very human influenza of 1918 infamy. From 1930–1998 the pig version evolved only slightly. But starting in 1998, the virus was subjected to a series of reassortment events (Garten et al. 2009). In North America, an aggressive swine H1N1 emerged with internal genes of a human H3N2 virus and an avian influenza. That virus subsequently spread across pig populations. In early 2009, a previously undocumented influenza, what we now know as swine flu H1N1 (2009), emerged in humans in central Mexico to spread around the world as a new pandemic strain. Three of the new virus segments appeared to be from the classical swine influenza (HA, NP, NS), three from the North American H3N2-avian-swine recombinant we just described (PB2, PB1, PA), and two from a Eurasian swine recombinant (NA, M) that originated in birds. That is, every one of the new H1N1's genetic segments proved most closely related to those of influenzas circulating among swine.

Given the US polio example, the form of the domestic 'traffic' dependence of H1 spread and evolution is of particular interest. As Nelson et al. (2011) put it,

> Millions of swine are transported year-round from the southern United States into the corn-rich Midwest, but the importance of these movements in the spatial dissemination and evolution of the influenza virus in swine

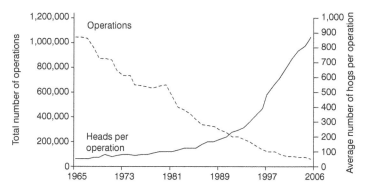

Figure 9.11 Annual numbers of US swine operations and average hogs per operation, 1965–2005 (Myers et al. 2006).

is unknown. Using a large data set of influenza virus sequences, collected in North American swine during 2003–2010, we investigated the spatial dynamics of two influenza viruses of the H1 subtype that were introduced into swine from humans around 2003. Employing recently developed Bayesian phylogeography methods, we find that the spread of this influenza virus follows the large-scale transport of swine from the South to the Midwest. Based on this pattern of viral migration, we suggest that the genetic diversity of swine influenza viruses in the Midwest is continually augmented by the importation of viruses from source populations in the South. Understanding the importance of long-distance pig movements in the evolution and spatial dissemination of influenza virus in swine may inform future strategies for the surveillance and control of influenza, and perhaps other swine pathogens.

Figure 9.12 redisplays Table 2 from Nelson et al. (2001) showing Markov jump counts between US regions vs. swine flows – number of exchanged swine – for 2009. The counts, showing estimated migration events across three US regions, are inferred through a Bayesian phylogenetic tree for several hundred H1N1 and H1N2 genetic sequences: South Central, South-Eastern, and Midwest sections, as characterized by Nelson et al. (2011). The resulting migration matrix shows six data points of exchange. The vertical axis is the jump count index, and the horizontal axis is the natural log of the number of transported swine. The third point represents slightly more than 1 million, and the highest, nearly 18 million swine transported between regions.

That third point appears to mark a cross-sectional punctuated transition to large-scale genetic change roughly analogous to the transition at 350 billion VMT in Figure 9.7. The resulting variation may be merely a correlate of the extent of transport, but the introgression offers the kind of genetic subtrate from which new variants and reassortants may draw. Indeed, new swine-origin human H1N1v, H1N2v and H3N2v were recently documented in the summer and fall of 2012 across ten states, mainly in the Midwest (CDC 2013).

9.7 Discussion and conclusions

The variables scientists include in their models embody a social decision. What researchers choose to make internal or external to their model, including which data to concatenate (or exclude), can have a significant impact on both its meaning and application. The same can be said of the formalisms developed here. We have presented a class of statistical models characterizing coevolutionary and mosaic disease dynamics (and attendant management strategies) from first principles. We extend evolutionary theory via necessary conditions imposed by the asymptotic limit theorems of communication theory, including a 'thermal' critical point for path dependency: from organisms (and environments) characterized by deep-time historical constraints to, we propose, pathogens with much greater leeway to explore their evolutionary space (e.g., Burdon and Thrall 2008).

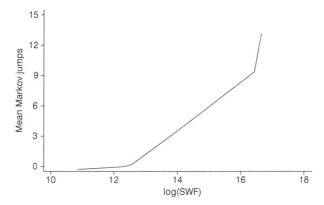

Figure 9.12 Markov jump counts between US regions vs. the log of swine flows, 2009 (Nelson et al. 2011). The counts are inferred through the phylogenetic tree for several hundred H1N1 and H1N2 genetic sequences.

The effects landscape dynamics impose on viral evolution and control efforts, appear fundamental. As Burdon and Thrall put the matter,

> [I]t seems highly likely that heterogeneity in agro-ecological interactions across geographical ranges could result in novel disease dynamics (e.g., shifts from 'boom-and-bust' to more endemic situations and vice versa) as well as spatial variation in the likelihood of disease emergence and the evolution of new virulence. From an applied evolution perspective, therefore one research issue of clear importance has to do with understanding how agricultural management (e.g., crop spatial arrangement and extent, rotational sequences) in rural landscapes might influence host-pathogen population dynamics ... Is it possible to use mosaic management approaches to landscapes to control disease? Overall, it is becoming increasingly clear that managing biological interactions in fragmented landscapes requires studying coevolution in a community context.

Beyond the traditional purview of evolutionary theory and even applied epizoology, the environmental origins of such dynamics extend into the history of human populations.

Western commentators have widely painted indigenous societies as populated by ignorant savages who needed civilizing (Said 1977; Young 1990). Western colonial power – military, financial, and otherwise – was thus rationalized for seizing resources and deculturing non-Western societies, producing a kind of hollowed-out socioeconomy in which psychological and behavioral pathologies become manifest (Fanon 1966; Memmi 1967). Similarly damaging polices have continued under rubrics of globalization and structural adjustment fundamentally changing the nature of the underlying ecology, and often aided and abetted by NGOs based in Western nations (Petras 1999; Hearn 2007).

The detrimental effects of dismembering traditional human socioeconomies in the name of progress have long included triggering pandemics (Watts 1999). Outbreaks are now repeatedly broadcast out of the exploited outbacks of the world, following the travel and trade patterns of exploitation back into cities at the heart of the industrialized West, much as have AIDS (Wallace et al. 1999; Wallace 2011b) and now the near-annual spillovers of novel influenza recombinants (Wallace et al. 2014).

However, while monocropping and other exploitative practices bear grave responsibility in the current epizootic crises, we risk the prelapsarian fantasy that pitches traditional approaches as inherently more sustainable. The archaeological strata are replete with dead civilizations that farmed themselves into extinction (Diamond 2011). In turn, there are many new approaches outside the control of the agribusiness model supporting sustainable production by, among other means, geographic heterogeneity. Wallace and Kock (2012) review examples in community-controlled agroforestry, grain and grass banking, cooperatives numbering tens of thousands of farmers, and a variety of experiments around nutrient management, conservation tillage, cover cropping, trap cropping, contour cropping, aquaculture, water harvesting, watershed restoration, scales of farming, and mixed crop-livestock systems, all integrated into local social matrices.

As Wallace and Kock describe,

> Farmers are daily devising and applying new innovations in organic agriculture to solve today's problems in growing plants and raising livestock, and in climatic and economic contexts of a particular historical moment Sustainability arises in part from communal ownership of the problem of integrating food and ecology, including recycling physical and social resources for the next season, year, or generation. Such communities are almost by definition unlikely, even unable, to engage in the kinds of 'spatial fixes' routinely undertaken by agribusinesses, which, with little compulsion otherwise, are able to move their operations out of a region they've environmentally ruined or even geographically 'surf' their own wave of destruction.

The blowback from individual and collective decisions on automobile ownership and usage in the UK and the US appears to have included unleashing polio epidemics among populations that were previously screened from infection by relative isolation. The public health consequences of individual and collective decisions regarding inexpensive animal protein threaten to be far more serious. Absent fundamental political change supporting such efforts as described by Wallace and Kock, and reversing the exploitative relationships instantiating current global policies, the blowback harvests of infection will likely continue to accrue until one of the more virulent of strains now evolving wipes out a good portion of humanity.

9.8 Summary

By their diversity in time, space, mode, and genetic heritage, traditional and conservation agricultures can create barriers limiting pathogen evolution and spread analogous to a sterilizing temperature. Large-scale monocropping and confined animal feeding lot operations remove such barriers, resulting, above agroecologically specific thresholds, in the development and wide propagation of novel disease strains. We apply a newly developed class of necessary conditions statistical models of evolutionary process, first using the theory on an evolutionarily stable viral pathogen vulnerable to vaccine treatment: post-WW II poliomyelitis emerged in the UK and the US from sudden widespread adoption of automobile ownership and usage. We then examine an evolutionarily variable pathogen, swine influenza in North America. The model suggests epidemiological blowback from globalizing intensive husbandry and the raising and shipping of monoculture livestock across increasing expanses, is likely to be far more consequential, driving viral selection for greater virulence and lowered response to biomedical intervention.

10 Escaping the howling wilderness

Firms instantiate processes of distributed cognition that take cues from the embedding environment to produce behavioral responses consonant with their historical trajectory, available resources, and cultural milieu, roughly analogous to a kind of epigenetic catalysis. Modes of behavioral expression having adaptive value can become fixed in the cultural heritage of the firm by learning or selection: systems requiring too much 'energy' for phenotypic adaptation to environmental demands will fail. Such evolutionary dynamics in simple Schumpeterian market economies will remain self-dynamic, self-referential, continually bootstrapping phenomena. In effect, Schumpeterian economies are 'languages that speak themselves,' largely independent of the needs or wishes of those embedded in them.

But a socioeconomic system, unlike possible biological counterparts, is a cultural artifact. There is nothing 'natural' to any particular such construct, although, again, large-scale dynamics remain constrained by resource availability in the context of historical trajectory and other cultural factors. Within those riverbanks, the socioeconomic stream can flow according to its own inherently unstable dynamics, or it can be subject to rigorous cultural channeling, as described by the fatal counterexamples of Chapters 7, 8, and 9. The metaphors of hunter-gatherer vs. farmer are not inappropriate.

In accordance with the Data Rate Theorem, farmed ecosystems can be inherently more productive, from a human perspective, than what can be gathered from raw nature. The transition from literal hunter-gatherer societies to neolithic farming enabled the subsequent construction of rich human ecosystems, including cities, city-states, and more elaborate structures. However, as Chapters 7, 8, and 9 show, and has been well known, improper farming can devastate the land, creating a dust bowl.

At present, in the US, neoliberal ideologies of unregulated 'free markets' – modified by the literally inhuman 'planning' of Pentagon capitalism, mass incarceration, and plantation agribusiness – have given unfettered reign to an enormous structure with self-dynamic 'large deviations' that possess a grammar and syntax whose internal logic is unaffected by human needs or concerns. Globally, as a consequence of the victory of these neoliberal ideologies, some billions of us ride a rampant, rapidly evolving, socioeconomic engine that has neither engineer nor conductor. We are, very essentially, a tribe of primitive hunter-gatherers at the mercy of an unstable ecological monstrosity that we do not have the political will to control, except in the preparation for mass suicide: the draconian modes of various national versions of Pentagon Capitalism have not been directed at improving living and working conditions. Emerging from the present howling wilderness of 'planning' for global war in the context of a predatory social capitalism that privatizes profits while socializing costs, will require a more carefully farmed economic ecosystem, a large-scale 'agricultural' economics that must be culturally tailored to local conditions. As with language, music, art, and all the rest, there can be no one, fixed farmed economy that will fit all needs at all times.

The theoretical approach of this work has, overall, focused on asymptotic limits for which mathematical modeling is straightforward. Holling (1973, 1992), however, asserts that ecosystems are highly organized at intermediate scales, and introduced the idea of a 'keystone' mesoscale level whose dynamics resonate both upward and downward, driving lower and higher levels of organization, as discussed at the end of Chapter 6.

That is, real socioeconomies seem to involve complex hierarchical forms of interacting individual keystones that, organized as one or more *keystone systems* linked by crosstalk, drive smaller and larger dynamics. Identifying and reconstructing such keystone systems would provide a means of direct farming for an economic ecology. As said, this approach would involve a difficult set of empirical questions whose resolution must vary greatly by both embedding culture and local historical trajectory.

There is, of course, a cautionary note regarding the highly formal approach taken here. Pielou (1977, p. 106) warns that mathematical models in biology and ecology are only useful as subordinate partners in a continuing dialog with data: models can only recommend perspectives for subsequent empirical test that, in turn, can be used to correct the models. Simply replacing the intellectual straightjacket of one set of economic formalisms with another will not address the spectrum of problems now facing the study of economic pattern and process. These will yield only to data-based empirical study in which mathematical models are only one among many possible tools: the word is not the thing.

11 Mathematical appendix

11.1 The Shannon coding theorem

Messages from a source, seen as symbols x_j from some alphabet, each having probabilities P_j associated with a random variable X, are 'encoded' into the language of a 'transmission channel', a random variable Y with symbols y_k, having probabilities P_k, possibly with error. Someone receiving the symbol y_k then retranslates it (without error) into some $x_{k'}$ which may or may not be the same as the x_j that was sent.

More formally, the message sent along the channel is characterized by a random variable X having the distribution

$$P(X=x_j)=P_j, j=1, ..., M.$$

The channel through which the message is sent is characterized by a second random variable Y having the distribution

$$P(Y=y_k)=P_k, k=1, ..., L.$$

Let the joint probability distribution of X and Y be defined as

$$P(X=x_j, Y=y_k)=P(x_j, y_k)=P_{j,k}$$

and the conditional probability of Y given X as

$$P(Y=y_k|X=x_j) = P(y_k|x_j).$$

Then the Shannon uncertainty of X and Y independently and the joint uncertainty of X and Y together are defined respectively as

$$H(X) = -\sum_{j=1}^{M} P_j \log(P_j)$$

$$H(Y) = -\sum_{k=1}^{L} P_k \log(P_k) \tag{11.1}$$

$$H(X,Y) = -\sum_{j=1}^{M} \sum_{k=1}^{L} P_{j,k} \log(P_{j,k})$$

The *conditional uncertainty* of Y given X is defined as

$$H(Y \mid X) = -\sum_{j=1}^{M} \sum_{k=1}^{L} P_{j,k} \log[P(y_k \mid x_j)] \tag{11.2}$$

For any two stochastic variates X and Y, $H(Y) \geq H(Y|X)$, as knowledge of X generally gives some knowledge of Y. Equality occurs only in the case of stochastic independence.

Since $P(x_j, y_k) = P(x_j)P(y_k|x_j)$, we have $H(X|Y) = H(X,Y) - H(Y)$.

The information transmitted by translating the variable X into the channel transmission variable Y – possibly with error – and then retranslating without error the transmitted Y back into X is defined as

$$I(X|Y) \equiv H(X) - H(X|Y) = H(X) + H(Y) - H(X,Y) \tag{11.3}$$

See, for example, Ash (1990), Khinchin (1957) or Cover and Thomas (2006) for details. The essential point is that if there is no uncertainty in X given the channel Y, then there is no loss of information through transmission.

In general this will not be true, and herein lies the essence of the theory.

Given a fixed vocabulary for the transmitted variable X, and a fixed vocabulary and probability distribution for the channel Y, we may vary the probability distribution of X in such a way as to maximize the information sent. The capacity of the channel is defined as

$$C \equiv \max_{P(X)} I(X / Y) \tag{11.4}$$

subject to the subsidiary condition that $\Sigma P(X) = 1$.

The critical trick of the Shannon Coding Theorem for sending a message with arbitrarily small error along the channel Y at any rate $R < C$ is to encode it in longer and longer 'typical' sequences of the variable X; that is, those sequences whose distribution of symbols approximates the probability distribution $P(X)$ above which maximizes C.

If $S(n)$ is the number of such 'typical' sequences of length n, then $\log[S(n)] \approx n H(X)$, where $H(X)$ is the uncertainty of the stochastic variable defined above. Some consideration shows that $S(n)$ is much less than the total number of possible messages of length n. Thus, as $n \to \infty$, only a vanishingly small fraction of all possible messages is meaningful in this sense. This observation, after some considerable development, is what allows the Coding Theorem to work so well. In sum, the prescription is to encode messages in typical sequences, which are sent at very nearly the capacity of the channel. As the encoded messages become longer and longer, their maximum possible rate of transmission without error approaches channel capacity as a limit. Again, Ash (1990), Khinchin (1957), and Cover and Thomas (2006) provide details.

11.2 The 'tuning theorem'

Telephone lines, optical wave guides and the tenuous plasma through which a planetary probe transmits data to earth may all be viewed in traditional information-theoretic terms as a *noisy channel* around which we must structure a message so as to attain an optimal error-free transmission rate.

Telephone lines, wave guides and interplanetary plasmas are, relatively speaking, fixed on the timescale of most messages, as are most sociogeographic networks. Indeed, the capacity of a channel, according to Equation 11.4, is defined by varying the probability distribution of the 'message' process X so as to maximize $I(X|Y)$.

Suppose there is some message X so critical that its probability distribution must remain fixed. The trick is to fix the distribution $P(x)$ but *modify the channel* – i.e. tune it – so as to maximize $I(X|Y)$. The *dual* channel capacity C^* can be defined as

$$C^* \equiv \max_{P(Y),P(Y/X)} I(X/Y) \tag{11.5}$$

But $C^* = \max_{P(Y), P(Y|X)} I(Y|X)$, since $I(X|Y)=H(X)+H(Y)-H(X,Y)=I(Y|X)$.

Thus, in a purely formal mathematical sense, *the message transmits the channel* and there will indeed be, according to the Coding Theorem, a channel distribution $P(Y)$ which maximizes C^*.

One may do better than this, however, by modifying the channel matrix $P(Y|X)$. Since

$$P(y_j) = \sum_{i=1}^{M} P(x_i)P(y_j \mid x_i)$$

$P(Y)$ is entirely defined by the channel matrix $P(Y|X)$ for fixed $P(X)$ and

$$C^* = \max_{P(Y),P(Y|X)} I(Y|X) = \max_{P(Y|X)} I(Y|X).$$

Calculating C^* requires maximizing the complicated expression

$$I(X|Y)=H(X)+H(Y)-H(X,Y)$$

which contains products of terms and their logs, subject to constraints that the sums of probabilities are 1 and each probability is itself between 0 and 1. Maximization is done by varying the channel matrix terms $P(y_j|x_i)$ within the constraints. This is a difficult problem in nonlinear optimization requiring Lagrange multiplier methods. However, for the special case $M = L$, C^* may be found by inspection:

If $M = L$, then choose $P(y_j|x_i) = \delta_{j,i}$, where $\delta_{i,j}$ is 1 if $i = j$ and 0 otherwise. For this special case

$$C^* \equiv H(X)$$

with $P(y_k) = P(x_k)$ for all k. *Information is thus transmitted without error when the channel becomes 'typical' with respect to the fixed message distribution $P(X)$.* If $M < L$ matters reduce to this case, but for $L < M$ information must be lost, leading to Rate Distortion arguments explored more fully below.

Thus modifying the channel may be a far more efficient means of ensuring transmission of an important message than encoding that message in a 'natural' language which maximizes the rate of transmission of information on a fixed channel.

We have examined the two limits in which either the distributions of $P(Y)$ or of $P(X)$ are kept fixed. The first provides the usual Shannon Coding Theorem, and the second, hopefully, a tuning theorem variant. It seems likely, however, that for many important systems $P(X)$ and $P(Y)$ will 'interpenetrate,' to use Richard Levins' terminology. That is, $P(X)$ and $P(Y)$ will affect each other in characteristic ways, so that some form of mutual tuning may be the most effective strategy.

11.3 The Shannon-McMillan theorem

Not all statements – sequences of the random variable X – are equivalent. According to the structure of the underlying language of which the message is a particular expression, some messages are more 'meaningful' than others, that is, in accord with the grammar and syntax of the language. The other principal result from information theory, the Shannon-McMillan or Asymptotic Equipartition Theorem, describes how messages themselves are to be classified.

Suppose a long sequence of symbols is chosen, using the output of the random variable X above, so that an output sequence of length n, with the form

$$x_n = (\alpha_0, \alpha_1, ..., \alpha_{n-1})$$

has joint and conditional probabilities

$$P(X_0 = \alpha_0, X_1 = \alpha_1, ..., X_{n-1} = \alpha_{n-1})$$
$$P(X_n = \alpha_n \mid X_0 = \alpha_0, ..., X_{n-1} = \alpha_{n-1})$$

(11.6)

Using these probabilities we may calculate the conditional uncertainty

$$H(X_n | X_0, X_1, ..., X_{n-1})$$

The uncertainty of the *information source $H[\mathbf{X}]$*, is defined as

$$H[\mathbf{X}] \equiv \lim_{n \to \infty} H(X_n | X_0, X_1, ..., X_{n-1})$$

(11.7)

In general, $H(X_n | X_0, X_1, ..., X_{n-1}) \leq H(X_n)$.

Only if the random variables X_j are all stochastically independent does equality hold. If there is a maximum n such that, for all $m > 0$

$$H(X_{n+m} | X_0, ..., X_{n+m-1}) = H(X_n | X_0, ..., X_{n-1})$$

then the source is said to be of *order* n. It is easy to show that

$$H[\mathbf{X}] = \lim_{n \to \infty} \frac{H(X_0, ... X_n)}{n+1}$$

In general the outputs of the $X_j, j=0, 1, ..., n$ are *dependent*. That is, the output of the communication process at step n depends on previous steps. Such serial correlation, in fact, is the very structure which enables most of what is in this book.

Here, however, the processes are all assumed fixed, that is, the serial correlations do not change in time, and the system is *stationary.*

A very broad class of such self-correlated, stationary, information sources, the so-called *ergodic* sources for which the long-run relative frequency of a sequence converges stochastically to the probability assigned to it, have a particularly interesting property:

It is possible, in the limit of large n, to divide all sequences of outputs of an ergodic information source into two distinct sets, S_1 and S_2, having, respectively, very high and very low probabilities of occurrence, with the source uncertainty providing the splitting criterion. In particular the Shannon-McMillan Theorem states that, for a (long) sequence having n (serially correlated) elements, the number of 'meaningful' sequences, $N(n)$ – those belonging to set S_1 – will satisfy the relation

$$\frac{\log[N(n)]}{n} \approx H[\mathbf{X}] \tag{11.8}$$

More formally,

$$\lim_{n\to\infty} \frac{\log[N(n)]}{n} = H[\mathbf{X}]$$

$$= \lim_{n\to\infty} H(X_n \mid X_0,...,X_{n-1}) \tag{11.9}$$

$$= \lim_{n\to\infty} \frac{H(X_0,...,X_n)}{n+1}$$

The Shannon Coding theorem, by means of an analogous splitting argument, shows that for any rate $R < C$, where C is the channel capacity, a message may be sent without error, using the probability distribution for X which maximizes $I(X|Y)$ as the coding scheme. Using the internal structures of the information source permits *limiting attention only to meaningful sequences of symbols.* This restriction can greatly raise the maximum possible rate at which information can be transmitted with arbitrarily small error: if there are M possible symbols and the uncertainty of the source is $H[\mathbf{X}]$, then the effective capacity of the channel C, using this 'source coding,' becomes (Ash 1990)

$$C_E = C \frac{\log(M)}{H[\mathbf{X}]} \tag{11.10}$$

As $H[\mathbf{X}] \leq \log(M)$, with equality only for stochastically independent, uniformly distributed random variables,

$$C_E \geq C \tag{11.11}$$

Note that, for a given channel capacity, the condition $H[\mathbf{X}] \leq C$ always holds.

11.4 The rate distortion theorem

The Shannon-McMillan Theorem can be expressed as the 'zero error limit' of the Rate Distortion Theorem (Dembo and Zeitouni 1998; Cover and Thomas 2006). The theorem defines a splitting criterion that identifies high probability pairs of sequences. We follow closely the treatment of Cover and Thomas (2006).

The origin of the problem is the question of representing one information source by a simpler one in such a way that the least information is lost. For example, we might have a continuous variate between 0 and 100, and wish to represent it in terms of a small set of integers in a way that minimizes the inevitable distortion that process creates. Typically, for example, an analog audio signal will be replaced by a 'digital' one. The problem is to do this in a way which least distorts the *reconstructed* audio waveform.

Suppose the original stationary, ergodic information source Y with output from a particular alphabet generates sequences of the form $y^n = y_1, ..., y_n$.

These are 'digitized,' in some sense, producing a chain of 'digitized values' $b^n = b_1, ..., b_n$, where the b- alphabet is much more restricted than the y- alphabet.

b^n is, in turn, *deterministically retranslated* into a reproduction of the original signal y^n. That is, each b^m is mapped on to a unique n-length y-sequence in the alphabet of the information source Y:

$$b^m \rightarrow \hat{y}^n = \hat{y}_1, ..., \hat{y}_n$$

Note, however, that many y^n sequences may be mapped onto the *same* retranslation sequence $\hat{y}^n$, so that information will, in general, be lost.

The central problem is to explicitly minimize that loss.

The retranslation process defines a new stationary, ergodic information source, $\hat{Y}$.

The next step is to define a *distortion measure* $d(y, \hat{y})$, which compares the original to the retranslated path. For example, the *Hamming distortion* is

$$d(y, \hat{y}) = 1, y \neq \hat{y}$$
$$d(y, \hat{y}) = 0, y = \hat{y}$$

(11.12)

For continuous variates the *Squared error distortion* is

$$d(y, \hat{y}) = (y - \hat{y})^2$$

(11.13)

Possibilities abound.

The distortion between paths y^n and $\hat{y}^n$ is defined as

$$d(y^n, \hat{y}^n) = \frac{1}{n} \sum_{j=1}^{n} d(y_j, \hat{y}_j)$$

(11.14)

Suppose that with each path y^n and b^n– path retranslation into the y– language and denoted y^n, there are associated individual, joint, and conditional probability distributions $p(y^n)$, $p(\hat{y}^n)$, $p(y^n|\hat{y}^n)$.

The *average distortion* is defined as

$$D = \sum_{y^n} p(y^n) d(y^n, \hat{y}^n)$$

(11.15)

It is possible, using the distributions given above, to define the information transmitted from the incoming Y to the outgoing $\hat{Y}$ process in the usual manner, using the Shannon source uncertainty of the strings:

$$I(Y, \hat{Y}) \equiv H(Y)-H(Y|\hat{Y})=H(Y)+H(\hat{Y})-H(Y, \hat{Y})$$

If there is no uncertainty in Y given the retranslation $\hat{Y}$, then no information is lost.

In general, this will not be true.

The *information rate distortion function R(D)* for a source Y with a distortion measure $d(y, \hat{y})$ is defined as

$$R(D) = \min_{p(y,\hat{y}); \sum_{(y,\hat{y})} p(y)p(y|\hat{y})d(y,\hat{y}) \le D} I(Y,\hat{Y}) \tag{11.16}$$

The minimization is over all conditional distributions $p(y|\hat{y})$ for which the joint distribution $p(y,\hat{y})=p(y)p(y|\hat{y})$ satisfies the average distortion constraint (i.e., average distortion $\le D$).

The *Rate Distortion Theorem* states that *R(D) is the maximum achievable rate of information transmission which does not exceed the average distortion D.* Cover and Thomas (2006) or Dembo and Zeitouni (1998) provide details.

An important observation is that $R(D)$ is necessarily convex in D (Cover and Thomas 2006). This has profound implications for dynamic processes, since R can be interpreted as a free energy homolog, as it is a channel capacity measure.

It is also important to note that pairs of sequences $(y^n, \hat{y}^n)$ can be defined as *distortion typical* that is, for a given average distortion D, defined in terms of a particular measure, pairs of sequences can be divided into two sets, a high probability one containing a relatively small number of (matched) pairs with $d(y^n, \hat{y}^n) \le D$, and a low probability one containing most pairs. As $n \to \infty$, the smaller set approaches unit probability, and, for those pairs,

$$p(y^n) \ge p(\hat{y}^n|y^n)\exp[-nI(Y, \hat{Y})] \tag{11.17}$$

Thus, roughly speaking, $I(Y, \hat{Y})$ embodies the splitting criterion between high and low probability pairs of paths.

For the theory of interacting information sources, then, $I(Y, \hat{Y})$ can play the role of H in a generalized Onsager relations argument.

The rate distortion function can actually be calculated in many cases by using a Lagrange multiplier method – see Cover and Thomas (2006).

Glazebrook and Wallace (2009a, b) suggest using something like $s \equiv d(\hat{x}, x)$ as a metric in a geometry of information sources, e.g., when simple ergodicity fails, and $H(x) \ne H(\hat{x})$ for high probability paths $\hat{x}$ and x.

11.5 Groupoids

Following Weinstein (1996) closely, a groupoid, G, is defined by a base set A upon which some mapping – a morphism – can be defined. Note that not all possible pairs of states (a_j, a_k) in the base set A can be connected by such a morphism. Those that can define the groupoid element, a morphism $g=(a_j, a_k)$ having the natural inverse $g^{-1}=(a_k, a_j)$. Given such a pairing, it is possible to define 'natural' end-point maps $\alpha(g)=a_j$, $\beta(g)=a_k$ from the set of morphisms G into A, and an associative product in the groupoid g_1g_2 provided $\alpha(g_1g_2)=\alpha(g_1)$, $\beta(g_1g_2)=\beta(g_2)$, and $\beta(g_1)=\alpha(g_2)$. Then the product is defined, and associative, $(g_1g_2)g_3=g_1(g_2g_3)$.

In addition, there are natural left and right identity elements λ_g, ρ_g such that $\lambda_g g=g=g\rho_g$ (Weinstein 1996).

An orbit of the groupoid G over A is an equivalence class for the relation $a_j \sim G\, a_k$ if and only if there is a groupoid element g with $\alpha(g)=a_j$ and $\beta(g)=a_k$. Following Cannas da Silva and Weinstein (1999), we note that a groupoid is called transitive if it has just one orbit. The transitive groupoids are the building blocks of groupoids in that there is a natural decomposition of the base space of a general groupoid into orbits. Over each orbit there is a transitive groupoid, and the disjoint union of these transitive groupoids is the original groupoid. Conversely, the disjoint union of groupoids is itself a groupoid.

The isotropy group of $a \in X$ consists of those g in G with $\alpha(g)=a=\beta(g)$. These groups prove fundamental to classifying groupoids.

If G is any groupoid over A, the map $(\alpha, \beta){:}G \to A \times A$ is a morphism from G to the pair groupoid of A. The image of (α, β) is the orbit equivalence relation $\sim G$, and the functional kernel is the union of the isotropy groups. If $f{:}\ X \to Y$ is a function, then the kernel of f, $ker(f)=[(x_1,x_2)\in X \times X{:}f(x_1)=f(x_2)]$ defines an equivalence relation.

Groupoids may have additional structure. As Weinstein (1996) explains, a groupoid G is a topological groupoid over a base space X if G and X are topological spaces and α, β and multiplication are continuous maps. A criticism sometimes applied to groupoid theory is that their classification up to isomorphism is nothing other than the classification of equivalence relations via the orbit equivalence relation and groups via the isotropy groups. The imposition of a compatible topological structure produces a nontrivial interaction between the two structures. Above, we have introduced a metric structure on manifolds of related information sources, producing such interaction.

In essence, a groupoid is a category in which all morphisms have an inverse, here defined in terms of connection to a base point by a meaningful path of an information source dual to a cognitive process.

As Weinstein (1996) points out, the morphism (α, β) suggests another way of looking at groupoids. A groupoid over A identifies not only which elements of A are equivalent to one another (isomorphic), but *it also parameterizes the different ways (isomorphisms) in which two elements can be equivalent* i.e., in our context, all possible information sources dual to some cognitive process. Given the information theoretic characterization of cognition presented above, this produces a full modular cognitive network in a highly natural manner.

Brown (1987) describes the fundamental structure as follows:

A groupoid should be thought of as a group with many objects, or with many identities ... A groupoid with one object is essentially just a group. So the notion of groupoid is an extension of that of groups. It gives an additional convenience, flexibility and range of applications

EXAMPLE 1. A disjoint union [of groups] $G = \cup_\lambda G_\lambda, \lambda \in \Lambda\}$, is a groupoid: the product ab is defined if and only if a, b belong to the same G_λ, and ab is then just the product in the group G_λ. There is an identity 1_λ for each $\lambda \in \Lambda$. The maps α, β coincide and map G_λ to λ, $\lambda \in \Lambda$.

EXAMPLE 2. An equivalence relation R on [a set] X becomes a groupoid with α, $\beta:R \rightarrow X$ the two projections, and product $(x,y)(y,z)=(x,z)$ whenever $(x,y),(y,z) \in R$. There is an identity, namely (x,x), for each $x \in X$.

Weinstein (1996) makes the following fundamental point:

Almost every interesting equivalence relation on a space B arises in a natural way as the orbit equivalence relation of some groupoid G over B. Instead of dealing directly with the orbit space B/G as an object in the category S_{map} of sets and mappings, one should consider instead the groupoid G itself as an object in the category G_{htp} of groupoids and homotopy classes of morphisms.

The groupoid approach has become quite popular in the study of networks of coupled dynamical systems which can be defined by differential equation models, (e.g., Golubitsky and Stewart 2006).

11.6 Cost constraints

Let $Q(\kappa M) \geq 0$, $Q(0)=0$ represent a monotonic increasing function of the intensity measure of available free energy M, and C be the maximum channel capacity available to the cognitive processes of interest. One would expect

$$\hat{H} = \frac{\int_0^C H \exp[-H/Q]dH}{\int_0^C \exp[-H/Q]dH} = \frac{Q[\exp(C/Q)-1]-C}{\exp(C/Q)-1} \tag{11.18}$$

κ is an inverse energy intensity scaling constant that may be quite small indeed, a consequence of the typically massive entropic translation losses between the free energy consumed by the physical processes that instantiate information and any actual measure of that information.

Near $M = 0$, expand Q as a Taylor series, with a first term $Q \approx \kappa M$.

This expression tops out quite rapidly with increases in either C or Q, producing energy- and channel capacity-limited results

$$\hat{H} = Q(\kappa M), \; C/2 \tag{11.19}$$

Then, expanding Q near zero, the two limiting relations imply

$$Q(\kappa M_{X,Y}) < Q(\kappa M_X) + Q(\kappa M_Y) \rightarrow M_{X,Y} < M_X + M_Y,$$

$$C_{X,Y} < C_X + C_Y$$

(11.20)

The channel capacity constraint can be parsed further for a noisy Gaussian channel. Then (Cover and Thomas 2006)

$$C = 1/2 \log[1 + \mathcal{P}/\sigma^2] \approx 1/2\mathcal{P}/\sigma^2$$

(11.21)

for small $\mathcal{P}/\sigma^2$, where $\mathcal{P}$ is the 'power constraint' such that $E(X^2)$ and σ^2 is the noise variance. Assuming information sources X and Y act on the same scale, so that noise variances are the same and quite large, then, taking $\mathcal{P} = Q(\kappa M)$ – channel power is determined by available free energy – and

$$Q(\kappa M_{X,Y}) < Q(\kappa M_X) + Q(\kappa M_Y)$$

Both limiting inequalities are, then, free energy relations leading to a kind of 'reaction canalization' in which a set of lower level cognitive modules consumes less free energy if information crosstalk among them is permitted than under conditions of individual signal isolation.

11.7 Morse theory

Morse theory examines relations between analytic behavior of a function – the location and character of its critical points – and the underlying topology of the manifold on which the function is defined. We are interested in a number of such functions, for example a 'free energy' constructed from information source uncertainties on a parameter space and 'second order' iterations involving parameter manifolds determining critical behavior. These can be reformulated from a Morse theory perspective. Here we follow closely the elegant treatments of Pettini (2007).

The essential idea of Morse theory is to examine an $n-$ dimensional manifold M as decomposed into level sets of some function $f: M \rightarrow \mathbf{R}$ where $\mathbf{R}$ is the set of real numbers. The $a-$ level set of f is defined as

$$f^{-1}(a) = \{x \in M : f(x) = a\}$$

the set of all points in M with $f(x) = a$. If M is compact, then the whole manifold can be decomposed into such slices in a canonical fashion between two limits, defined by the minimum and maximum of f on M. Let the part of M below a be defined as

$$M_a = f^{-1}(-\infty, a] = \{x \in M : f(x) \leq a\}$$

These sets describe the whole manifold as a varies between the minimum and maximum of f.

Morse functions are defined as a particular set of smooth functions $f : M \rightarrow \mathbf{R}$ as follows. Suppose a function f has a critical point x_c, so that the derivative $df(x_c) = 0$, with critical value $f(x_c)$. Then f is a Morse function if its critical points are nondegenerate in the sense that the Hessian matrix of second derivatives at x_c, whose elements, in terms of local coordinates are

$$H_{i,j} = \partial^2 f / \partial x^i \, \partial x^j$$

has rank n, which means that it has only nonzero eigenvalues, so that there are no lines or surfaces of critical points and, ultimately, critical points are isolated.

The index of the critical point is the number of negative eigenvalues of H at x_c.

A level set $f^{-1}(a)$ of f is called a critical level if a is a critical value of f, that is, if there is at least one critical point $x_c \in f^{-1}(a)$.

Again, following Pettini (2007), the essential results of Morse theory are:

1   If an interval $[a,b]$ contains no critical values of f, then the topology of $f^{-1}[a,v]$ does not change for any $v \in (a, b]$. Importantly, the result is valid even if f is not a Morse function, but only a smooth function.

2   If the interval $[a, b]$ contains critical values, the topology of $f^{-1}[a,v]$ changes in a manner determined by the properties of the matrix H at the critical points.

3   If $f:M \to \mathbf{R}$ is a Morse function, the set of all the critical points of f is a discrete subset of M, i.e. critical points are isolated. This is Sard's Theorem.

4   If $f: M \to \mathbf{R}$ is a Morse function, with M compact, then on a finite interval $[a, b] \subset \mathbf{R}$, there is only a finite number of critical points p of f such that $f(p) \in [a, b]$. The set of critical values of f is a discrete set of $\mathbf{R}$.

5   For any differentiable manifold M, the set of Morse functions on M is an open dense set in the set of real functions of M of differentiability class r for $0 \le r \le \infty$.

6   Some topological invariants of M, that is, quantities that are the same for all the manifolds that have the same topology as M, can be estimated and sometimes computed exactly once all the critical points of f are known: Let the Morse numbers $\mu_i (i=1, \dots, m)$ of a function f on M be the number of critical points of f of index i, (the number of negative eigenvalues of H). The Euler characteristic of the complicated manifold M can be expressed as the alternating sum of the Morse numbers of any Morse function on M,

$$\chi = \sum_{i=0}^{m} (-1)^i \mu_i$$

The Euler characteristic reduces, in the case of a simple polyhedron, to

$$\chi = V - E + F$$

where V, E, and F are the numbers of vertices, edges, and faces in the polyhedron.

7   Another important theorem states that, if the interval $[a,b]$ contains a critical value of f with a single critical point x_c, then the topology of the set M_b defined above differs from that of M_a in a way which is determined by the index, i, of the critical point. Then M_b is homeomorphic to the manifold obtained from attaching to M_a an i–handle, i.e., the direct product of an i–disk and an $(m-i)$–disk.

Again, Pettini (2007) contains both mathematical details and further references. See, for example, Matsumoto (2002).

11.8 Universality class tuning

Biological renormalization

Equation (3.13) states that the information source and the correlation length, the degree of coherence on the underlying network, scale under renormalization clustering in chunks of size R as

$$H[K_R, J_R]/f(R)= H[J,K]$$

$$\chi[K_R, J_R]R = \chi(K, J)$$

with $f(1)=1$, $K_1=K$, $J_1=J$, where we have slightly rearranged terms.

Differentiating these two equations with respect to R, so that the right hand sides are zero, and solving for dK_R/dR and dJ_R/dR gives, after some consolidation, expressions of the form

$$dK_R / dR = u_1 d\log(f) / dR + u_2 / R$$
$$dJ_R / dR = v_1 J_R d\log(f) / dR + \frac{v_2}{R} J_R \tag{11.22}$$

The u_i, v_i, $i=1, 2$ are functions of K_R, J_R, but not explicitly of R itself.

We expand these equations about the critical value $K_R=K_C$ and about $J_R=0$, obtaining

$$dK_R / dR = (K_R - K_C)y d\log(f) / dR + (K_R - K_C)z / R$$
$$dJ_R / dR = w J_R d\log(f) / dR + x J_R / R \tag{11.23}$$

The terms $y=du_1/dK_R|_{KR}=K_C\}$, $z=du_2/dK_R|_{KR}=K_C\}$, $w=v_1(K_C,0)$, $x=v_2(K_C, 0)$ are constants.

Solving the first of these equations gives

$$K_R=K_C+(K-K_C)R^z f(R)^y \tag{11.24}$$

again remembering that $K_1=K$, $J_1=J$, $f(1)=1$.

Wilson's (1971) essential trick is to iterate on this relation, which is supposed to converge rapidly near the critical point, assuming that for K_R near K_C, we have

$$K_C/2 \approx K_C+(K-K_C)R^z f(R)^y \tag{11.25}$$

We iterate in two steps, first solving this for $f(R)$ in terms of known values, and then solving for R, finding a value R_C that we then substitute into the first of equations (3.13) to obtain an expression for $H[K, 0]$ in terms of known functions and parameter values.

The first step gives the general result

$$f(R_C) \approx \frac{[K_C / (K_C - K)]^{1/y}}{2^{1/y} R_C^{z/y}} \tag{11.26}$$

Solving this for R_C and substituting into the first expression of Equation (3.13) gives, as a first iteration of a far more general procedure (Shirkov and Kovalev 2001), the result

$$H[K,0] \approx \frac{H[K_C / 2,0]}{f(R_C)} = \frac{H_0}{f(R_C)}$$

$$\chi(K,0) \approx \chi(K_C / 2,0)R_C = \chi_0 R_C, \tag{11.27}$$

which are the essential relationships.

Note that a power law of the form $f(R)=R^m$, $m = 3$, which is the direct physical analog, may not be biologically reasonable, since it says that 'language richness' can grow very rapidly as a function of increased network size. Such rapid growth is simply not observed.

Taking the biologically realistic example of non-integral 'fractal' exponential growth,

$$f(R) = R^\delta \tag{11.28}$$

where $\delta > 0$ is a real number which may be quite small, we can solve Equation 11.26 for R_C, obtaining

$$R_C = \frac{[K_C / (K_C - K)]^{[1/(\delta y + z)]}}{2^{1/(\delta y + z)}} \tag{11.29}$$

for K near K_C. Note that, for a given value of y, one might characterize the relation $\alpha \equiv \delta y + z =$ constant as a 'tunable universality class relation' in the sense of Albert and Barabasi (2002).

Substituting this value for R_C back gives a complex expression for H, having three parameters: δ, y, z.

A more biologically interesting choice for $f(R)$ is a logarithmic curve that 'tops out', for example

$$f(R)= m\log(R)+1 \tag{11.30}$$

Again $f(1)=1$.

Using Mathematica 4.2 or above to solve Equation (11.25) for R_C gives

$$R_C = [\frac{Q}{\mathrm{Lambert}W[Q\exp(z / my)]}]^{y/z} \tag{11.31}$$

where

$$Q \equiv (z/my)2^{-1/y}[K_C/(K_C-K)]^{1/y}$$

The transcendental function Lambert $W(x)$ is defined by the relation

$$\mathrm{Lambert}W(x)\exp(\mathrm{Lambert}W(x))=x$$

It arises in the theory of random networks and in renormalization strategies for quantum field theories.

An asymptotic relation for $f(R)$ would be of particular biological interest, implying that 'language richness' increases to a limiting value with population growth. Taking

$$f(R)=\exp[m(R-1)/R] \tag{11.32}$$

gives a system which begins at 1 when $R=1$, and approaches the asymptotic limit $\exp(m)$ as $R \to \infty$. Mathematica finds

$$R_C = \frac{my \,/\, z}{\mathrm{Lambert}W[A]} \tag{11.33}$$

where

$$A \equiv (my/z)\exp(my/z)[2^{1/y}[K_C/(K_C-K)]^{-1/y}]^{y/z}$$

These developments indicate the possibility of taking the theory significantly beyond arguments by abduction from simple physical models, although the notorious difficulty of implementing information theory existence arguments will undoubtedly persist.

Universality class distribution

Physical systems undergoing phase transition usually have relatively pure renormalization properties, with quite different systems clumped into the same 'universality class,' having fixed exponents at transition (Binney et al. 1986). Biological and social phenomena may be far more complicated:

If the system of interest is a mix of subgroups with different values of some significant renormalization parameter m in the expression for $f(R, m)$, according to a distribution $\rho(m)$, then the first expression in Equation (3.13) should generalize, at least to first order, as

$$
\begin{aligned}
H[K_R,J_R] &=< f(R,m) > H[K,J] \\
&\equiv H[K,J]\int f(R,m)\rho(m)dm
\end{aligned}
\tag{11.34}
$$

If $f(R)=1+m\log(R)$ then, given any distribution for m,

$$<f(R)> = 1 + <m>\log(R) \tag{11.35}$$

where $<m>$ is simply the mean of m over that distribution.

Other forms of $f(R)$ having more complicated dependencies on the distributed parameter or parameters, like the power law R^δ, do not produce such a simple result. Taking $\rho(\delta)$ as a normal distribution, for example, gives

$$<R^\delta> = R^{<\delta>}\exp[(1/2)(\log(R^\sigma))^2] \tag{11.36}$$

where σ^2 is the distribution variance. The renormalization properties of this function can be determined from Equation (11.25), and the calculation is left to the reader as an exercise, and can be done in Mathematica.

Thus the information dynamic phase transition properties of mixed systems will not in general be simply related to those of a single subcomponent, a matter of possible empirical importance: if sets of relevant parameters defining renormalization universality classes are indeed distributed, experiments observing pure phase changes may be very difficult. Tuning among different possible renormalization strategies in response to external signals would result in even greater ambiguity in recognizing and classifying information dynamic phase transitions.

Important aspects of mechanism may be reflected in the combination of renormalization properties and the details of their distribution across subsystems.

In sum, real biological, social, or interacting biopsychosocial systems are likely to have very rich patterns of phase transition which may not display the simplistic, indeed, literally elemental, purity familiar to physicists. Overall mechanisms will, however, still remain significantly constrained by the theory, in the general sense of probability limit theorems.

Punctuated universality class tuning

The next step is to iterate the general argument onto the process of phase transition itself, producing a tunable punctuation.

As described, an essential character of physical systems subject to phase transition is that they belong to particular 'universality classes.' Again, this means that the exponents of power laws describing behavior at phase transition will be the same for large groups of markedly different systems, with 'natural' aggregations representing fundamental class properties (Binney et al. 1986).

It appears that biological or social systems undergoing phase transition analogs need not be constrained to such classes, and that 'universality class tuning,' meaning the strategic alteration of parameters characterizing the renormalization properties of punctuation, might well be possible. Here we focus on the tuning of parameters within a single, given, renormalization relation. Clearly, however, wholesale shifts of renormalization properties must ultimately be considered as well.

Universality class tuning has been observed in models of 'real world' networks. As Albert and Barabasi (2002) put it,

> The inseparability of the topology and dynamics of evolving networks is shown by the fact that [the exponents defining universality class] are related by [a] scaling relation , underlying the fact that a network's assembly uniquely determines its topology. However, in no case are these exponents unique. They can be tuned continuously.

Suppose that a structured external environment, itself an appropriately regular information source **Y**, 'engages' a modifiable system characterized by an information source. The environment begins to write an image of itself on the system in a distorted manner permitting definition of a mutual information $I[K]$ splitting criterion according to the Rate Distortion or Joint Asymptotic Equipartition Theorems. K is an inverse coupling parameter between system and environment. At punctuation – near some critical point K_C – the systems begin to interact very strongly indeed, and, near K_C, using a simple physical model, $I[K] \approx I_0[\frac{K_C - K}{K_C}]^\alpha$.

For a physical system α is fixed, determined by the underlying 'universality class.' Here we will allow α to vary, and, in the section below, to itself respond explicitly to imposed signals.

Normalizing K_C and I_0 to 1,

$$I[K] \approx (1 - K)^\alpha \tag{11.37}$$

The horizontal line $I[K]=1$ corresponds to $\alpha=0$, while $\alpha=1$ gives a declining straight line with unit slope which passes through 0 at $K=1$. Consideration shows there are progressively sharper transitions between the necessary zero value at $K=1$ and the values defined by this relation for $0 < K, \alpha < 1$. The rapidly rising slope of transition with declining α is of considerable significance:

The *instability* associated with the splitting criterion $I[K]$ is defined by

$$Q[K] \equiv -K \, d \, I[K]/dK = \alpha K (1 - K)^{\alpha - 1} \tag{11.38}$$

and is singular at $K=K_C=1$ for $0 < \alpha < 1$. Following earlier work (e.g., Wallace and Fullilove 2008), we interpret this to mean that values of $0 < \alpha \ll 1$ are highly unlikely for real systems, since $Q[K]$, in this model, represents a kind of barrier for 'social' information systems.

On the other hand, smaller values of α mean that the system is far more efficient at responding to the adaptive demands imposed by the embedding structured environment or regulatory authority, since the mutual information which tracks the matching of internal response to external demands, $I[K]$, rises more and more quickly toward the maximum for smaller and smaller α as the inverse coupling parameter K declines below $K_C=1$. That is, systems able to attain smaller α are more responsive to external signals than those characterized by larger values, in this model, but smaller values will be harder to reach, probably only at some considerable physiological or opportunity cost. Focused conscious action takes resources, of one form or another.

The more biologically or socially realistic renormalization strategies given above produce sets of several parameters defining the universality class, whose tuning gives behavior much like that of α in this simple example.

Formal iteration of the phase transition argument on this calculation gives a tunable regulation, focusing on paths of universality class parameters:

Suppose the renormalization properties of an information source at some 'time' k are characterized by a set of appropriately coarse-grained parameters

$A_k \equiv \alpha_1^k, ..., \alpha_m^k$. Fixed parameter values define a particular universality class for the renormalization. We suppose that, over a sequence of 'times', the universality class properties can be characterized by a path $x_n = A_0, A_1, ..., A_{n-1}$ having significant serial correlations which, in fact, permit definition of *another* adiabatically piecewise stationary ergodic information source associated with the paths x_n. Call that source **X**.

Suppose also, in the now-usual manner, that the set of external (or internal, systemic) signals impinging on the information source of basic interest is also highly structured and forms another information source **Y** that interacts not only with the system of interest globally, but specifically with its universality class properties as characterized by **X**. **Y** is necessarily associated with a set of paths y_n.

Pair the two sets of paths into a joint path, $z_n \equiv (x_n, y_y)$ and invoke an inverse coupling parameter, K, between the information sources and their paths. This leads, by the arguments above, to phase transition punctuation of $I[K]$, the mutual information between **X** and **Y**, under either the Joint Asymptotic Equipartition Theorem or under limitation by a distortion measure, through the Rate Distortion Theorem. The essential point is that $I[K]$ is a splitting criterion under these theorems, and thus partakes of the homology with free energy density which we have invoked above.

Activation of universality class tuning, the mean field model's version of attentional focusing, then becomes itself a punctuated event in response to increasing linkage between the organism and an external structured signal or some particular system of internal events.

This iterated argument exactly parallels the extension of the General Linear Model to the Hierarchical Linear Model in regression theory.

Another path to the fluctuating dynamic threshold might be through a second order iteration similar to that just above, but focused on the parameters defining the universality class distributions given above.

11.9 The large deviations formalism

It is of some interest to more explicitly carry through the program suggested by Campagnat et al. (2006) via a recapitulation of large deviations and fluctuation formalism.

Information source uncertainty, according to the Shannon-McMillan Theorem, serves as a splitting criterion between high and low probability sequences (or pairs of them) and displays the fundamental characteristic of a growing body of work in applied probability often termed the Large Deviations Program (LDP). This seeks to unite information theory, statistical mechanics, and the theory of fluctuations under a single umbrella.

Following Dembo and Zeitouni, (1998, p.2), let $X_1, X_2, ... X_n$ be a sequence of independent, standard Normal, real-valued random variables and let

$$S_n = \frac{1}{n} \sum_{j=1}^{n} X_j \qquad (11.39)$$

Since S_n is again a Normal random variable with zero mean and variance $1/n$, for all $\delta > 0$

$$\lim_{n \to \infty} P(|S_n| \geq \delta) = 0 \tag{11.40}$$

where P is the probability that the absolute value of S_n is greater or equal to δ. Some manipulation, however, gives

$$P(|S_n| \geq \delta) = 1 - \frac{1}{\sqrt{2\pi}} \int_{-\delta\sqrt{n}}^{\delta\sqrt{n}} \exp(-x^2/2) dx \tag{11.41}$$

so that

$$\lim_{n \to \infty} \frac{\log P(|S_n| \geq \delta)}{n} = -\delta^2/2 \tag{11.42}$$

This can be rewritten for large n as

$$P(|S_n| \geq \delta) \approx \exp(-n\delta^2/2) \tag{11.43}$$

That is, for large n, the probability of a large deviation in S_n follows something much like the asymptotic equipartition relation of the Shannon-McMillan Theorem, so that meaningful paths of length n all have approximately the same probability $P(n) \propto \exp(-n\,H[\mathbf{X}])$.

Questions about meaningful paths appear suddenly as formally isomorphic to the central argument of the LDP which encompasses statistical mechanics, fluctuation theory, and information theory into a single structure (Dembo and Zeitouni 1998).

Again, the cardinal tenet of large deviation theory is that the rate function can, under proper circumstances, be expressed as a mathematical entropy having the standard form

$$-\sum_k p_k \log p_k \tag{11.44}$$

for some set of probabilities p_k.

Next we briefly recapitulate part of the standard treatment of large fluctuations (e.g., Onsager and Machlup 1953; Fredlin and Wentzell 1998).

The macroscopic behavior of a complicated physical system in time is assumed to be described by the phenomenological Onsager relations giving large-scale fluxes as

$$\sum_i C_{i,j} dK_j / dt = \partial S / \partial K_i \tag{11.45}$$

where the $C_{i,j}$ are appropriate constants, S is the system entropy, and the K_i are the generalized coordinates which parametize the system's free energy.

Entropy is defined from free energy F by a Legendre transform – more of which follows below:

$$S \equiv F - \sum_j K_j \partial F / \partial K_j,$$

where the K_j are appropriate system parameters.

Neglecting volume problems for the moment, free energy can be defined from the system's partition function Z as

$F(K)=\log[Z(K)]$

The partition function Z, in turn, is defined from the system Hamiltonian – defining the energy states – as

$$Z(K) = \sum_j \exp[-KE_j]$$

where K is an inverse temperature or other parameter and the E_j are the energy states.

Inverting the Onsager relations gives

$$dK_i / dt = \sum_j L_{i,j} \partial S / \partial K_j = L_i(K_1,...,K_m,t) \equiv L_i(K,t) \qquad (11.46)$$

The terms $\partial S / \partial K_i$ are macroscopic driving forces dependent on the entropy gradient.

Let a white Brownian noise $\varepsilon(t)$ perturb the system, so that

$$dK_i / dt = \sum_j L_{i,j} \partial S / \partial K_j + \epsilon(t)$$
$$= L_i(K,t) + \epsilon(t) \qquad (11.47)$$

where the time averages of ε are $< \varepsilon(t) >=0$ and $<\varepsilon(t)\varepsilon(0)>=D\delta(t)$. $\delta(t)$ is the Dirac delta function, and we take K as a vector in the K_i.

Following Luchinsky (1997), if the probability that the system starts at some initial macroscopic parameter state K_0 at time $t=0$ and gets to the state $K(t)$ at time t is $P(K, t)$, then a somewhat subtle development (e.g., Feller 1971) gives the forward Fokker-Planck equation for P:

$$\partial P(K,t)/\partial t =-\nabla \cdot (L(K,t)P(K,t))+(D/2)\nabla^2 P(K,t) \qquad (11.48)$$

In the limit of weak noise intensity this can be solved using the WKB (i.e., the eikonal) approximation, as follows. Take

$$P(K,t)=z(K,t)\exp(-s(K,t)/D) \qquad (11.49)$$

$z(K,t)$ is a prefactor and $s(K,t)$ is a classical action satisfying the Hamilton–Jacobi equation which can be solved by integrating the Hamiltonian equations of motion. The equation reexpresses $P(K,t)$ in the usual parametized negative exponential format.

Let $p \equiv \nabla s$. Substituting and collecting terms of similar order in D gives

$$dK / dt = p + L,$$
$$dp / dt = -\partial L / \partial Kp \qquad (11.50)$$

and

$$-\partial s / \partial t \equiv h(K, p,t) = pL(K,t) + \frac{p^2}{2} \qquad (11.51)$$

with $h(K,t)$ the Hamiltonian for appropriate boundary conditions.

Again following Luchinsky (1997), these Hamiltonian equations have two different types of solution, depending on p. For $p=0$, $dK/dt = L(K, t)$, describing the system in the absence of noise. We expect that with finite noise intensity the system will give rise to a distribution about this deterministic path. Solutions for which $p \neq 0$ correspond to *optimal paths* along which the system will move with overwhelming probability.

These results can, however, again be directly derived as a special case of a Large Deviation Principle based on generalized entropies mathematically similar to Shannon's uncertainty from information theory, bypassing the Hamiltonian formulation entirely.

11.10 The data rate theorem for the natural channel

The Rate Distortion Function for the natural channel is

$$R(D)=\sigma^2/D \tag{11.52}$$

leading to the 'entropy'

$$S(D)=R(D)-D\,dR/dD = 2\,\sigma^2/D \tag{11.53}$$

This gives, as the simplest 'Onsager' equation,

$$dD/dt=-\mu\,dS(D)/dD=2\mu\sigma^2/D^2 \tag{11.54}$$

having the solution

$$D(t)=(6\mu\sigma^2 t)^{1/3} \tag{11.55}$$

Recall that, for the Gaussian channel, $D(t) \propto \sqrt{t}$.
The canonical SDE then becomes

$$D_t=[2\mu\sigma^2/D_t^2-G(M)]dt+\beta\,D_t\,dW_t \tag{11.56}$$

Carrying through the Ito chain rule for $Y_t=D_t^2$ finds the stability criterion for the variance driven by the discriminant of a cubic equation in D_t, so that

$$R_{nss} \geq \frac{\sigma}{\sqrt{2\mu}}\sqrt{(3/2)(\beta^4\mu\sigma^2)^{1/3}} \tag{11.57}$$

References

Adami, C. and N. Cerf, 2000, Physical complexity of symbolic sequences, *Physica D,* 137:62–69.

Adami, C., C. Ofria, and T. Collier, 2000, Evolution of biological complexity, *Proceedings of the National Academy of Sciences,* 97:4463–4468.

Adorno, S. and F. Salla, 2007, Organized criminality in prisons and the attacks of the PCC, *Estudos Avancados,* 21, December:7–29.

Albert, R. and A. Barabasi, 2002, Statistical mechanics of complex networks, *Reviews of Modern Physics,* 74:47–97.

Aldrich, H., G. Hodgson, D. Hull, T. Knudsen, J. Mokyr, and V. Vanberg, 2008, In defense of generalized Darwinism, *Journal of Evolutionary Economics,* 18:577–596.

Alexander, M., 2010, *The New Jim Crow: Mass Incarceration in the Age of Color-blindness,* New York: The New Press.

Arana, A., 2005, How the street gangs took Central America, *Foreign Affairs,* May/June, 98–111.

Ash, R., 1990, *Information Theory,* New York: Dover.

Atiyah, M. and I. Singer, 1963, The index of elliptical operators on compact manifolds, *Bulletin of the American Mathematical Society,* 69:322–433.

Atlan, H. and I. Cohen, 1998, Immune information, self-organization and meaning, *International Immunology,* 10:711–717.

Baars, B., 1988, *A Cognitive Theory of Consciousness,* New York: Cambridge University Press.

Baars, B., 2005, Global workspace theory of consciousness: toward a cognitive neuroscience of human experience, *Progress in Brain Research,* 150:45–53.

Baars, B. and S. Franklin, 2003, How conscious experience and working memory interact, *Trends in Cognitive Science,* 7:166–172.

Bartolozzi M., A. Leinweber, and A. Thomas, 2006, Symbiosis in the Bak-Sneppen model for biological evolution with economic applications, *Physica A,* 365:499–508.

Beck, C. and F. Schlogl, 1993, *Thermodynamics of Chaotic Systems: An Introduction,* Cambridge: Cambridge University Press.

Becker, G.S., 1968, Crime and punishment: an economic approach, *Journal of Political Economy,* 76:169–217.

Beinhocker, E., 2006, *The Origin of Wealth: Evolution, Complexity, and the Radical Remaking of Economics,* Cambridge, MA: Harvard Business School Press.

Bennett, C., 1988, Logical depth and physical complexity. In R. Herkin (ed.), *The Universal Turing Machine: A Half-Century Survey,* pp. 227–257, New York: Oxford University Press.

Binney, J., N. Dowrick, A. Fisher, and M. Newman, 1986, *The Theory of Critical Phenomena*, Oxford: Clarendon Press.

Black, F. and M. Scholes, 1973, The pricing of options and corporate liabilities, *Journal of Political Economy*, 81:637–654.

Blaug, M., 1997, Ugly currents in modern economics, *Opinions Politiques*, September, 3–8.

Boccaletti, S., V. Latora, Y. Moreno, M. Chavez, and D. Hwang, 2006, Complex networks: structure and dynamics, *Physics Reports*, 424:175–208.

Bonvillian, W., 2013, Advanced manufacturing policies and paradigms for innovation, *Science*, 342:1173–1175.

Boschma, R. and R. Martin, 2010, *The Handbook of Evolutionary Economic Geography*, Cheltenham: Edward Elgar.

Brown, R., 1987, From groups to groupoids: a brief survey, *Bulletin of the London Mathematical Society*, 19:113–134.

Burch, D., 2005, Production, consumption and trade in poultry: corporate linkages and North-South supply chains. In N. Fold and W. Prichard (eds), *Cross-Continental Food Chains*, pp. 66–78, London: Routledge.

Burdon, J. and P. Thrall, 2008, Pathogen evolution across the agro-ecological interface: implications for management, *Evolutionary Applications*, 1:57–65.

Byers, N., 1999, E. Noether's discovery of the deep connection between symmetries and conservation laws, *Israel Mathematical Conference Proceedings*, 12, ArXiv physics/9807044.

Caccioli, F., M. Marsilli, and P. Vivo, 2009, Eroding market stability by proliferation of financial instruments, *European Journal of Physics B*, 71:467–479.

Cannas DaSilva, A. and A. Weinstein, 1999, *Geometric Models for Noncommutative Algebras*, Providence, RI: American Mathematical Society.

Capuano, C. and F. Purificato, 2012, The macroeconomic impact of organized crime: a neo-Kaleckian perspective, MPRA paper 40077, http://mpra.ub.uni-muenchen.de/40077/.

Carlaw, K. and R. Lipsey, 2012, Does history matter?: Empirical analysis of evolutionary versus stationary equilibrium views of the economy, *Journal of Evolutionary Economics*, 22: 735–766. doi 10.1007/s00191–012–0282–4.

CDC (Centers for Disease Control and Prevention), 2013, Influenza activity – United States, 2012–2013; Season and composition of the 2013–2014 influenza vaccine, *Morbidity and Mortality Report* (*MMWR*), June 14, 62(23):473–479.

Champagnat, N., R. Ferriere, and S. Meleard, 2006, Unifying evolutionary dynamics: from individual stochastic processes to macroscopic models, *Theoretical Population Biology*, 69:297–321.

Chiang, M. and S. Boyd, 2004, Geometric programming duals of channel capacity and rate distortion, *IEEE Transactions on Information Theory*, 50:245–255.

Christie, N., 1982, *Limits to Pain,* New York: John Wiley and Sons.

Coase, R., 1999, Interview with Ronald Coase, *Newsletter of the International Society of New Institutional Economics*, 2(1) (Spring), 3–10.

Cohen, I., 2000, *Tending Adam's Garden: Evolving the Cognitive Immune Self*, New York: Academic Press.

Cover, T. and J. Thomas, 2006, *Elements of Information Theory*, second edition, New York: Wiley.

Csete, M. and J. Doyle, 2002, Reverse engineering of biological complexity, *Science*, 295:1664–1669.

de Groot, S. and P. Mazur, 1984, *Non-Equilibrium Thermodynamics*, New York: Dover.

Dechenaux, E. and A. Samuel, 2012, Preemptive corruption, *Economica,* 79:258–283.

Dembo, A. and O. Zeitouni, 1998, *Large Deviations and Applications*, second edition, New York: Springer.

Derman, E. and N. Taleb, 2005, The illusions of dynamic replication, *Quantitative Finance,* 5:323–326.

Derrida, B., 2007, Nonequilibrium steady states, *Journal of Statistical Mechanics: Theory and Experiment*, P07023. doi:10.1088/1742-5468/2007/07/P07023.

Diamond, J., 1997, *Guns, Germs and Steel: The Fates of Human Societies*, New York: Norton.

Diamond, J., 2011, *Collapse: How Societies Choose to Fail or Succeed*, New York: Penguin Books.

Dickens, C., 1853, *Bleak House*, London: Bradbury and Evans.

Diekmann, U. and R. Law, 1996, The dynamical theory of coevolution: a derivation from stochastic ecological processes, *Journal of Mathematical Biology,* 34:579–612.

Dumas, L., 1986, *The Over-Burdened Economy*, Los Angeles, CA: UCLA Press.

Durham, W., 1991, *Coevolution: Genes, Culture and Human Diversity*, Stanford, CA: Stanford University Press.

Ehrlich, I., 1973, Participation in illegitimate activities: a theoretical and empirical investigation, *Journal of Political Economy*, 81:521–565.

El Gamal, A. and Y. Kim, 2010, Lecture Notes on Network Information Theory, ArXiv:1001.3404v4.

Eldredge, N. and S. Gould, 1972, Punctuated equilibrium: an alternative to phyletic gradualism. In T. Schopf (ed.), *Models in Paleobiology*, pp. 82–115, San Francisco, CA: Freeman, Cooper and Co.

Ellis, R., 1985, *Entropy, Large Deviations, and Statistical Mechanics*, New York: Springer.

Emery, M., 1989, *Stochastic Calculus in Manifolds*, New York: Springer.

English, T., 1996, Evaluation of evolutionary and genetic optimizers: no free lunch. In L. Fogel, P. Angeline and T. Back (eds), *Evolutionary Programming V: Proceedings of the Fifth Annual Conference on Evolutionary Programming*, pp. 163–169, Cambridge, MA: MIT Press.

Erdos, P. and A. Renyi, 1960, On the evolution of random graphs, *Publications of the Mathematical Institute of the Hungarian Academy of Sciences*, 5, 17–61.

Erwin, D. and J. Valentine, 2013, *The Cambrian Explosion: The Construction of Animal Biodiversity*, Greenwood Village, CO: Roberts and Company.

Ewens, W., 2004, *Mathematical Population Genetics*, New York: Springer.

Executive Office of the President, 1998, *Economic Report of the President*, Washington, DC: US Government Printing Office.

Fanon, F., 1966, *The Wretched of The Earth*, New York: Grove Press.

Felbab-Brown, V. and J. Forest, 2012, Political violence and the illicit economies of West Africa, *Terrorism and Political Violence*, 24:787–806.

Feller, W., 1971, *An Introduction to Probability Theory and its Applications*, New York: John Wiley and Sons.

Feynman, R., 2000, *Lectures on Computation*, New York: Westview Press.

Fodor, J. and M. Piatelli-Palmarini, 2010, *What Darwin Got Wrong*, New York: Farrar, Straus, and Giroux.

Fredlin, M. and A. Wentzell, 1998, *Random Perturbations of Dynamical Systems*, New York: Springer.

Friedman, M., 1999, Conversation with Milton Friedman. In B. Snowdon and H. Vane (eds), *Conversations with Leading Economists: Interpreting Modern Macroeconomics*, pp. 124–144, Cheltenham: Edward Elgar.

Fullbrook, E. (ed.), 2009, *Ontology and Economics: Tony Lawson and His Critics*, New York: Routledge.

Fullilove, M. and R. Wallace, 2011, Serial forced displacement in American cities, 1916–2010, *Journal of Urban Health*, 88:381–389.

Gabora, L. and D. Aerts, 2005, Evolution as a context-driven actualization of potential: Toward an interdisciplinary theory of change of state, *Interdisciplinary Science Reviews*, 30:69–88.

Gabora, L. and D. Aerts, 2007, A cross-disciplinary framework for the description of contextually mediated change, *Electronic Journal of Theoretical Physics*, 4(15):1–22.

Gamarekian, B., 1986, Where have all the inventors gone? *New York Times,* June 20.

Garland, D., 2001, *Mass Imprisonment,* London: Sage Publications.

Garoupa, N., 2007, Optimal law enforcement and criminal organization, *Journal of Economic Behavior and Organization*, 63:461–474.

Garten, R., et al., 2009, Antigenic and genetic characterization of swine-origin 2009 A(H1N1) influenza viruses circulating in humans, *Science*, 325:197–201.

Glazebrook, J.F. and R. Wallace, 2009a, Rate distortion manifolds as models for cognitive information, *Informatica*, 33:309–345.

Glazebrook, J.F. and R. Wallace, 2009b, Small worlds and red queens in the global workspace: an information-theoretic approach, *Cognitive Systems Research*, 10:333–365.

Goldenfeld, N. and C. Woese, 2010, Life is physics: evolution as a collective phenomenon far from equilibrium. ArXiv:1011.4125v1 [q-bio.PE].

Golubitsky, M. and I. Stewart, 2006, Nonlinear dynamics and networks: the groupoid formalism, *Bulletin of the American Mathematical Society*, 43:305–364.

Gorky, M., 1972 [1906], *The City of the Yellow Devil*, Moscow: Progress Publishers.

Gould, S., 2002, *The Structure of Evolutionary Theory*, Cambridge, MA: Harvard University Press.

Gould, S. and R. Lewontin, 1979, The spandrels of San Marco and the Panglossian paradigm: A critique of the adaptationist programme, *Proceedings of the Royal Society of London, B*, 205:581–598.

Granovetter, M., 1973, The strength of weak ties, *American Journal of Sociology*, 78:1360–1380.

Guerrero-Gutierrez, E., 2011, *Security, Drugs, and Violence in Mexico: A Survey*, Mexico City: Lantia Consultores, S.C.

Gumbel, E., 1958, *Statistics of Extremes*, New York: Columbia University Press.

Gunderson, L., 2000, Ecological resilience in theory and application, *Annual Reviews of Ecological Systematics*, 31:425–439.

Halbfinger, D., 1998, In Washington Heights, drug war survivors reclaim their stoops, *New York Times*, May 18.

Haldane, A., R. May, 2011, Systemic risk in banking ecosystems, *Nature* 469:351–355.

Hanski, I., G. Zurita, M.I. Bellocq, and J. Rybicki, 2013, Species-fragmented area relationship, *Proceedings of the National Academy of Sciences*, 110:12715–12720. doi 10.1073/pnas. 1311491110.

Hartl, D. and A. Clark, 2006, *Principles of Population Genetics*, Sunderland, MA: Sinaur Associates.

Haug, E. and N. Taleb, 2011, Option traders use (very) sophisticated heuristics, never the Black–Scholes–Merton formula, *Journal of Economic Behavior and Organization*, 77:97–106.

Hazewinkel, M., 2002, Index formulas, *Encyclopedia of Mathematics*, New York: Springer.

Hearn, J., 2007, African NGO's: the new comparadors? *Development and Change*, 38:1095–1110.

Heine, S.J., 2001, Self as cultural product: an examination of East Asian and North American selves, *Journal of Personality*, 69:881–906.

Hodgson G., 1993, *Economics and Evolution: Bringing Life Back into Economics*, Ann Arbor, MI: University of Michigan Press.

Hodgson, G. and T. Knudsen, 2010, *Darwin's Conjecture: The Search for General Principles of Social and Economic Evolution*, Chicago, IL: University of Chicago Press.

Hollan, J., J. Hutchins, and D. Kirsch, 2000, Distributed cognition: toward a new foundation for human-computer interaction research, *ACM Transactions on Computer–Human Interaction*, 7:174–196.

Holling, C., 1973, Resilience and stability of ecological systems, *Annual Reviews of Ecological Systematics*, 4:1–23.

Holling, C., 1992, Cross-scale morphology, geometry and dynamics of ecosystems, *Ecological Monographs*, 62:447–502.

Hong, B.Y., 1979, *Inflation under Cost Pass-along Management*, New York: Praeger, New York.

Horsthemeke, W. and R. Lefever, 2006, *Noise-induced Transitions*: *Theory and Applications in Physics, Chemistry, and Biology*, New York: Springer.

Hugh-Jones, E., 1955, Industrial productivity: The lessons of Fawley, *Journal of Industrial Economics*, 3:73–183.

J.M.C., 1913. Possible complications of the compensated dollar, *The American Economic Review*, 3:576–588.

Johnson, N., 2011, Proposing policy by analogy is risky, *Nature*, 469:302–303.

Kauffman, S., 1996, *At Home in the Universe: The Search for the Laws of Self-Organization and Complexity*, New York: Oxford University Press.

Khasminskii, R., 2012, *Stochastic Stability of Differential Equations*, second edition, New York: Springer.

Khinchin, A., 1957, *Mathematical Foundations of Information Theory*, New York: Dover.

Kitano, H., 2004, Biological robustness, *Nature: Genetics*, 5:826–837.

Knight, F., 1921, *Risk, Uncertainty, and Profit*, Boston, MA: Schaffner and Marx.

Krebs, P., 2005, Models of cognition: neurological possibility does not indicate neurological plausibility. In B. Bara, L. Barsalou, and M. Buddiarelli (eds), *Proceedings of CogSci2005*, pp. 1184–1189, Stresa, Italy. Available at http://cogprints.org/4498/.

Krugman, P., 1979, A model of innovation, technology transfer, and the world distribution of income, *The Journal of Political Economy*, 87:253–266.

Kumar, V. and S. Skaperdas, 2009, On the economics of organized crime. In N. Garoupa (ed.), *Criminal Law and Economics*, Northampton, MA: Edward Elgar.

Landau, L. and E. Lifshitz, 2007, *Statistical Physics, Part I*, third edition, New York: Elsevier.

Langton, C., 1992, Life at the edge of chaos. In C. Langton, C. Taylor, J. Farmer, and S. Rasmussen (eds), *Artificial Life II*, pp. 41–90, Reading, MA: Addison-Wesley.

Law, M.J., 2012, 'The car indispensable': the hidden influence of the car in inter-war suburban London, *Journal of Historical Geography*, 38:424–433.

Lawson, T., 2006, The nature of heterodox economics, *Cambridge Journal of Economics*, 30:483–505.

Lawson, T., 2009a, The current economic crisis: its nature and the course of academic economics, *Cambridge Journal of Economics*, 33:759–788.

Lawson, T., 2009b, Contemporary economics and the crisis, *Real-World Economics Review*, 50:122–131.

Lawson, T., 2010, Really reorienting modern economics, INET Conference, London, April 8–11.

Lawson, T., 2012, Mathematical modelling and ideology in the economics academy: competing explanations of the failings of the modern discipline? *Economic Thought*, 1:3–22.

Leibler, J., et al., 2009, Industrial food animal production and global health risks: exploring the ecosystems and economics of avian Influenza, *EcoHealth,* 6:58–70.

Leontief, W., 1982, Letter, *Science*, 217:104–107.

Levin, S. 1989, Ecology in theory and application. In S. Levin, T. Hallam, and L. Gross (eds), *Applied Mathematical Ecology*, Biomathematics Texts 18, New York: Springer.

Lewontin, R., 2000, *The Triple Helix: Gene, Organism, and Environment*, Cambridge, MA: Harvard University Press.

Lewontin, R., 2010, Not so natural selection, *New York Review of Books*, May 27. Available at: http://www.nybooks.com/articles/archives/2010/may/27/not-so-natural-selection/

Liepert, C., 1989, *Die Heimlischen Kosten des Fortschritts*, Frankfurt: S. Fischer.

Lowenstein, R., 2000, *When Genius Failed: The Rise and Fall of Long Term Capital Management*, New York: Random House.

Luchinsky, D., 1997, On the nature of large fluctuations in equilibrium systems: observations of an optimal force, *Journal of Physics A*, 30:L577-L583.

Mansour, A., N. Marceau, and S. Mongrain, 2006, Gangs and crime deterrence, *Journal of Law, Economics, and Organization*, 22:315–339.

Markus, H. and S. Kitayama, 1991, Culture and the self-implications for cognition, emotion, and motivation, *Psychological Review*, 98:224–253.

Marshall, C., 2006, Explaining the Cambrian 'explosion' of animals, *Annual Reviews of Earth and Planetary Science*, 34:355–384.

Martin, B., 1978, The selective usefulness of game theory, *Social Studies of Science*, 8:85–110.

Masuda, T. and R. Nisbett, 2006, Culture and change blindness, *Cognitive Science*, 30:381–399.

Matsumoto, Y., 2002, *An Introduction to Morse Theory*, Providence, RI: American Mathematical Society.

May, R., 1973, *Stability and Complexity in Model Ecosystem*s, Princeton, NJ, Princeton University Press.

Melman, S., 1961, *The Peace Race*, New York: Ballantine Books.

Melman, S., 1971, *The War Economy of the United States: Readings in Military Industry and Economy*, New York: St. Martin's Press.

Melman, S., 1983, *Profits Without Production*, New York: Knopf.

Melman, S., 1988, Economic consequences of the arms race: the second-rate economy, *AEA Papers and Proceedings*, 78:55–59.

Melman, S., 1993, *What Else Is There To Do?*, Washington DC: National Commission for Economic Conversion and Disarmament (ECD).

Melman, S., 1997, From private to state capitalism: how the permanent war economy transformed the institutions of American capitalism, *Journal of Economic Issues*, 31:311.

Memmi, A., 1967, *The Colonizer and the Colonized,* Boston, MA: Beacon Press.

Messinger, S. and A. Ostling, 2009, The consequences of spatial structure for pathogen evolution, *American Naturalist*, 174:441–454.

Minero, P., M. Franceschetti, S. Dey, and G. Nair, 2009, Data Rate Theorem for stabilization over time-varying feedback channels, *IEEE Transactions on Automatic Control*, 54:243–255.

Mitter, S., 2001, Control with limited information, *European Journal of Control*, 7:122–131.

Mochan, H., S. Billups, and J. Overland, 2005, A dynamic model of differential human capital and criminal activity, *Economica*, 72:655–681.

Moynihan, D.P., 1998, *Secrecy*, New Haven CT: Yale University Press.

Myers, K., et al., 2006, Are swine workers in the United States at increased risk of infection with zoonotic influenza virus? *Clinical Infection and Disease*, 42:14–20.

NACDD, 1968, *Report of the National Advisory Commission on Civil Disorders*, Washington, DC: US Government Printing Office.

Nair, G., F. Fagnani, S. Zampieri, and R. Evans, 2007, Feedback control under data rate constraints: an overview, *Proceedings of the IEEE*, 95:108–137.

Nelson, R., 1995, Recent evolutionary theorizing about economic change, *Journal of Economic Literature*, 33:48–90.

Nelson, M., et al., 2011, Spatial dynamics of human-origin H1 influenza A virus in North American swine, *PLos Pathogens* 7:e1002077.

Nelson, R. and S. Winter, 1982, *An Evolutionary Theory of Economic Change*, Cambridge, MA: Harvard University Press.

Newman, J., 1997, A model of mass extinction, *Journal of Theoretical Biology*, 189:235–252.

Nisbett, R. and Y. Miyamoto, 2005, The influence of culture: holistic versus analytic perception, *Trends in Cognitive Science*, 9:467–473.

Nisbett, R., K. Peng, C. Incheol, and A. Norenzayan, 2001, Culture and systems of thought: holistic vs. analytic cognition, *Psychological Review*, 108:291–310.

Nocedal, J. and S. Wright, 1999, *Numerical Optimization,* New York: Springer.

Oden, M.D., 1988, *A Military Dollar Really is Different*, Lansing, MI: Employment Research Associates.

Odling-Smee, F., K. Laland, and M. Feldman, 2003, *Niche Construction: The Neglected Process in Evolution*, Princeton, NJ: Princeton University Press.

Office of the Controller, City of New York, 1998, *Dilemma in the Millennium*, August. New York: City of New York.

Ofria, C. Adami, and T. Collier, 2003, Selective pressures on genomes in molecular evolution, *Journal of Theoretical Biology*, 222:62–69.

Onsager, L. and S. Machlup, 1953, Fluctuations and irreversible processes, *Physical Review*, 91:1505–1512.

Pappas, G., 1989, *The Magic City*, Ithaca, NY: Cornell University Press.

Parenti, C., 2000, *Lockdown America: Police and Prisons in the Age of Crisis*, New York: Verso.

Petras, J., 1999, NGO's: in the service of imperialism, *Journal of Contemporary Asia*, 29:429–435.

Pettini, M., 2007, *Geometry and Topology in Hamiltonian Dynamics and Statistical Mechanics*, New York: Springer.

Pew Center on States, 2009, http://www.pewstates.org/uploadedFiles/PCS_Assets/2009/PSPP_1in31_report_FINAL_WEB_3–26–09.pdf.

PIE Report, 2013, http://web.mit.edu/press/images/documents/pie-report.pdf.

Pielou, E., 1977, *Mathematical Ecology*, New York: John Wiley and Sons.

Plowden, W., 1973, *The Car and Politics in Britain*, London: Pelican Books.

Protter, P., 1990, *Stochastic Integration and Differential Equations*, New York: Springer.

Reuter, P., 1983, *Disorganized Crime*, Cambridge, MA: MIT Press.

Roca, C., J. Cuesta, and A. Sanchez, 2009, Evolutionary game theory: temporal and spatial effects beyond replicator dynamics, *Physics of Life Reviews*, 6:208–249.

Rockafellar, R., 1970, *Convex Analysis*, Princeton, NJ: Princeton University Press.

Rollason, K., 2009, Flying pigs a good sign: flight of Boeing 777 from city shows CentrePort's potential, *Winnipeg Free Press*, May, article 46214312.

Rubenstein, A., 1995, John Nash: the master of economic modelling, *Scandinavian Journal of Economics*, 97:9–13.

Saegert, S., D. Fields, and K. Libman, 2011, Mortgage foreclosures and health disparities: serial displacement as asset extraction in African American populations, *Journal of Urban Health*, 88:390–402.

Sahai, A., 2004, The necessity and sufficiency of anytime capacity for control over a noisy communication link, *Decision and Control, 43rd IEEE Conference on CDC*, Vol. 2, pp. 1896–1901.

Sahai, A. and S. Mitter, 2006, The necessity and sufficiency of anytime capacity for control over a noisy communication link Part II: vector systems, http://arxiv.org/abs/cs/0610146.

Said, E.,1977, *Orientalism*, London: Penguin.

Schinazi, R., 2005, Mass extinction: an alternative to the Allee effect, *Annals of Applied Probability*, 15:984–991.

Sereno, M., 1991, Four analogies between biological and cultural/linguistic evolution, *Journal of Theoretical Biology*, 151:467–507.

Sergent, C. and S. Dehaene, 2004, Is consciousness a gradual phenomenon? Evidence for an all-or-none bifurcation during the attentional blink, *Psychological Science*, 15:720–725.

Shannon, C., 1959, Coding theorems for a discrete source with a fidelity criterion, *Institute of Radio Engineers International Convention Record*, 7, 142–163.

Shirkov, D. and V. Kovalev, 2001, The Bogoliubov renormalization group and solution symmetry in mathematical physics, *Physics Reports*, 352:219–249.

Simons, A. and D. Tucker, 2007, The misleading problem of failed states: a 'socio-geography' of terrorism in the post-9/11 era, *Third World Quarterly*, 28:387–401.

Skaperdas, S., 2001, The political economy of organized crime: providing protection when the state does not, *Economics of Governance*, 2:173–202.

Skarbek, D., 2011, Governance and prison gangs, *American Political Science Review*, 105:702–716.

Smallman-Raynor, M. and A. Cliff, 2013, Abrupt transition to heightened poliomyelitis epidemicity in England and Wales 1947–1957, associated with a pronounced increase in the geographical rate of disease propagation, *Epidemiology and Infection*, 142: 577–591. doi:10.1017/S0950268813001441.

Spenser, J., 2010, The giant component: the golden anniversary, *Notices of the AMS*, 57:720–724.

Sung, H.E., 2004, State failure, economic failure and predatory organized crime: a comparative analysis, *Journal of Research in Crime and Delinquency*, 41:111–129.

Taleb, N., 2007, *The Black Swan: The Impact of the Highly Improbable*, New York: Random House.

Tatikonda, S. and S. Mitter, 2004, Control over noisy channels, *IEEE Transactions on Automatic Control*, 49:1196–1201.

Taylor, P. and L. Jonker, 1978, Evolutionarily stable strategies and game dynamics, *Mathematical Biosciences*, 40:145–156.

Thompson, H., 2010, Why mass incarceration matters: rethinking crisis, decline, and transformation in postwar American history, *Journal of American History*, 39:703–754.

Tirman, J., 1984, *The Militarization of High Technology*, Cambridge, MA: Ballinger.

Trevelyan, B., M. Smallman-Raynor, and A. Cliff, 2005, The spatial dynamics of poliomeyelitis in the United States: from epidemic emergence to vaccine-induced retreat, 1910–1971, *Annals of the Association of American Geographers*, 95:269–293.

Ullmann, J.E., 1970, Conversion and the import problem: a confluence of opportunities, *IEEE Spectrum*, 7(4):55–62.

Ullmann, J.E., 1978, Tides and shallows. In L. Benton (ed.), *Management for the Future*, New York: McGraw-Hill.

Ullmann, J.E., 1985, *The Prospects of American Industrial Recovery*, Westport, CT: Quorum Books.

Ullmann, J.E., 1988, *The Anatomy of Industrial Decline*, Westport, CT: Greenwood-Quorum.

Ullmann, J.E., 1989, *Economic Conversion: Indispensable for America's Economic Recovery*, Briefing Paper 3, Washington DC: National Commission for Economic Conversion and Disarmament (ECD).

Ullmann, J.E., 1993, A national high speed rail system: The task for engineers, *IEEE Technology and Society*, Winter, 12(4):13–20.

Ullmann, J.E., 1994, Conversion: The prospects for Long Island, *Hofstra Business Review*, April, 1.

Ullmann, J.E., 1997a, Ronald Reagan and the illusion of victory in the Cold War. In A. Ugrinsky, E. Schmertz, and N. Datlof (eds), *President Reagan and the World*, pp. 109ff. Westport CT: Greenwood Press.

Ullmann, J.E., 1997b. Defense Cuts, base closings and conversion: slow reaction and missed opportunities, Paper at Conference on 'George Bush: Leading in a New World,' 10th Presidential Conference, Hofstra University, Hempsted, NY, April 17–19.

US Congress, Joint Economic Committee, 1986, *The US Trade Position in High Technology, 1980–1986*, Washington, DC: US Government Printing Office.

US Department of Commerce, 1991, *1990 Statistical Abstract of the United States*, Washington, DC: US Government Printing Office.

US Department of Commerce, 1997, *1998 Statistical Abstracts of the United States*, Washington, DC: US Government Printing Office.

Van den Broeck, C., J. Parrondo, and R. Toral, 1994, Noise-induced nonequilibrium phase transition, *Physical Review Letters*, 73:3395–3398.

Van den Broeck, C., J. Parrondo, R. Toral, and R. Kawai, 1997, Nonequilibrium phase transitions induced by multiplicative noise, *Physical Review E*, 55:4084–4094.

Vijaykrishna, V. et al., 2011, Long-term evolution and transmission dynamics of swine influenza A virus, *Nature*, 473:519–523.

Von Neumann, J., 1966, *Theory of Self-Reproducing Automata*, Urbana, IL: University of Illinois Press.

Vulliamy, E., 2011, How a big US bank laundered billions from Mexico's murderous drug gangs, *The Guardian*, April 2.

Wacquant, L., 2001, Deadly symbiosis: when ghetto and prison meet and mesh, *Punishment and Society*, 3:95–134.

Wallace, R., 1989, Homeless, contagious housing destruction and municipal service cuts in New York City: I Demographics of a housing deficit, *Environment and Planning A*, 21:1585–1602.

Wallace, R., 1990a, Homeless, contagious housing destruction and municipal service cuts in New York City: II Dynamics of a housing famine, *Environment and Planning A*, 22:5–15.

Wallace, R., 1990b, Urban desertification, public health and public order: planned shrinkage, contagious housing destruction and AIDS in the Bronx, *Social Science and Medicine*, 31:801–816.

Wallace, R., 2000, Language and coherent neural amplification in hierarchical systems: renormalization and the dual information source of a generalized spatiotemporal stochastic resonance, *International Journal of Bifurcation and Chaos*, 10:493–502.

Wallace, R., 2002, Adaptation, punctuation and information: a rate-distortion approach to non-cognitive 'learning plateaus' in evolutionary process, *Acta Biotheoretica*, 50:101–116.

Wallace, R., 2005, *Consciousness: A Mathematical Treatment of the Global Neuronal Workspace Model*, New York: Springer.

Wallace, R., 2007, Culture and inattentional blindness: a global workspace perspective, *Journal of Theoretical Biology*, 245:378–390.

Wallace, R., 2009a, Metabolic constraints on the eukaryotic transition, *Origins of Life and Evolution of Biospheres*, 38:165–176.

Wallace, R.G., 2009b, Breeding influenza: the political virology of offshore farming, *Antipode*, 41:916–951.

Wallace, R., 2010a, Expanding the modern synthesis, *Comptes Rendus Biologies*, 333:701–709.

Wallace, R., 2010b, Structure and dynamics of the 'protein folding code' inferred using Tlusty's topological rate distortion approach, *BioSystems*, 103:18–26.

Wallace, R., 2011a, A formal approach to evolution as self-referential language, *BioSystems*, 106:36–44.

Wallace, R., 2011b, Forced displacement of African-Americans in New York City and the international diffusion of multiple-drug-resistant HIV. In O. Kahn and G. Pappas (eds), *Megacities and Public Health*, American Public Health Association.

Wallace, R., 2012, Consciousness, crosstalk, and the mereological fallacy: An evolutionary perspective, *Physics of Life Reviews*, 9:426–453.

Wallace, R., 2013a, A new formal approach to evolutionary processes in socioeconomic systems, *Journal of Evolutionary Economics*, 23:1–15.

Wallace, R., 2013b, Cognition and biology: perspectives from information theory, *Cognitive Processing*, 15(1): 1–12. doi:10.1007/s10339-013-0573-1.

Wallace, R., 2014, A new formal perspective on 'Cambrian Explosions' *Comptes Rendus Biologies*, 337:1–5. doi 10.1016/j.crvi.2013.11.002.

Wallace, R. and M. Fullilove, 2008, *Collective Consciousness and its Discontents*, New York: Springer.

Wallace, R.G. and R. Kock, 2012, Whose food footprint? Capitalism, agriculture and the environment, *Human Geography*, 5:63–83.

Wallace, D. and R. Wallace, 1998, *A Plague on Your Houses*, New York: Verso.

Wallace, R. and R.G. Wallace, 2008a, On the spectrum of prebiotic chemical systems: an information-theoretic treatment of Eigen's Paradox, *Origins of Life and Evolution of Biospheres*, 38:419–455.

Wallace, R. and D. Wallace, 2008b, Punctuated equilibrium in statistical models of generalized coevolutionary resilience, *Transactions on Computational Systems Biology* IX LNBI 5121 23–85.

Wallace, R. and D. Wallace, 2009, Code, context and epigenetic catalysis in gene expression, *Transactions on Computational Systems Biology* XI, LNBI 5750 283–334.

Wallace, R. and D. Wallace, 2010, *Gene Expression and its Discontents: The Social Production of Chronic Disease*, New York: Springer.

Wallace, D. and R. Wallace, 2011, Consequences of massive housing destruction: the New York City fire epidemic, *Building Research and Information*, 39:395–411.

Wallace, R. and R.G. Wallace, 2014, Blowback: new formal perspectives on agriculturally driven pathogen evolution, *Epidemiology and Infection*. doi 10.1017/S0950268814000077.

Wallace, R., M. Fullilove, and A. Flisher, 1996, AIDS, violence and behavioral coding: information theory, risk behavior and dynamic process on core-group sociogeographic networks, *Social Science and Medicine*, 43:339–352.

Wallace R., J.E. Ullmann, D. Wallace, and H. Andrews, 1999, Deindustrialization, inner city decay and the hierarchical diffusion of AIDS in the US: how neoliberal and cold war policies magnified the ecological niche for emerging infections and created a national security crisis, *Environment and Planning A*, 31:113–139.

Wallace, R., D. Wallace, and R.G. Wallace, 2009, *Farming Human Pathogens: Ecological Resilience and Evolutionary Process*, New York: Springer.

Wallace, R. G., L. Bergmann, R. Kock, M. Gilbert, L. Hogerwerf, R. Wallace, and M. Holmberg, 2014, The dawn of Structural One Health: a new science tracking disease emergence along circuits of capital, *Social Science and Medicine*. doi: 10.1016/j.socscimed.2014.09.047

Watts, S., 1999, *Epidemics and History: Disease, Power, and Imperialism*, New Haven, CT: Yale University Press.

Weinstein, A., 1996, Groupoids: unifying internal and external symmetry, *Notices of the American Mathematical Association*, 43:744–752.

West-Eberhard, M., 2003, *Developmental Plasticity and Evolution*, New York: Oxford University Press.

Whittington, H., 1985, *The Burgess Shale*, New Haven, CT: Yale University Press.

Wilson, K., 1971, Renormalization group and critical phenomena. I Renormalization group and the Kadanoff scaling picture, *Physics Reviews B*, 4:3174–3183.

Wolpert, D. and W. MacReady, 1995, No free lunch theorems for search, Santa Fe Institute, SFI-TR-02-010.

Wolpert, D. and W. MacReady, 1997, No free lunch theorems for optimization, *IEEE Transactions on Evolutionary Computation*, 1:67–82.

Wymer, C., 1997, Structural nonlinear continuous-time models in econometrics, *Macroeconomic Dynamics,* 1:518–548.

You, K. and L. Xie, 2013, Survey of recent progress in networked control systems, *Acta Automatica Sinica*, 39:101–117.

Young, R., 1990, *White Mythologies: Writing History and the West*, New York: Routledge.

Yu, S. and . P. Mehta, 2010, Bode-like fundamental performance limitations in control of nonlinear systems, *IEEE Transactions on Automatic Control*, 55:1390–1405.

Zhu, R., A. Rebirio, D. Salahub, and S. Kaufmann, 2007, Studying genetic regulatory networks at the molecular level: delayed reaction stochastic models, *Journal of Theoretical Biology,* 246:725–745.

Zurek, W., 1985, Cosmological experiments in superfluid helium? *Nature*, 317:505–508.

Zurek, W., 1996, The shards of broken symmetry, *Nature*, 382:296–298.

Index

For Product Safety Concerns and Information please contact our EU
representative GPSR@taylorandfrancis.com Taylor & Francis Verlag GmbH,
Kaufingerstraße 24, 80331 München, Germany

Printed and bound by CPI Group (UK) Ltd, Croydon, CR0 4YY

01/05/2025

01858359-0007